THE
WEATHER
BOOK

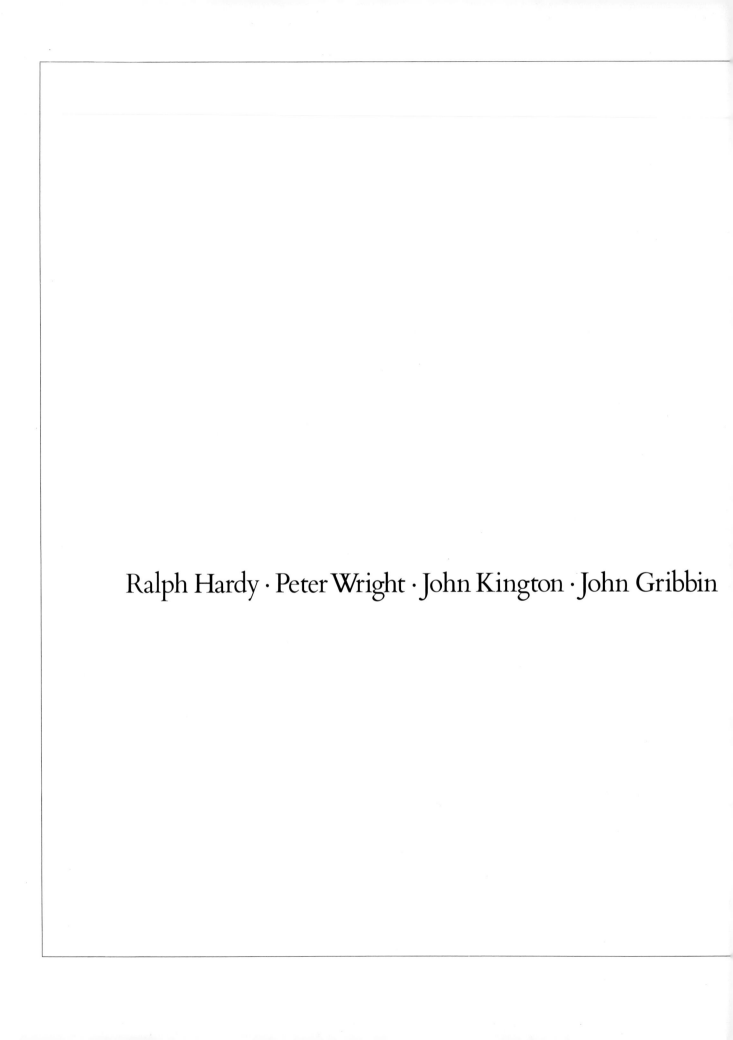

Ralph Hardy · Peter Wright · John Kington · John Gribbin

THE WEATHER BOOK

Little, Brown and Company

Boston · Toronto

First published in 1982 by
Little, Brown and Company
34 Beacon Street, Boston,
Massachusetts 02106

Edited, designed and produced by
Harrow House Editions Limited,
7a Langley Street, Covent Garden, London WC2H 9JA

Library of Congress Catalog card number: 81-84683
First American edition.
ISBN 0-316-34623-3

Phototypeset in Bembo 270 by
Tameside Filmsetting Ltd., Ashton-under-Lyne, England
Illustrations originated by
Scan Studios Ltd., Dublin, Eire
Printed and bound by Artes Graficas, Toledo, Spain
D. L. TO.: 116-1982

CONTENTS

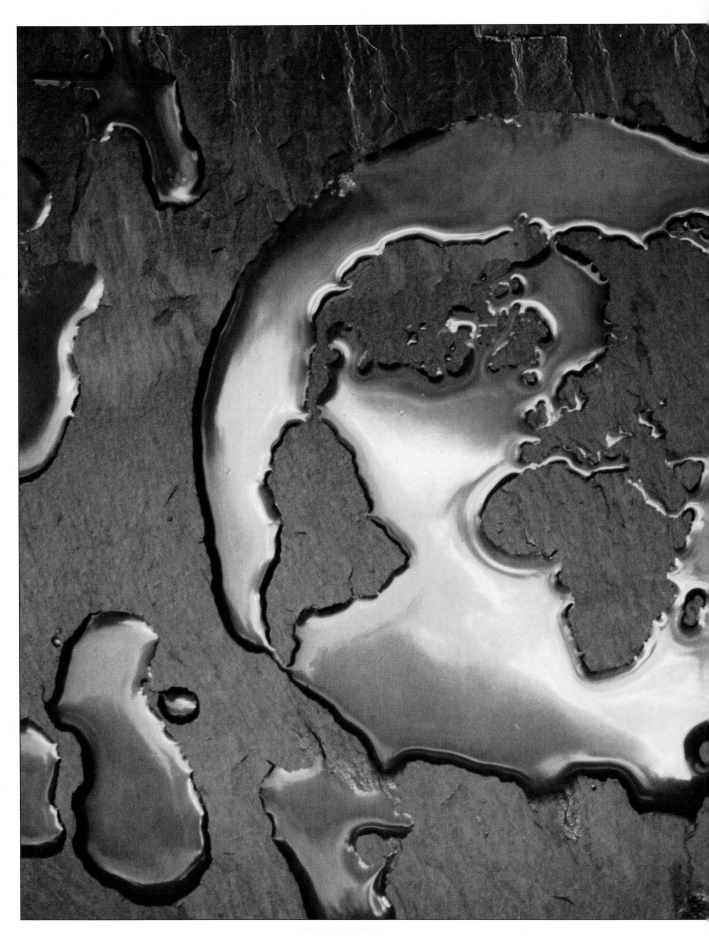

FOREWORD

The one true wilderness left for most of us in a man-made world is the ever-changing, often annoying and some-times deadly action of the weather. Dreamers of artificial cities that may one day orbit in space have wit enough to visualize running their miniature weather systems by a programme of random numbers, in order to retain a little of the unexpectedness that helps to save us from boredom. In similar vein a leading meteorologist opposes schemes for controlling the weather on Earth, not because he considers them altogether unpractical, but because he insists that coping with the vagaries of the climate helps to keep us human. I think, too, of weathermen in Tokyo who told me why they objected to well-meaning American experiments aimed at taming the typhoons that ravage so many places around the Pacific: the Japanese rely on the occurrence of these fearsome storms for much of their annual rainfall.

Certain it is that climatic adversity during the long-playing cycles of the ice ages accelerated the emergence of our species; certain, too, that hikers, climbers, flyers and sailors feel an urge to go out and face the elements, as something more manly or womanly to do than watching the television. And in my own small boat anything that I may know about the science of the weather is swept aside by a wholesome awe, when the sky goes dark at noon, the squall snatches at the sails and the waves attack like angry beasts.

At home my window offers me a non-stop motion picture where those flying freezers that we call clouds drift or stampede across the landscape. Learn a little of their types and meanings, and you can soon find in the clouds a source of fascination and prognostication, and learn to keep an eye on what my wife calls "the naughty parts of the sky". Even when the atmosphere clears and the Sun blazes on a summer's day, you may watch optical ripples on the hot road, where small springs of rising air pour warmth and moisture into the sky. Adding enough of them together may build a thundercloud, still capable of scaring quite sophisticated people. And sometimes, most disconcertingly of all, the window-picture goes blank, as fog takes charge and I hear silence settle on a busy airport nearby.

Then is the time to recall more ominous silences – for instance among sand dunes in northwest India, where you can kick up desert dust in a region that, 4000 years ago, was lush with cereal crops and shady trees. That was before the climate changed and the monsoon broke its promise to the peoples of the Indus civilization. And in Manhattan, of all places, I found myself in a quite different kind of noiseless desert, after a heavy fall of snow that smothered the city and emptied the streets. It was like a preview of the next ice age, when New York's Hudson River will revert to being a glacier – unless, defying the injunctions of my meteorologist friend, human beings contrive to control the climate and become sufficiently skilful to ward off the ice.

The sciences of weather and climate have matured with astonishing rapidity during the past 20 years. They have gone through their greatest transformation since the invention of the barometer and thermometer in the seventeenth century, and this book reflects the surer knowledge, the sharper questions and the bolder guesses that characterize invigorated research. For forecasters and theorists alike the weather satellites afford unprecedented views and soundings of the atmosphere, as it manufactures the weather in swirling engines of air and water powered by the Sun. Even the most powerful computers available are barely able to model this global machinery adequately or keep pace with its changes, yet meteorologists have shown great initiative in using computers both for practical forecasting and as aids to comprehending intricate processes of weather and the longer-term patterns of climatic change.

Another revolution has occurred with the rise of historical climatology and with the realization – reluctant, I should say, in some quarters – that our generation is not exempt from the variability of climate that provides a background to the history of previous generations. The reasons for climatic change from century to century are still difficult to pin down and competing theories jostle for attention, with current researches pointing towards the Sun itself as the most likely culprit.

For longer timescales, though, one recent achievement has been a decision between dozens of rival ice-age theories, favouring in the end an astronomical explanation for the comings and goings of the ice. In the new perspective, severe icing is normal nowadays, but sometimes, as in our present warm interval, the ice retreats for a while. And the repeated burials of huge tracts of land – the whole of Canada and northern Europe for instance – under thick ice-sheets like those which burden Greenland and Antarctica even now, are the grossest insults to the natural environment known to us from the recent geological past. Meteorology and climatology are the most highly developed and thought-provoking of all the environmental sciences.

The very food we eat reflects the adaptations of plants and animals to different climatic conditions and ten thousand years of deliberate selection. Farmers in prosperous countries run a science-based industry replete with mechanical and chemical aids, yet they take almost as big a gamble on the season's weather as any peasant. Drought or flood, heavy rain or hail, early or late frosts, or any of the pests or diseases that may be encouraged by unusual weather – these can wipe out a harvest. And for peoples living on the knife-edge of hunger, or exposed to the most severe fluctuations, weather and climate are a matter of life and death.

For those who can safely separate themselves from the weather, behind windows or windscreens, it is more a matter of fun and fascination – and the occasional unexpected drenching. The invitation from the author-experts of this book is to a keener awareness of the daily drama in which all of us participate willy-nilly. They explain basic principles and tour the boundaries of present understanding, so if you wish you knew how clouds and low-pressure systems work, how forecasts are made, or what the difference is between a "big ice age" and a "little ice age", here is an opportunity to find out painlessly. Why, you won't even get wet.

Nigel Calder

NIGEL CALDER is a science writer and winner of the UNESCO Kalinga prize for the popularization of science.

INTRODUCTION

The story of weather is the story of mankind. It has controlled his most fundamental activities – that of providing food and a need for shelter – and has dictated the patterns of growth of civilization. In its most extreme manifestations of drought and flood, it has condemned whole societies while in its most balanced and generous forms has allowed others to flourish. No accident of genetics has determined that one region – the temperate – should assume its dominant role while others, loosely called 'the Third World', have languished. An understanding of meteorology – of those mercurial changes in the weather and of the greater patterns of which they are the result – is a step towards understanding the story of life and mankind on earth.

The book is divided into five chapters. In the first chapter, *What Makes Weather,* the Earth is shown as part of the solar system, a planet travelling on its yearly orbit around the Sun with clockwork regularity, spinning daily on its tilting axis to produce the seasonal variations experienced between the tropics and the poles. The Earth is composed of spheres of rocky elements and has a liquid hydrosphere cocooned in layers of vapour shielding life from the harmful rays of the Sun, yet allowing its warmth to penetrate.

The unique properties of the components of this atmosphere interact to produce our weather. Heat from the Sun initiates physical changes in states of matter, which, being ruled by fundamental scales of temperature and their interrelated universal changes of pressure, form the driving forces behind the continual motion of the atmosphere. The different kinds of precipitation and the infinite combinations of winds and weather are modified by the effect of the Earth's rotation in space and the patterns of continents, mountains and seas.

Having described the unchanging global parameters that govern the dynamics of our weather, the second chapter of the book, *Natural Phenomena,* unveils the scenic beauty that is created by, for example, the ground-level clouds shrouding mountain valleys in summer, morning mists and iridescent drops of dew and frost that decorate the dawn, and the experience of the gentle quietness of a falling flake of snow or the raging power of hail. It captures the fairy-like effects of the 'brockenspectre', the reward of many mountain climbers and the rippling patch of reflected sky sparkling in the sand – the mirage that has brought despair to many a desert traveller. It explains how and why minute droplets of vapour, suspended in a cloud, coalesce to form a drop of rain – a mystery that has baffled scientists for centuries. But it tells also of other mysteries that remain unsolved even at a time when modern methods of modifying the weather by creating rain or diffusing the power of a hurricane are available.

The wonders of the atmosphere – its brilliant light shows, twilights, sunrises, sunsets and surprises – which are so often taken for granted, are all part of the daily pattern, a pattern which, if viewed over a period of months or years, presents a portrait of climate. Climate and climatic zones, described in the third chapter, *World*

Weather, have affected the course of evolution, the course of history and have been a factor in moulding civilizations and directing the migrations of various peoples since the world began. Evolutionary adaptations to the climate have helped Man to survive the rigours of the wide diversity of environments that he inhabits. The well-rounded shape of eskimos (similar to the seals and polar bears that also live in the Arctic) is due to a special layer of fat that protects them against bitter cold. In contrast, jungle people have evolved a slight build, which helps them to lose heat more easily to withstand humidities that people of temperate latitudes find uncomfortable and enervating. Climate accounts for the variations in culture and life-style in different parts of the world, and ancient customs evolved, for example, to conserve moisture or heat, today form the basis of modern techniques that allow people to live and work in the frigid wastes of the Antarctic, or to explore the rarefied atmosphere of Himalayan peaks.

While the seasons and prevailing winds are predictable within limits, it is essential to realize that we live in a small span of the Earth's lifetime which has already experienced innumerable ice ages, punctuated by brief interglacial periods of warmth and flourishing life. In the fourth chapter, *The Changing Climate,* climatic patterns are explained in terms of the cyclical changes in the way that the Earth tilts and wobbles as it moves around the Sun. But other factors – cycles of sunspot activity, phases of magnetic activity and planetary conjunctions which subtly change the centre of mass of the solar system – all operate simultaneously through different scales of time and they may well synchronize and initiate a sudden ice age. But, interwoven in this complex mesh of opposing forces is the human element that offsets all other possible natural causes of climatic change. In recent decades, Man has created a layer of polluting dust in the atmosphere which has coincided with a recent global surge of volcanic activity – producing more dust. The dust layer acts like glass in a greenhouse, trapping the Earth's heat, which may overwhelm all the other natural forces that work to throw us back into the oppressive heat of another dinosaur age. Whichever way this climatic knife-edge turns, the effects of even minute temperature changes have alarming implications and threaten our present delicately balanced world economy, making the future of weather forecasting vital to us all.

The final chapter of the book, *Forecasting,* explains how both short- and long-term climatic changes, whether they are induced by Man or not, are made. Forecasting has always been dependent on human experience and despite modern-day supercomputers and satellites, predicting the weather ultimately remains in the hands of the human forecaster, an art as much as a science. Without the gradual accumulation of weather knowledge by countless generations of philosophers and scientists and the painstaking efforts of innumerable amateur meteorologists, it would not be possible to provide the regular daily forecasts that we take for granted today.

WHAT MAKES WEATHER

"Water has merely leapt out of vapor and thin nothingness in the night sky to array itself in form. There is no logical reason for the existence of a snowflake any more than there is for evolution. It is an apparition from that mysterious shadow world beyond nature, that final world which contains – if anything contains – the explanation of men and catfish and green leaves."

Loren Eiseley – *The Immense Journey* 1957

An understanding of the weather we experience every day of our lives needs a knowledge of the basic principles that govern the atmosphere. As far as meteorology is concerned the position of the Earth in the solar system and its speed and angle of rotation are of equal importance to the composition and structure of the atmosphere. Together they account for the seasons of the year, the global distribution of climates and the daily variation in weather seen particularly in the temperate regions of the world. "What makes weather" shows how meteorology's many components interact to produce the commonplace and extraordinary facets of the world's weather.

The midnight sun, seen in June from Rikgransen in Norway – a location well within the Arctic Circle.

Our weather can be seen as an extraordinary jigsaw puzzle. Extraordinary because the largest pieces – the Sun, the orbiting and rotating Earth, the oceans and continents – are each interlocked and made up of smaller pieces, the basic building block of all substances being the molecule. The peculiar structure of the water molecule has an important influence on weather: water vapour can absorb heat which would otherwise be lost to space and, furthermore, changes of state from liquid to gas and liquid to ice are vital in redistributing energy from the Sun between the oceans, continents and atmosphere. Without exploring every intricacy in mathematical detail, we will try to fit the main pieces together, enough to appreciate the entire complex yet beautiful picture.

The Seasons

The fundamental cause of weather, and therefore our own logical starting point, is the Sun and the position of the Earth in the solar system. Quite naturally our perspective as Earth-dwellers is coloured by what we see and experience. Only during the last few generations have we come to realize that we live within a thin layer of atmosphere on a small planet orbiting a rather modest star – one of many billions in a galaxy which is itself one among innumerable others. But our planet does seem to be unique in one way – it supports life; as yet there is no positive evidence of life elsewhere in the universe.

The ability to sustain life is dependent on many factors. The Earth's size governs the strength of gravity and ensures that our atmosphere neither floats off into space nor exerts a crushing force upon us. The Earth's position in the solar system is such that the planet as a whole neither freezes nor boils. Our sun may be small in terms of the universe, but with a diameter of 1,390,473 kilometres (864,000 miles) it is nine times bigger than the Earth. The Sun's surface temperature, over 6000°C (10,832°F), is maintained by nuclear reactions in the interior. The energy produced by these reactions is continually radiated into space, but only a minute fraction of this energy is intercepted by the Earth; without it, not only weather but also life itself would cease.

The seasons occur because the Earth's axis is tipped with respect to its plane of revolution around the Sun. When the north pole is tilted towards the Sun (A) the Northern Hemisphere has its summer, while at the same time the Southern Hemisphere has its winter. Six months later, the opposite situation occurs (B), when the Southern Hemisphere is inclined towards the Sun. The arrow, representing the Sun's rays, indicates that solar intensity is equal in both (A) and (B), but because of the different angles of incidence and day length, a given area receives much more energy in summer, as shown above (C).

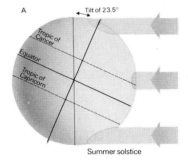

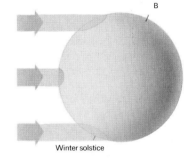

Summer solstice

Winter solstice

The ecliptic is the plane within which the Earth's orbit traces an elliptical path around the Sun. The distance from the Earth to the Sun is an unimportant factor in determining the seasons; in fact, we are at perihelion – closest to the Sun, at a distance of about 146·4 million kilometres (91·5 million miles) – during winter in the Northern Hemisphere. At aphelion the distance reaches its maximum, approximately 151·2 million kilometres (94·5 million miles).

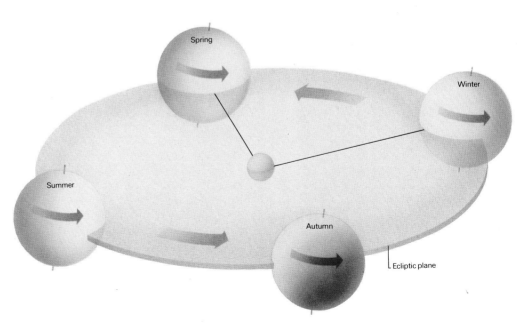

The Earth orbits the Sun once every 365 days 5 hours 48 minutes and 46 seconds and our 365-day calendar is kept in step with this motion by making leap years and end-of-century adjustments; everybody knows that every fourth year is a leap year, except at the change of a century, but many people do not realize that every 400 years the end of a century is a leap year because it is divisible by 400 and so – as part of the normal Gregorian leap year system – the year AD 2000 will be a leap year. The Earth's orbit is neither perfectly circular nor is it perfectly constant with time. Recent calculations have indicated cyclic variations in the Earth's orbit with time-scales of 97,000, 40,000 and 21,000 years – variations which may go a long way towards explaining past ice ages. Fortunately the annual variation of total incoming energy from the Sun due to the slight eccentricity of the Earth's orbit is small. If the orbit was more elongated, the summers in the Southern Hemisphere would be much hotter with correspondingly colder winters, while the differences between seasons in the Northern Hemisphere would be less pronounced than they are at present.

The seasonal variations we experience have no connection with the shape of the Earth's orbit; they result entirely from the way the Earth's axis of rotation is tilted in relation to the plane of the Earth's orbit round the Sun – known as the ecliptic. The Earth's axis has a tilt of 23.5 degrees, which remains fixed in space as the Earth travels round the Sun. This tilt is responsible for month-by-month changes in the amount of solar radiation reaching each part of the Earth, and hence the variation in the length of daylight throughout the year at different latitudes and the seasonal weather cycle.

Each year the areas lying near the north and south poles have at least one complete 24-hour period of darkness and one complete 24-hour period of daylight. In theory the poles themselves have six months of darkness followed by six months of daylight. In fact, because the Sun is not a point source of light but a sizeable disc, and because light tends to bend towards the Earth as it passes through the atmosphere, there is a twilight zone and the nights are slightly shorter than they otherwise would be.

The 23.5-degree tilt also accounts for the positions of the tropics – the Tropic of Cancer at 23.5°N and the Tropic of Capricorn at 23.5°S. Here the Sun is overhead at midday on the solstices, 21–22 June and 22–23 December. At these times the heat from the Sun reaches its maximum strength

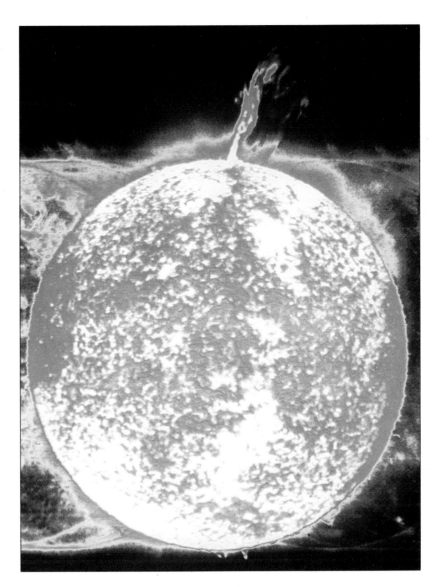

in the Northern and Southern Hemispheres respectively. Another feature that influences the weather is the Earth's roughly spherical shape, which creates sharp temperature differences because the Sun's rays strike with greater intensity on some parts of the Earth than on others. Also, at the polar regions, more of the Sun's rays are absorbed by the atmosphere before reaching the Earth.

It is interesting to speculate what marked differences would result if the Earth's axis was orientated differently with respect to the ecliptic. If it lay in the plane of the ecliptic the poles would have sizzling summers with the Sun virtually directly overhead night and day for weeks on end, while the winter hemisphere would be much colder. If on the other hand it was perpendicular to the ecliptic, there would be 12-hour days everywhere except at the poles all year long and no seasons at all.

The Sun is our nearest star and the source of all our heat and light. This picture, taken by Skylab's solar telescope, has been enhanced by computer, enabling subtle brightness differences to be seen on the star's surface.

13

Sensors on the Meteostat satellite take pictures in three different wavelengths simultaneously. In this image of the Earth (*right*), the visible spectrum is represented in green and black; the infra-red, showing the temperature of the Earth, is represented in red – the colder surfaces being the brightest – and water vapour in the troposphere appears blue.

The atmosphere can conveniently be divided into horizontal layers according to its temperature structure (*below*). The air is usually warmer in the lower troposphere than elsewhere in the lowest 100 kilometres (60 miles) of the atmosphere and the very rarefied layers of the thermosphere are hot.

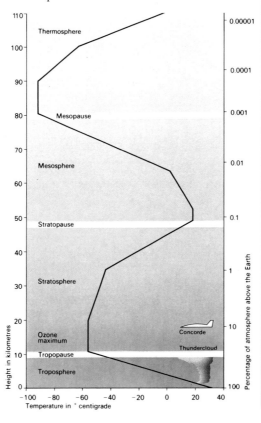

The Atmosphere

The heart of our weather, and indeed our very existence, may be the relationship between Sun and Earth, but the Earth's atmosphere is equally essential and may be regarded as the lungs by which the Earth breathes and lives. In comparison with the Earth's average diameter, 12,640 kilometres (7,900 miles), the lower atmosphere forms a very thin skin indeed. All our weather is produced in this layer, which is called the troposphere, and on average varies in depth from less than 10 kilometres (6 miles) near the poles to 20 kilometres (12 miles) at the tropics. The boundary between the troposphere and the layer above it, the stratosphere, is called the tropopause. In the troposphere there is an overall though rarely uniform decrease of temperature with height, whereas in the stratosphere temperatures are either constant or increase with height.

In depth the troposphere is shallower than the stratosphere, but when the weight or amount of air in each layer rather than the depth is considered, the picture is reversed – on average 75 per cent of the total atmosphere lies below the tropopause. This is because air is compressible; therefore near the Earth's surface it is much more dense than in higher layers. As the different layers of the atmosphere are not separated by physical barriers, there is a continual transfer of air.

Air is a mixture of gases and not a gas in its own right. The composition and relative amounts of gases comprising the atmosphere have gradually changed over millions of

respect of weather, and especially climate, carbon dioxide has additional importance in its effect on the Earth's radiation balance. Carbon dioxide is transparent to incoming solar radiation, but readily absorbs the Earth's outgoing radiation – the so-called "greenhouse effect" – and so any change in the amount of atmospheric carbon dioxide has an effect on the climate of the Earth. (The term "greenhouse effect" can be misleading because in fact a large part of the heating in a greenhouse is due to the prevention of external air currents mixing with and cooling the air inside.)

Recent estimates show that the amount of carbon dioxide in the Earth's atmosphere is increasing by about 0.5 per cent of its present concentration each year. The effect of this increase on the Earth's temperature is uncertain; some experiments suggest a 10 per cent increase may raise the average temperature by less than half of one degree centigrade. Nevertheless a continual increase may eventually lead to a shift of climatic zones, with consequences beneficial or otherwise far greater than this small change in average temperature suggests.

Unlike other gases the distribution of ozone varies considerably with height; it is almost entirely absent near the Earth's surface – which is fortunate because it is poisonous – and has its maximum concentration between 20 and 25 kilometres (12 and 15 miles) above the Earth's surface. Its importance lies in its ability to absorb harmful ultraviolet radiation from the Sun – this process has continued unobserved through countless centuries and Man has only recently become aware of its existence. At present scientists are investigating whether certain propellent gases used in modern aerosol sprays are eroding the ozone layer. However, in contrast to carbon dioxide, ozone concentration in the atmosphere is of little importance to the weather.

So far pure air, which can only exist under controlled laboratory conditions, has been considered. In reality dust particles, sufficiently small to be suspended in air, are universal. They are chiefly particles of smoke, salt, fine sand and volcanic ash. Large particles, with a radius greater than about 10 microns (one-hundredth of a millimetre), tend not to remain airborne. They either slowly fall to the surface simply due to gravity or are washed out by rain. Smaller particles remain suspended in the atmosphere and exist in colossal numbers; a concentration of 5,000,000 per litre (5000 per cubic centimetre) is not uncommon, but this figure may be reduced by 90 per cent over a calm sea or

Green plants, having the unique capacity to convert solar energy into food by the process of photosynthesis, provide the food that sustains all other forms of life. The leaves of these primitive Hawaiian tree ferns compete to trap the maximum amount of sunlight.

years – in the same way as the geography of the Earth and life itself have evolved with time. However, as far as we are concerned air can be regarded as constant both in time and space, but with two important exceptions. Firstly the burning of fossil fuels such as oil, coal and gas by Man is slowly but inexorably increasing the proportion of carbon dioxide in the Earth's atmosphere. Secondly, the concentration of the gas ozone, mostly in the stratosphere.

All animals and plants respire by taking in oxygen and giving out carbon dioxide, and therefore these two gases are vital to all forms of life. In photosynthesis, green plants utilize the energy of sunlight, together with carbon dioxide from the atmosphere and water from the soil, and give out oxygen. In

15

COMPOSITION OF THE ATMOSPHERE

Air is composed of a mixture of nitrogen, oxygen and carbon dioxide with minute traces of other gases

GAS	SYMBOL	VOLUME PER CENT	ROLE
NITROGEN	N_2	78·08	Cycled through Man's activities and through the action of micro-organisms on animal waste.
OXYGEN	O_2	20·94	Cycled mainly through the breathing of animals and plants and through the action of photosynthesis.
CARBON DIOXIDE	CO_2	0·03	Cycled through respiration and photosynthesis in the opposite sense to oxygen. It is also a product of burning fossil fuels.
ARGON	Ar	0·093	Inert and unimportant.
NEON	Ne	0·0018	Inert and unimportant.
HELIUM	He	0·0005	Inert and unimportant.
KRYPTON	Kr	Trace	Inert and unimportant.
XENON	Xe	Trace	Inert and unimportant.
OZONE	O_3	0·00006	A product of oxygen molecules split into single atoms by the Sun's radiation and unaltered oxygen molecules.
HYDROGEN	H_2	0·00005	Unimportant.

Aerosols, the heterogeneous collection of microscopic particles (*below*) that are suspended in the atmosphere, are mostly composed of sea-salt, dust, organic matter and smoke and are derived from both man-made and natural sources.

increased tenfold over dry, windy deserts. These myriad minute, unseen particles perform a vital function in the formation of cloud – another surprising piece of the weather jigsaw.

Just as pure air is an abstraction so is dry air. All air contains water in the form of water vapour, and its unique properties are vital in influencing weather and climate. Water vapour, itself a gas, is present throughout the atmosphere, but, unlike most other constituents of air, the amount varies considerably with height, temperature and place. Approximately two-thirds of the Earth's surface is covered by water, and huge tracts of land – such as the tropical forests of Asia, Africa and South America – are almost permanently moist. Water vapour, continually being formed by evaporation from plants and water surfaces, is taken by turbulence into the upper troposphere. It has been calculated that over a period of a year up to 200 centimetres (79 inches) of water evaporates from the western Pacific and central Indian Oceans, and even over land surfaces in temperate latitudes, such as the United Kingdom, evaporation can reach 50 centimetres (20 inches) per year. As water vapour is largely transparent to short-wave solar radiation but absorbs some of the Earth's long-wave radiation, its variability in space and time is an important influence on the radiation balance between the Sun and Earth; this determines whether the temperature is rising or falling at a particular place and time.

Radiation from Sun and Earth

Everybody is familiar with life-giving sunshine or heat from the Sun, but it is not widely realized that the Earth and its atmosphere radiate an amount of heat equal to that received back into space. If this were not the case our planet would become increasingly hot and would soon become barren. Of course, some heat does reach the Earth's surface from its interior by way of hot springs and volcanoes, but this is negligible in terms of the total radiation balance. Solar heating at the Earth's surface is largely concentrated at low latitudes, but on the other hand outgoing radiation from the Earth is much more uniform; this imbalance is the underlying cause of the major systems of winds and ocean currents, which take excess heat from tropical regions towards the poles. The global system of winds is known as "the general circulation of the atmosphere". The correction of imbalance, at different latitudes, between incoming solar and outgoing terrestrial radiation is connected with heat.

SOLAR POWER

The Sun is an increasingly appealing source of safe, clean and abundant energy, but its power is difficult to use because of local and seasonal variations in weather, especially in the amount of cloud. Several methods of collecting and converting solar energy are being developed: arrays of mirrors can reflect the energy to a central collector or, to avoid the vagaries of the weather, solar energy collectors on satellites facing the Sun can continuously transmit the energy back to Earth.

High up in the French Pyrennees at Odeillo, an experimental solar power station (*right*) reflects sunlight from a group of 63 flat movable mirrors on to a huge parabolic reflector, 40 metres (130 feet) high and composed of 9500 mirrors. These concentrate the sunlight on to a "target" 18 metres (60 feet) away.

Heat is transferred from a hot object by conduction, convection or electromagnetic radiation. Conduction is direct transfer by touch and so it is relatively unimportant in meteorology. Convection is the process by which a liquid or gas heated from below mixes because of the increased buoyancy of the lower layers, thereby distributing the heat through a greater depth. This process is very important in oceans and the atmosphere. The transfer of heat by electromagnetic radiation – gamma, X-, ultraviolet, light and infra-red rays plus radio waves – is unique insofar as energy in this form can travel through a vacuum, including interplanetary space. Although all electromagnetic radiation travels at the same speed, at 299,400 kilometres (186,000 miles) per second, it ranges over a wide span of wavelengths from innocuous long radio waves to potentially harmful gamma rays.

Everything radiates and also absorbs or reflects incoming radiation, but the wavelength of the radiation varies depending on the temperature and the composition of the surface. An object radiating at the maximum rate for a particular temperature is called "a black body". This is a misleading term because, although dull dark colours usually absorb and lose heat most readily, this is not always the case; for example, the Sun is a "black body" radiator and so is fresh snow.

The basic building blocks of all matter are atoms and molecules. They are in a constant state of turmoil or vibration, and it is the level of this kinetic energy that is measured as temperature. Common scales of temperature use the freezing and boiling points of water under specified conditions as bench marks – for example, 0 degrees centigrade (32°F) and 100 degrees centigrade (212°F) respectively. A less commonly used scale takes the point where, in theory, all molecular motion ceases and there is no internal energy as its zero value. This happens at −273.16°C, which is the zero point of the Kelvin (K) scale, named after Lord Kelvin (1824–1927).

If temperature is measured in degrees Kelvin there are two simple but remarkable relationships between the temperature and the radiation output of any black body. The first is Stefan's Law, which states that if the temperature doubles, the intensity of outgoing radiation doubles four times (that is, it is multiplied by 16). The second is Wien's Law, which states that if the temperature doubles, the wavelength of maximum radiation emission is halved. These two simple scientific laws explain the tremendous difference between incoming solar radiation and outgoing radiation from the Earth. The difference is entirely due to the contrast between solar and terrestrial temperatures and forms the driving force of the circulation of the atmosphere. The difference in radiation is even more remarkable when it is realized that only about two thousand millionths (two thousand billionths, US) of the total solar radiation is intercepted by the Earth, and almost one-third of that is reflected back into space.

As the surface temperature of the Sun is more than 6000°C (10,832°F), much of its radiation lies in the narrow band of wavelengths visible to the human eye; of course, this is unlikely to be a coincidence. Similarly, when an iron bar is heated until it is red hot, its radiation is simply shifted, in line with the temperature relationship of Wien's Law, into the visible part of the spectrum. Below the visible band of solar radiation that reaches us as light, solar radiation also includes a small proportion of dangerous short waves in the X-ray and ultraviolet parts of the spectrum, but fortunately the photochemical reactions that occur in the ozone layer in the outer part of the atmosphere shield us from them. Outside the visible band, about 50 per cent of the Sun's radiation lies in the wide infra-red section, together with nearly all long-wave terrestrial radiation.

If the short-wave solar radiation reaching each point on Earth was immediately balanced by the same amount, in terms of energy, of long-wave outgoing radiation, then simple equilibrium would be maintained. Fortunately for all life on Earth that is not the case; in terms of Absolute temperature the application of Stefan's Law shows that the polar regions of the Earth lose heat at about two-thirds the rate of tropical regions when equal areas are considered. On the same basis the polar regions receive heat over the course of a year at less than one-third of the rate near the equator. Conversely there is an excess of incoming heat energy in low latitudes.

It might be thought that the greater distance solar radiation must travel to reach the poles would explain this, but in fact this accounts for less than one-ten thousandth part of the difference. Indeed, at the solstices, when one pole receives 24 hours of daylight, more

solar radiation reaches the outer atmosphere over the polar areas than over a similar area at the equator. The polar deficit is mainly due to the low angle of the Sun in the sky. In high latitudes, even in midsummer, the Sun is invariably near the horizon, and its rays only penetrate the atmosphere and strike the surface at a shallow angle. This not only means that the energy reaching a given area of the outer atmosphere at the poles is reduced by reflection and absorption over the additional depth of atmosphere it has to pass through, but also that it is spread over a larger area.

The different climatic zones of the Earth, such as desert, forest, prairie and ice-field, are all the result of the general atmospheric circulation, which is driven by this geographical imbalance between incoming and outgoing radiation. It might well be regarded as the breathing of the Earth, without which the planet would die.

The General Circulation
Day-to-day weather changes in middle latitudes are often so great that it appears inconceivable that there is any overall global pattern to weather. Nevertheless, over the major part of the Earth's surface there are large-scale wind circulations that are persistent and hence predictable.

The general circulation may be regarded as the world-wide system of winds by which the necessary transport of heat from tropical to polar latitudes is accomplished in order to maintain global temperatures as they are. Perhaps the first question to be answered is why hotter air in low latitudes does not simply flow towards the poles, to be directly replaced by colder air from high latitudes and so compensate for the imbalance in incoming solar energy? The general circulation would then comprise a single cell in each hemisphere with hot air rising in the tropics and flowing polewards, sinking in polar regions and returning towards the equator. This type of circulation is known as the Hadley cell, after the Englishman G. Hadley, who first explained it in 1735. The increased buoyancy of hot equatorial air heated from below would ensure a poleward flow in the upper atmo-

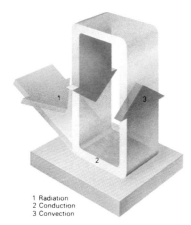

1 Radiation
2 Conduction
3 Convection

The Sun's heat reaches the Earth by radiation, conduction and convection. In radiation (1), solar energy travels through the vacuum of space, from the Sun to the Earth, in the form of electromagnetic waves and heats the Earth's surface. In conduction (2), air in the thin layer of the atmosphere in contact with the Earth is heated directly by the Earth's hot surface. In convection (3), the heated surface air expands, and being lighter than the air above, it rises to be replaced by cooler air.

Visible light is only a small proportion of the electromagnetic radiation that we receive from the Sun. Beyond the blue end of the visible spectrum are the progressively shorter wavelengths of the ultraviolet, X- and gamma-rays. Beyond the red end are the longer infra-red rays and radio waves.

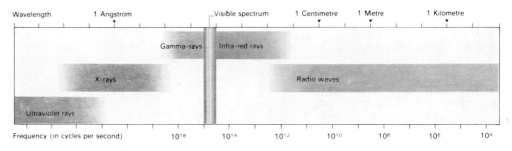

sphere, while the returning surface winds would be northerlies in the Northern Hemisphere and southerlies in the Southern Hemisphere (a wind direction is always given as that from which the wind is blowing.) But this simple picture does not exist because of the effect of the Earth's rotation and the distribution of oceans, continents, mountain ranges, deserts, forests, snow and ice, all of which interact with and influence large-scale atmospheric motion; thus major circulation patterns in the real atmosphere are much more complicated.

The Intertropical Convergence Zone (ITCZ) is a narrow zone, varying in width from a few kilometres to about a hundred kilometres near the equator. Surface winds blow towards the ITCZ from both north and south, so that in general it is an area of ascending air. Its position varies from day to day and week to week, but it usually lies within the summer hemisphere. It is associated with some of the heaviest rainfall areas in the world – the equatorial forests and jungles of South America and Asia. Its seasonal wanderings north and south of the equator bring monsoon rainfall to southern Asia and parts of Africa, where it draws in moisture-laden winds from the Indian Ocean.

On the other hand, although the ITCZ is made more active by mountain ranges in hot, continental interiors, where there is little moisture, the atmosphere in the vicinity of the ITCZ may be completely cloud free. Over the oceans the ITCZ is often much broader and loses its identity, giving rise to broad regions of little or no wind – known as the doldrums.

THE EARTH'S ALBEDO

The albedo of any surface is the proportion of incident solar radiation reflected by it and is an important factor in the heating of the atmosphere and its general circulation. The value of any albedo varies, depending on the nature and scattering properties of different terrestrial surfaces. The incident angle of solar radiation is also important: water has a low albedo of around 5 per cent when the Sun is high in the sky, but acts like a mirror and reflects up to 70 per cent of solar radiation when the Sun's rays strike obliquely. Satellites have enabled more accurate global measurements to be made and effects due to the amount of snow cover or any changes induced by Man's activities such as forest clearance on climate can now be determined. But, as the Earth's albedo is made up of many components that vary with time and place, it is still inadequately understood.

Forests (*below*) reflect about 7 per cent of the Sun's radiation and use most of the incoming heat in evaporation.

As fresh snow (*above*) reflects 90 per cent of the Sun's radiation, little heat is available to raise the temperature.

As sandy deserts (*below*) reflect only about 25 per cent of solar radiation the daily rise in temperature is considerable.

The theoretical Hadley type of circulation (A), where hot equatorial air rises and flows polewards to be replaced by cold air, does not exist because the combined effects of the Coriolis force and the conservation of angular momentum both prevent this simple north–south movement. However, what are known as Hadley cells do exist in the tropics and often near the poles (B). The Hadley cells at the tropics are responsible for the trade winds, the Intertropical Convergence Zone and the doldrums. Between these two Hadley cells lies a zone of settled weather in the subtropics where high pressure predominates, and in higher latitudes a zone of changeable weather. The polar front marks the boundary between air of polar and tropical origins.

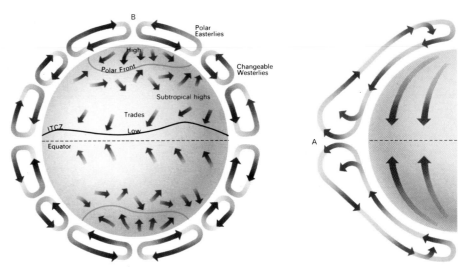

"Day after day, day after day,
We stuck, nor breath nor motion;
As idle as a painted ship
Upon a painted ocean" – the quote from the poem "The Ancient Mariner" by Samuel Taylor Coleridge vividly invokes the feeling of being becalmed in the Pacific Ocean by the doldrums.

Islands and east-facing coastlines situated in subtropical high-pressure belts (*right*) make perfect holiday resorts because the continuous sunshine is modified by gentle sea breezes which blow from the cool sea surface on to land where warm air is rising.

In both hemispheres there are zones of more or less steady surface winds blowing towards the equator, from the northeast or southeast. They extend roughly between 25°N and 25°S and were as well known to the skippers of sailing vessels hundreds of years ago as were the doldrums near the equator. They constitute the returning flow of the tropical Hadley cells.

Areas of high pressure, where air from the tropical Hadley cell descends, are centred between 20° and 30° latitude from the equator. For the most part these are regions of clear skies and light winds and almost all the major deserts of the world lie in these latitudes. Many of the islands and east-facing coastlines which lie within these regions benefit from occasional or regular showers created by sea breezes. These climates are therefore much more favourable than those of continental interiors and their locations provide some of the most popular holiday resorts in the world.

The temperate areas, sometimes called the zones of changeable westerlies, lie between the tropical and polar Hadley cells and are situated between 30° or 40° and 60° or 70° of latitude. Winds and weather in these regions are very variable, especially in the Northern Hemisphere, where the continents, and in particular the Rocky mountains, induce great oscillations in the weather pattern. The predominant winds in these latitudes are westerlies because of the rotation of the Earth. In this zone the transport of heat polewards is effected by pulses of warm air rather than by the steady, even flow of trade winds. As one might expect the movement of cold air towards the equator takes place in a similar way. The polar front marks the quasi-permanent boundary between air of cold polar origin and that warm tropical regions, and varies in intensity and position.

The polar Hadley cells, especially the one at the north pole, are neither as permanent nor as intense as those near the equator. Nevertheless, high pressure, descending air and quiet weather can persist in polar regions. At such times southeast or northeast winds – the polar easterlies – predominate on the cold side of the polar front.

The Earth's Rotation

The reluctance of the atmosphere to adopt the simple, single Hadley cell circulation in each hemisphere with direct northerly and southerly winds in favour of a much more complex circulation system is almost entirely due to the Earth's rotation. Although this rotation has an effect on all movement on Earth, we are not normally conscious of it; an archer, for example, would be surprised to know that his arrows veer off course to the right as the Earth rotates. To take this motion into account, the aim of long-range artillery, with trajectories of 32 kilometres (20 miles) or more, have been adjusted ever since the First World War. Every wind that blows is also affected by the Earth's rotation, except those near the equator.

The effect of the rotation of the Earth is termed the Coriolis effect, and takes the form of an apparent deflection of a freely moving object or fluid to the right in the Northern Hemisphere and to the left in the Southern Hemisphere. For convenience scientists have introduced the concept of a fictitious force to relate, mathematically, the size of the deflection to latitude.

The Coriolis effect explains the lack of northerly and southerly winds in the Hadley cells; the northeast and southeast trades and the polar easterlies all owe their westward deflection to the Earth's rotation, or the Coriolis effect.

The scientific maxim that energy is neither created nor destroyed is beautifully demonstrated by the behaviour of the atmosphere. The rotational energy of an object – the angular momentum – is dependent on the radius of the circle involved: the larger the radius the greater the energy. For example, when an ice-skater spins with his arms extended he spreads his weight over a much wider area than he would do if they were at his side. However, when he draws them in, his rate of spin increases so that his angular momentum can be maintained, as by the laws of physics it must be. In this way his faster rate of rotation compensates for the decrease in energy needed for each rotation. Similarly, because the radius of latitude circles decreases with distance towards the poles, the farther winds blow from the equator the greater their westerly component becomes. At low latitudes the change in radius of rotation with distance is small and so, therefore, is the increase in the westerly component. But from the subtropics polewards, this effect can lead to strong, high-level westerly winds or "jet-streams".

The variability in location of the jet-streams in middle latitudes is notorious and, since they are intimately related to the weather systems and are themselves important in aircraft operations, it is necessary to forecast their future positions. At times a jet-stream can encircle the whole globe at about 55° with little north-to-south deviation; this is termed the low index phase. It then begins to

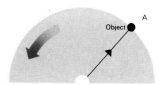

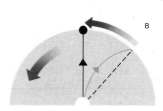

—— Observed path of ball

The Coriolis force can best be understood by imagining a man standing at the centre of a rotating disc facing an object at the rim (A). When he throws a ball at the object, the ball travels on in a straight line and misses the moving object. To the man who is rotating with the object, however, the ball has moved in a curved path away from the object (B). Similarly, because of the Earth's rotation, winds flowing from high to low pressure are always deflected.

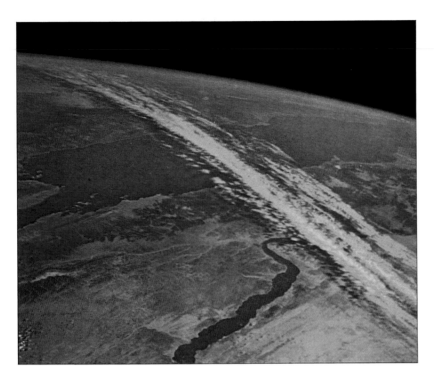

For several reasons, the amount of heat received and reradiated does not normally balance out on a daily basis; the season, the character of the land surface, degree of cloudiness and strength of the wind are each important factors, and a closer look at these influences gives some insight into day-by-day weather differences.

In temperate latitudes the temperature on calm, cloudless days would be expected to increase over 24 hours in summer and decrease in winter due to the excess or deficit of incoming solar radiation compared with heat radiated by the Earth. But other factors operate to counteract this day-by-day rise or fall in temperature.

The proportion of solar radiation reflected by a horizontal surface, known as its albedo, greatly influences daytime temperatures. Albedos vary greatly from no less than 80 per cent for fresh snow (when the Sun is low in the sky) to a mere 10 per cent for tropical forests and other dense vegetation in low latitudes. Deserts reflect about 30 per cent, whereas for fields and grassland the figure is around 20 per cent. When surfaces are wet from rain, less heat is reflected, but because some is used in evaporating the water, the temperature rise is less than it would otherwise be. Water surfaces are different again: their albedo may range from about 3 per cent when the Sun is low in the sky to over 50 per cent; a stormy sea reflects less solar radiation than calm water.

Over land, the differences between day and night temperatures can in exceptional circumstances approach 30°C (86°F) and often reach 20°C (68°F), whereas over deep sea surfaces this variation is almost always less than 1°C (1.8°F) and the daytime heating of the oceans is spread through a layer hundreds of metres deep by the mixing action of winds and waves. The oceans serve as vast reservoirs of heat, which is why the Southern Hemisphere, with about twice the area of ocean as the Northern Hemisphere, has warmer winters and cooler summers. With land surfaces, heating or cooling can only spread downwards very slowly by conduction – literally the transmission of energy from molecule to molecule – and therefore differences of temperature between winter and summer affect only the surface layer.

A thick layer of cloud can dramatically influence temperature changes at the Earth's surface. It acts as a blanket, reflecting up to 60 per cent of the radiation it receives and can absorb a further 20 per cent. Thus in cloudy conditions the difference between daytime and night-time temperatures is minimal. The

High-level winds or jet-streams are often marked in satellite pictures by bands of high cloud circling the globe (*above*). In the high index phase, A (*below*), they have little north–south movement and give changeable weather. The low index phase, B, produces lows and may develop further, C, until the waves disrupt into a stationary cellular pattern called "blocking", which can produce either good or bad weather.

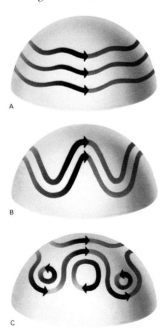

undulate, with waves moving west to east. If the waves continue to grow they become slow moving, developing into almost stationary, persistent and largely unconnected cells between which a weaker, fragmented jet-stream threads its way. In this situation, known as the high index phase, weather systems stagnate and the sector is said to be "blocked". Blocking is a feature of most severe winters and scorching summers in middle and high latitudes. These large-scale atmospheric motions operate over time scales of weeks or months, transporting heat polewards. However, locally the radiation balance changes hour by hour, causing temperature changes over the course of a day.

Solar radiation is reflected, absorbed and scattered by the atmosphere. Blue light, because its wavelength is at the shorter end of the visible spectrum, is scattered much more than red light, hence the Sun's disc appears as yellow orange and the sky appears blue. When the Sun is low in the sky, or even below the horizon, the scattered blue light is out of sight, leaving the sky with a reddish hue. This is marked when there is a haze layer, which is particularly efficient at scattering light in the red end of the spectrum. On average, about 47 per cent of solar radiation entering the outer atmosphere eventually reaches the ground. Of this 47 per cent, about one-third is radiated back into space via the troposphere; another third heats the lower atmosphere and the remainder is expended in evaporating water.

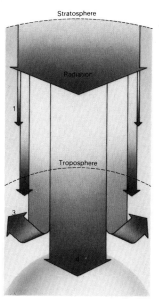

Of the energy from the Sun that is intercepted by the Earth, 3 per cent is absorbed by the stratosphere (1), 15 per cent is absorbed by the gas and dust in the troposphere (2) and 35 per cent is reflected back into the stratosphere (3), mostly by clouds. Less than half of the total radiation from the Sun, on average about 47 per cent (4), reaches the Earth.

The crescent and full shape of the Moon is outlined because, although the Sun is hidden below the horizon, its rays continue to illuminate layers of air above our heads. This picture, taken in Mombasa, Africa on 25 November 1976, also shows the planet Venus in the Scorpio region of the sky.

The temperature varies through every 24-hour period, largely as the daily balance between incoming radiation from the Sun and outgoing terrestrial radiation changes seasonally. In the idealized conditions shown below, the temperature shows a net rise over 24 hours in summer and a fall in winter. On a calm, cloudless, sunny day, for example, at a latitude of about 50°N, the temperature rises rapidly from soon after dawn, or a little later if dew has formed. The Earth's radiation grows until by mid-afternoon it equals incoming solar heating – the point of maximum temperatures. Thereafter, as the Sun sinks, the temperature falls and the rate of radiation drops progressively until a balance is reached again soon after sunrise – the time of minimum temperatures. In winter, as the Sun is always at a low angle, the temperature rise is typically confined to the middle of the day in these idealized conditions.

timing of cloud formation or dispersal is important because it strongly influences subsequent temperatures, but it remains a difficult forecasting problem.

Wind is associated with turbulence and mixing of air in the lowest layers. In this way heating or cooling occurring at the ground is spread through the lowest layers of the atmosphere. Wind also has the effect of smoothing out differences between day and night temperatures, and a strong wind may cause the diurnal temperature variation to be reduced by 90 per cent.

The convection currents set up in a pan of water, when it is heated from the base, are familiar to all. In the atmosphere the existence and depth of any convection current is almost entirely dependent on the variation of temperature with height. If the air aloft is warm enough to inhibit convection, it is said to be "stable" and only surface air temperatures rise. If, on the other hand, the air above the surface layer is cool, convection currents are set up when surface temperatures exceed a certain value. The atmosphere then becomes

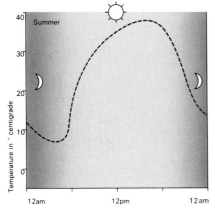
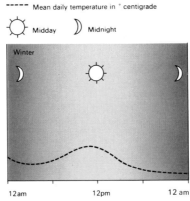

- - - - - Mean daily temperature in ° centigrade

☼ Midday ☽ Midnight

Satellite pictures provide regular photographs of the entire surface of the Earth, enabling the various weather systems – jet-streams, areas of fog and sea-ice – to be identified by characteristic shapes and shading. The picture (*right*) shows the development of two tropical hurricanes.

unstable and subsequent solar heating is spread throughout the depth of the instability, sometimes giving rise to clouds if the unstable layer is of sufficient depth.

The variety of factors such as season, surface characteristics, cloud, wind and stability that determine the temperature at any point gives some idea of the difficulties of forecasting. There are still further factors concerned with the movement and development of weather systems, but to consider these it is necessary to gain an insight into the most useful tool for both the amateur and professional meteorologist alike – the relationship between atmospheric pressure, wind, humidity and the weather.

Atmospheric Pressure

Antique barometers provide ample evidence that the existence of a connection between air pressure and weather has been widely known for well over 100 years. Atmospheric pressure is literally the weight of the atmosphere, but because air is fluid as opposed to solid, the pressure it exerts, roughly equivalent to 10,000 kilograms (10 tons) over each square metre (11 square feet) of the Earth, is exerted in all directions. Household barometers usually measure air pressure in terms of the length of a column of mercury – about 76 centimetres (29.9 inches) of mercury weighs the same as an equivalent column of air through the whole of the atmosphere.

A meteorologist uses units of pressure called millibars – 1000 millibars are equivalent to 76 centimetres (29.9 inches) of mercury – to study patterns of atmospheric pressure both at the Earth's surface and at higher levels in the troposphere, in order to determine the intensity and future movements of weather systems, and whether they are likely to intensify or relax. These pressure patterns are shown on charts as isobars – lines joining places of equal pressure. In the last 20 years or so computers have made it possible to predict atmospheric motion using complex mathematical models. The relationship between air pressure, wind, temperature and water vapour is fairly straightforward and forms a basis for an understanding of weather.

Winds, Temperature and Pressure

Continents tend to be cold in winter with high pressure and warm in summer with low pressure. If these relationships were universally true, they would be most valuable in forecasting weather. Unfortunately, although a volume of cold air is heavier than the same volume of warm air, the atmosphere is so deep that high pressure aloft does not necessarily correspond with cold air at the Earth's surface. In the same way low pressure can often accompany cold weather.

Normally air would be expected to flow from high pressure to low pressure until the difference is evened out – just as a punctured tyre will lose air until its pressure is equal to that outside. The atmosphere is subjected to other factors, such as differences in surface heating and cooling and, most importantly, the Coriolis force, which is due to the rotation of the Earth. Only within the tropics, where the effect of the Earth's rotation is almost entirely in the vertical plane, can simple airflow patterns from high to low pressure be found.

Heating near the equator warms the air through a considerable depth, causing it to expand and rise. As more air lies in the upper atmosphere in these areas, pressure is greater than normal at higher levels and consequently flows "outwards" towards the poles. This outflow reduces pressure near the surface so that at low levels the air motion is towards the equator or, more accurately, towards the ITCZ. In middle and high latitudes, a more complex interaction between airflow at high levels and the development of areas of low pressure – depressions – and areas of high pressure – anticyclones – takes place.

If a situation where the isobars are straight and parallel (with high pressure always on one side and low pressure always on the other) is considered, it would seem reasonable to expect air to flow across them until all pressure differences had been removed. But, because of the Earth's rotation, as soon as the air begins to flow it is deflected to the right in the Northern Hemisphere and to the left in the Southern Hemisphere. The combined effects of the atmospheric pressure gradient and the Coriolis force is an airflow called the geostrophic wind, parallel to the isobars. This remarkable effect, discovered in the middle of the nineteenth century, is summarized by Buys Ballot's Law – "If you stand with your back to the wind in the Northern Hemisphere, low pressure is on your left." Conversely in the Southern Hemisphere, low pressure is on your right.

Using charts showing atmospheric pressure at the Earth's surface, the relationship between the spacing of isobars, the pressure gradient and the geostrophic wind enables wind speeds to be deduced. However, as isobars are rarely straight, centrifugal forces deflect the wind slightly across the isobars towards low pressure at the centre of a depression or outwards from a high-pressure area. Both these effects are enhanced by

A mercury barometer (*below*) is basically a vertical tube, closed at the top, and standing in a reservoir of mercury open to the atmosphere. The tube is initially filled with mercury and inverted so that there is no air above the mercury. In operation, the column of mercury is balanced by the external air pressure alone and varies in length with changes of atmospheric pressure.

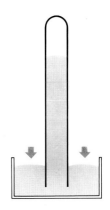

The aneroid barometer (*below*) consists of a closed container with flexible sides. Because the container is sealed, any change in pressure alters the size of the "can".

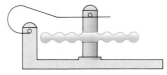

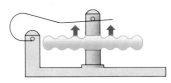

The changes are magnified by a system of levers, connected to a pointer on a dial or a digital read-out device.

25

friction, which acts to reduce the wind speed and hence the Coriolis force.

Winds in the upper atmosphere behave similarly to those at low levels and are subjected to similar forces except for friction, which is minimal at high levels. In looking at high-level winds, however, it is more convenient to consider the average temperature up to the level concerned rather than the pressure at that height. At high levels in the Northern Hemisphere winds blow with cold air on the left, and when the temperature gradient is greatest the winds are at their strongest. Jet-streams mark the boundaries between deep, cold air of polar origin and warmer air from low latitudes, and are important indicators of likely areas for low-pressure development.

It might be expected that a low-pressure area would be quickly filled by the inflow or convergence of air towards it, and that the outflow, or divergence, would collapse an area of high pressure. However, provided that the pressure pattern at upper levels is such that there is divergence above areas of low surface pressure and convergence above areas of high pressure, this does not happen. This factor emphasizes how the surface pressure field is intimately related to the positions and intensity of jet-streams and highs and lows in the upper atmosphere. Before the advent of computers the study of developments in the upper air provided the basis for forecasting the movement and development of surface pressure systems.

A most important feature of the three-dimensional circulation of air within low-pressure and high-pressure systems is that air must rise over lows and descend over anti-cyclones. The rates of ascent or descent are much smaller than the speed at which wind blows horizontally and are typically only one or two centimetres per second (less than one-tenth of a mile per hour). Nevertheless, this vertical motion leads directly to the formation of widespread cloud and rain in association with a low-pressure area, and often to clear skies in anticyclones. This connection between pressure and the formation of cloud and rain is dependent on a small but vital piece of the weather jigsaw – water.

Water, Ice and Water Vapour

In an age when fuel oil sometimes seems all-important, water, fundamental to all life, may often be regarded as uninteresting and unremarkable. Water is the only substance to occur naturally in the atmosphere as a solid, liquid and gas and the energy absorbed or released during its changes from one state to

The aberrant behaviour of water as it cools causes ice to float on the surface of the sea, where it acts as an insulating barrier, allowing diatoms (*above*) as well as numerous other life forms to exist (at depth) in polar seas. If ice did sink, the polar seas would be permanently frozen, with far-reaching effects on ocean life and world climate.

another not only plays an important part in the local weather but also in the general circulation of the atmosphere. Water has a further unique property: liquids generally decrease in volume as they are cooled, but below 3.98°C (39°F) water expands, and a given volume of water is therefore heaviest at this temperature. This anomalous behaviour, due to the peculiar molecular structure of water, is vital because it means that ice forms on top of water, not only allowing marine life to continue beneath it but, because it is a poor conductor of heat and does not mix with underlying water, reduces the rate of subsequent cooling.

The molecules in liquid water at 0°C (32°F) are in continuous random motion and therefore have more internal energy than ice at the same temperature. When water freezes this hidden or latent energy is liberated as heat in quantities sufficient to raise the temperature of the same amount of water as that being frozen by over 80°C (176°F). At the other end of the scale the change from

Humidity levels in the cloud forests of the foothills of Mt Mulu in Indonesia are among the highest in the world; the air here is hot and is capable of holding the large amounts of water vapour that are readily available from the vegetation.

liquid water to vapour also requires a large amount of heat – the latent heat of vaporization. In this case the latent heat is sufficient to raise the temperature of the same amount of water as that vaporizing by no less than 256°C (493°F). Both changes of state, solid to liquid and liquid to gas, and the reverse transformations, are important in the formation of clouds, rain and snow.

The least familiar phase – water vapour – is perhaps the most important in the atmosphere. Water vapour is a gas and is not to be confused with steam fog, commonly called simple steam, which is liquid water in the form of minute droplets. All air contains varying amounts of water vapour. As water vapour is lighter than air, moist air is lighter than dry air; thus the evaporation of water into air makes the air more buoyant, which is important in the formation of clouds. As water evaporates into air there comes a point at which the air is unable to hold any more; it is then said to be saturated. The water vapour content of air is termed its humidity,

and when expressed as a percentage of the maximum possible, at a particular pressure and temperature, it is referred to as its relative humidity. The relative humidity varies from 100 per cent in most cloud and fog to 10 per cent or less over deserts during the day.

As the temperature increases, air can hold more water vapour, and if the water content is unaltered, the humidity of the air therefore decreases. This is the principle of the clothes tumble-drier which uses heated air to evaporate more moisture. On the other hand decreasing the temperature of air reduces its moisture-holding capacity until eventually saturation point is reached. Continued cooling beyond this point leads to condensation of liquid water, either on to surfaces in the form of dew or as suspended droplets or cloud.

The dew point temperature is the temperature to which cooling needs to proceed for air to become saturated, and is used by meteorologists in forecasting cloud and fog. Humidity is measured most commonly by the wet and dry bulb hygrometer.

27

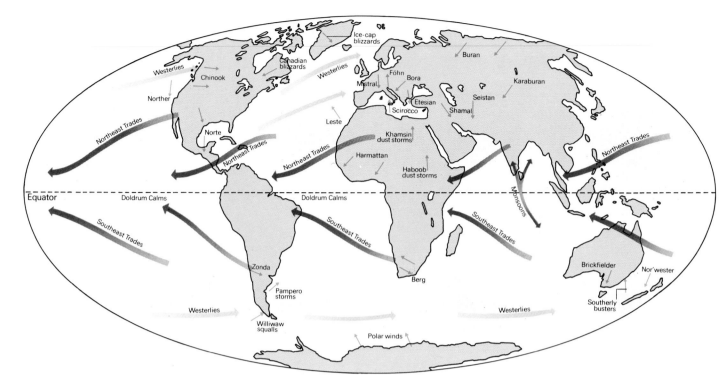

The world's winds are created by differences in the amount of solar radiation (and hence surface pressure), the distribution of oceans and continents and the rotation of the Earth. The major winds are the trade winds, which blow towards the tropics, and the westerlies, which predominate in high latitudes, except near the poles. In many areas there are local winds caused by heating differences due to land, sea or mountains.

Although dew forms readily as surface air cools below its dew point, small particles of dust or salt (condensation nuclei) are necessary for the condensation of droplets in free air. It is possible to cool very pure air to a state of super-saturation reaching 400 per cent and hence these nuclei play an important part in the genesis of cloud. All clouds form by condensation of water droplets in rising air. The governing factor is the close relationship between humidity, pressure and temperature. To understand what takes place in the interior of a cloud it is best to consider what happens when a bubble of moist air at ground level rises without mixing with its surroundings, and without heat transfer into or out of the bubble, that is adiabatically.

As the bubble of air slowly ascends, the atmospheric pressure around it gradually decreases – at approximately 6000 metres (20,000 feet) it will have decreased by half. Under reduced pressure the bubble expands, thus reducing its internal pressure and maintaining equilibrium. The energy needed for this expansion can only come from within the bubble itself in the form of heat, resulting in a fall in temperature. The rate of loss of temperature with height is approximately 1°C per 100 metres (1.8°F per 300 feet) and is called the dry adiabatic lapse rate (DALR). If the cooling bubble continues to ascend it eventually reaches saturation point. Above this level, further ascent and cooling is accompanied by condensation of water

droplets and the consequent release of latent heat, causing the temperature to subsequently fall much more slowly. This slower rate, the saturated adiabatic lapse rate (SALR) varies according to the actual quantity of water condensing in the air; at low levels the lapse rate is about half that for dry air, but high in the atmosphere, where little water vapour remains, the lapse rates for both dry and saturated air are almost equal.

Not only is moist air more buoyant than dry air, but once saturation is reached it becomes more buoyant still. This explains the association of cloud with slowly ascending air in low-pressure systems. On the other hand in an area of high pressure, where descending air is warmed by compression, clouds evaporate and clear skies prevail.

Most clouds extend to levels where the temperature is less than 0°C (32°F), at which water droplets might be expected to freeze. However, cloud droplets rarely freeze at this temperature and observations in the free atmosphere, together with laboratory experiments, have shown that, provided there are no external influences, clouds remain predominantly composed of water droplets down to temperatures of −20°C (−4°F). Below −40°C (−40°F), however, few if any of these "supercooled" droplets persist. The reason for this strange but important phenomenon is complex, but is largely explained by the latent heat of fusion released when a droplet freezes. Unless temperatures are very

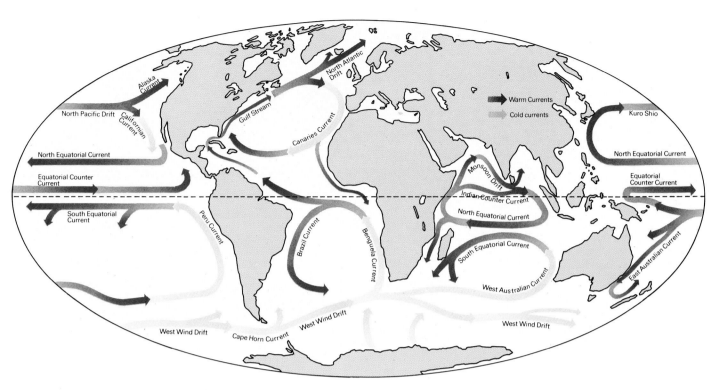

low, this heat is not easily absorbed by the immediate surroundings and inhibits freezing. However, impact with an ice crystal or dust particle in a supercooled cloud induces instantaneous freezing – hence the build-up of rime ice in freezing fog and aircraft icing.

Water droplets range from between 0·002 (0·00008 inch) and 0·03 millimetre (0·001 inch) in diameter in clouds but between 1 and 5 millimetres (0·04 and 0·2 inch) diameter in the case of rain. Drizzle is an intermediate stage composed of droplets mainly between 0·05 and 0·5 millimetre (0·002 and 0·02) in diameter. Cloud droplets are so small and weigh so little that they are unable to overcome air resistance and remain suspended in the atmosphere. The question that arises is how the smallest cloud droplets increase in volume, 100 million times, to become even a small raindrop? Further gradual condensation on to a cloud droplet may produce drizzle within 12 to 24 hours, but could not possibly lead to rain, which nevertheless is frequently observed to fall within one hour of the cloud's formation. Droplets in a cloud are rarely of uniform size and the larger ones can "sweep up" or coalesce with others as they fall; even so, the smallest droplets are unaffected and are swept aside without collision.

By far the most important process of raindrop growth is due to yet another strange property of water in air, known after its discoverers as the Bergeron-Findeison process: when no further water can evaporate

into air, the air is said to be saturated, which means that the rate at which water molecules leave the water surface (evaporate) is the same as the rate at which they return (condense). Thus there is a balance or equilibrium. However, if ice is present at the same temperature in the saturated vapour, fewer molecules evaporate from the ice surface than from the water droplets, but the same number still condense. In other words the vapour is supersaturated with respect to ice. This situation exists inside a refrigerator and is the

Ocean currents circulate in the same general direction as the winds. There are two large clockwise gyres in the Northern Hemisphere – in the North Atlantic and North Pacific – and three anticlockwise gyres in the Southern Hemisphere oceans.

On contact, supercooled water droplets freeze instantaneously to form a deposit of rime.

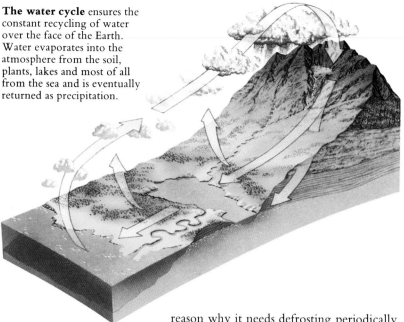

The water cycle ensures the constant recycling of water over the face of the Earth. Water evaporates into the atmosphere from the soil, plants, lakes and most of all from the sea and is eventually returned as precipitation.

An approaching warm front is typically heralded by the altocumulus clouds in the foreground (*centre right*) and these merge into a thin layer of altostratus.

reason why it needs defrosting periodically. In a cloud, where ice crystals and water droplets co-exist, as saturation point is approached with respect to water the ice crystals grow, which tends to reduce the humidity, leading to continual evaporation from the water droplets. Eventually the large ice crystals start to fall, colliding with others to form snowflakes and at warmer lower levels melt to become rain.

This theory forms the basis of most rain-making experiments in which the growth of large ice crystals, eventually to become rain-drops, is stimulated by introducing dry ice or similar crystals into clouds of supercooled water droplets. Having pieced together this small, but surprisingly complex, piece of the weather jigsaw it is possible to place a much larger piece, the water cycle.

The Water Cycle

Of the total moisture in the atmosphere, about 84 per cent evaporates from the oceans; the remainder is derived from moist land surfaces and transpiration from vegetation. However, only 75 per cent of the total falls on the oceans – much less water than actually evaporates, the balance being preserved by rivers returning water to the sea.

All together oceans contain approximately 97 per cent of the water on the globe; about three-quarters of the rest is locked up in ice-sheets and glaciers and the remainder is stored mainly in the soil and underground reservoirs. The atmosphere contains only about one part in ten thousand of all global water. Although it accounts for such a small proportion, atmospheric moisture is re-cycled, that is it is rained out and replaced on

average every ten days. At this rate the total water content of the oceans would take over one million years to pass through the atmosphere. The accumulation of ice near the poles due to excess precipitation over evaporation in high latitudes is counter-balanced by the spreading of ice-sheets, the formation of glaciers and the breaking away and the eventual melting of icebergs. In temperate or tropical coastal areas the complete hydrological cycle can be as short as one hour, but in the icy Arctic wastes it can take tens of thousands of years.

Weather Systems

Ever since the earliest charts of sea-level pressure were constructed it was apparent that particular patterns in pressure fields frequently recurred in association with similar types of weather, hence the popularity and usefulness of the domestic barometer. It was not until comparatively recently, however, that the physical reasons for these associations were discovered.

Because near the Earth's surface winds blow out from an anticyclone, a high-pressure area, air lying at high level over the anticyclone centre slowly subsides to take its place. Having some insight into humidity and cloud formation, this subsidence can be seen to be associated with dissolving cloud and clear skies. Anticyclones are therefore usually large areas of fine weather, typically

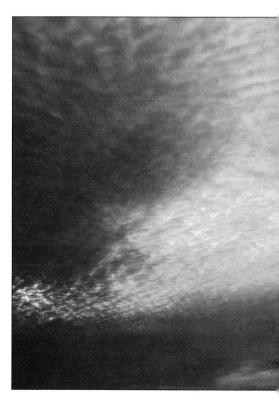

1600 kilometres (1000 miles) across. In summer, surface temperatures are often at their highest and in winter at their lowest during anticyclonic conditions. Winter highs form over cold continents, where the air is relatively dense. If the air is dry, clear skies lead to further cooling because daytime solar heating cannot compensate for the outgoing radiation. If the surface air is moist, as is often the case in temperate coastal regions, then fog is likely, sometimes persisting for several days. Usually the warming of air in an anticyclone, due to subsidence, does not extend to the surface and a situation is reached where temperatures a few thousand metres up are higher than those at ground level. In extreme cases the difference can exceed 20°C (68°F). This temperature inversion acts as a lid, preventing dust and smoke from dispersing upwards and is responsible for hazy conditions and pollution in cities.

Two or three times in most years in the Northern Hemisphere the eastward progression of weather systems is halted by an intense high-latitude anticyclone which displaces low-pressure areas well to the south of their normal path. These so-called "blocking anticyclones" lead to extremes of weather, especially in winter, when cold north and northeast winds bring Arctic air to western and southern Europe and the southern USA.

The most important weather system in temperate latitudes as far as rainfall is concerned is the warm sector depression, which is formed in conjunction with the belt of strong upper winds, known as the polar front, that surrounds the globe, marking the zone of maximum north-to-south temperature gradient. Sometimes there are two of these zones, in which case the one nearer the pole is termed the arctic front. These fronts vary in width, position and intensity, but when waves form on them they can develop into vigorous low-pressure systems, bringing wet and windy weather to large areas.

While the role of the low-pressure system, in the context of the large-scale circulation of the atmosphere, is to transport heat polewards, it produces prolonged and quite heavy rain and gale-force winds over a broad swathe of countryside, typically some 4800 kilometres (3000 miles) in length and 480 kilometres (300 miles) in breadth as it travels eastwards during its life of five or six days.

Weather Fronts

Although rather like snowflakes or finger prints, no two fronts are identical, they do nevertheless share some broad characteristics. The most important feature is that warm air, being less dense, tends to override the colder air at both the warm and cold front. Each frontal surface therefore slopes quite gradually. Beyond the warm front, cloud can extend more than 400 kilometres (240 miles) ahead of the point where no cold air remains

A frontal depression is initiated by a zone of strong temperature gradients with westerly winds (A). Any perturbation (B) leads to a low-pressure zone, and air flowing into this low is deflected (C) and becomes intensified (D), forming fronts.

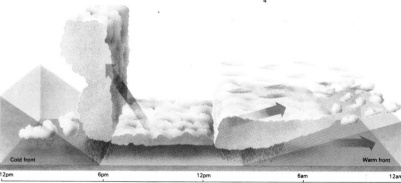

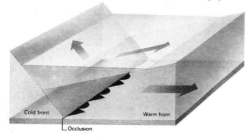

Frontal surfaces (*below*) slope gently because cold air is heavier than warm air. Ahead of a warm front (A), warm air overrides cold air, whereas in (B) cold air lies behind the cold front. If warm air is lifted, the front is occluded (C).

In a warm front (*above*), warm air overrides the colder air ahead of it, forming cloud which often produces steady and prolonged rain ahead of the surface warm air. In the cold front, cold air undercuts and lifts warm air ahead of the front, creating cloud and a short spell of heavy rain. It is usually followed by much brighter, showery weather. An occluded front often has the characteristics of a warm front, but is usually followed by brighter weather.

31

The Mistral is a dry, cold northwesterly or northerly wind that funnels violently down the Rhône Valley in France (*right, centre*).

Monsoons develop most dramatically in India and Southeast Asia, where intense heating of the land in summer causes low pressure, bringing warm, moist air from tropical oceans across the heated continents. In turn, this air rises due to mountain barriers and further heating, giving widespread torrential rain.

near the ground, and on an active cold front a band of thick cloud, often 150 kilometres (90 miles) wide, is present. The increase of cloud and winds, and the onset of rain ahead of a warm front, are gradual, typically taking place over a period of 12 hours or so.

Cold fronts can be dramatic, sometimes being accompanied by squalls, thunderstorms and even tornadoes in some parts of the world. Behind the cold front, the weather can either be showery if the low pressure remains over the area concerned or fine if a ridge of high pressure follows to take its place. The zone of weather associated with an occluded warm sector, where the warm air has been entirely lifted off the Earth's surface, is narrower and less intense than in the early stages of a low-pressure system. Although the warm sector depression and its associated fronts are the major rain-producing features of temperate latitudes, there are other types of low-pressure systems which are also important.

Intense heating over continents in summer can lead to quite large, quasi-permanent areas of low pressure – "heat-lows" – often associated with a complete absence of bad weather. Although the air within the heat-low is ascending, the circulation is usually weak and the air dry, so that no cloud forms. Forecasters are only too well aware of the critical and narrow threshold between weather situations giving hot, dry weather and those where widespread thunderstorms develop, either due to the injection of moist, buoyant air at low levels or of colder air at high levels. The junior relation of the heat-low is the sea breeze – a local effect induced by the difference in heating over adjacent areas of land and sea; the senior relation is the monsoon, found over large areas of Asia, where convergence due to continental heating and mountains results in copious rainfall.

The winter equivalent of the heat low, the "polar low", is peculiar to countries bordering oceans in middle or high latitudes, particularly where warm sea currents lie adjacent to land masses. In a cold Arctic airstream, heated strongly from below by a relatively warm sea, strong upward motion is induced, resulting in a small area of low pressure, typically some 320 kilometres (200 miles) across. Polar lows can result in heavy snowfall and are notoriously difficult to predict, though in recent years satellites have enabled them to be detected earlier than was possible from the rather sparse network of surface observations that are available.

When a stream of water flows round or over an obstacle, an eddy or small whirlpool

forms downstream of the obstruction. A similar situation occurs in the atmosphere, where a jet-stream or prevailing wind flowing through a substantial depth of the atmosphere crosses a mountain. The disruption of the air stream generates a low-pressure area which is usually static, a lee low or orographic low found downwind of mountains. Downslope winds associated with lee lows, in the lee of mountains, are often hot and dry due to adiabatic warming and therefore produce warm, cloud-free weather. This phenomenon, the Föhn effect, accounts for warm winds such as the Chinook winds of the eastern Rockies and the Mistral of the Rhône Valley, typical of mountain areas.

Often on weather charts there is an area lying between two highs and two lows in which there are few isobars and therefore little wind. This slack area, known as a "col", is seldom persistent and, depending on the surface humidity and winds higher in the atmosphere, can produce foggy weather in

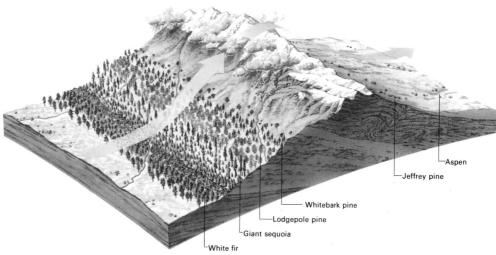

White fir
Giant sequoia
Lodgepole pine
Whitebark pine
Jeffrey pine
Aspen

AIR MASSES

There are two main types of air mass – polar and tropical – and they are classified according to their place of origin and their temperature. As the air moves away from its source region, it travels over sea or over land and becomes modified with maritime or continental characteristics. Climatologists have developed the following nomenclature for identification.

cP (continental polar) is cold, stable and dry in winter, whereas in summer it is cool and dry but not very stable.

mP (maritime polar) is found over high-latitude oceans and tends to be moist and unstable.

cT (tropical continental) originates over tropical land masses and so becomes hot, dry and unstable.

mT (maritime tropical) is the rain-bearing air from tropical oceans and tends to be warm, moist and fairly unstable.

The windward side of the mountains in the Sierra Nevada (*above*) supports a rich variety of trees that form bands according to the amount of rain they receive. As warm, moist air is forced to rise over the mountain barrier, water vapour condenses into clouds and rain or snow falls in quantity on the mountain peak. As the air descends on the leeward side of the range, its temperature rises and the cloud disperses or evaporates, leaving a dry zone.

winter and thundery conditions in summer. Always when deducing or forecasting weather from charts it is helpful to have some knowledge of the broad characteristics of the air concerned. This knowledge can be gained by studying the air's area of origin, and how it is likely to have been modified during its journey – air mass analysis.

There are wide areas of the globe where surface conditions are largely homogenous, for example the oceans, Arctic snowfields and the interiors of some continents. If the circulation in the lower atmosphere is slack over those regions, the air mass will be modified gradually by the underlying surface until it has almost uniform characteristics.

An air mass by definition covers a wide area, typically 1,000,000 square kilometres (386,000 square miles) and comprises quasi-homogenous air; its area of origin is the source region. The air has to be slow moving in this region for many days so that it can attain uniform characteristics, hence the large, almost stationary, subtropical belts of high pressure, polar highs and winter continental anticyclones are favourable climatic zones for air masses to form.

Air masses are classified mainly according to the geography of the surrounding area, continent or ocean, and the latitude. It is, however, also necessary to take the season into account, because the contrast between the interior of a large continent in winter and summer is so great that, depending on the time of year, the air mass can be considered to be either polar or tropical.

The weather jigsaw is not complete, and perhaps never will be, despite the great advances in understanding its complexities. But at least it has been possible to assemble the main outline: the seasonal cycle, the general atmospheric circulation, effects of rotation, weather systems and not least the vital and fascinating properties of water, which has such an important part to play – be it beneficial or otherwise – in the lives of us all.

33

NATURAL PHENOMENA

"The rising or settin' orb of day,
The clouds that flit, or slowly float away,
Nature in all the various shapes she wears,
Frowning in storms, or breathing gentle airs,
The snowy robe her wintry state assumes,
Her summer heats, her fruits, and her perfumes . . ."
William Cowper – *Retirement*

The weather, at least in temperate climes, is endowed with characteristics which make it possible for the poet to describe it in terms of human behaviour (and vice versa, for a person might commonly be said to have a sunny temperament). Cowper's Nature wears robes and frowns, breathes gentle airs and is perfumed. There are times when changes in the weather seem formless and arbitrary – sunshine is obscured in an instant, and a cold flurry of wind disturbs an otherwise calm day – but whatever images are used, the changes are meteorological phenomena, the tangible signs of great forces at work and the active clues to an understanding of meteorology.

Platelets of frost, 100 times their natural size, were formed by cool, dense air flowing down into a hollow.

The elements

The unmistakable signatures of wind and water, heat and cold are indelibly stamped as a permanent record on the Earth's rocks; so clearly in fact that evidence of not only past climatic regimes but even individual weather phenomena can be read with ease.

The origins of the water on the Earth's surface are by no means fully understood, but the most widely accepted theories suggest that a large proportion of the water now present in the oceans, in the atmosphere and as lake, river and ground water was released as vapour from the newly forming rocks of the primitive Earth more than 4000 million (or 4 billion in the US) years ago. At about that time the Earth was approaching a temperature at which water could exist in the liquid state and so pools would have formed and coalesced into lakes and lakes would have joined up to form the first oceans.

The primitive atmosphere developing over the still–hot surface of the Earth was still unstable and the first cycles of evaporation, condensation, precipitation and run-off would almost certainly have taken place in a near-constant barrage of thunderstorms. Fuelled by the heat and gaseous outpourings from centres of volcanic activity, the churning clouds of gas and vapour must have lashed the surface with torrential downpours of rain and mud in storms of a violence that we can only guess at.

No sooner was water available on the surface of the Earth than it began the fundamental processes of weathering, transportation and deposition which, through the agencies of wind and waves, ice and running water, chemical reactions and temperature extremes are continually sculpting and remodelling the Earth's surface.

From the heat and moisture of that primitive Earth there gradually developed a whole range of climatic regimes, encircling the Earth in a series of bands lying roughly parallel to the equator. The zones themselves have waxed and waned during the course of time and the landmasses too have shifted over the surface of the globe, but at any given time, and at any given place, events have

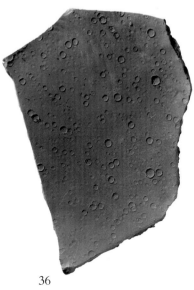

Ancient imprints of plant leaves, such as these 75-million-year-old ferns (*above*) found within the Arctic Circle on Alexander Island, indicate that warm, humid weather prevailed here in the past.

The oceans (*right*), formed in primeval times from centuries of torrential rain and which today interact with the atmosphere to give rise to clouds, snow and rain, also modify our weather.

Modern imprints of rain in mud (*left*) will in time become relics fossilized in mudstone and form clues of the rains that once occurred in this region.

left their imprint in the rocks: polygonal patterns of deep cracks, later filled with sand, mark the sun-baked bed of a parched and dried-up lake bed. Raindrops spattering a soft, muddy surface leave their unmistakable pattern of tiny impact craters – sometimes preserved in such detail that it is possible to determine the direction of the wind that blew a violent squall across the mud-flats of some ancient river estuary. Glacier scour marks, shoreline ripples, fossilized coral reefs, lagoons and deltas, tell-tale chemicals and animal and plant remains all combine to record a history of constant environmental change.

Huge thicknesses of cross-bedded sandstones with wind-polished grains tell of harsh desert conditions in areas that perhaps a few tens of millions of years earlier had been warm and mild, clothed in dense coastal swamp forest in which were laid down layers of shale and mudstone, sandstone and clay and vast accumulations of organic debris that would eventually become coalfields that are so vital to some societies today.

So detailed is the record that for more recent times it is possible to reconstruct the landscapes over which our ancestors roamed and hunted. Nearly one million years ago, the flora and climate of the Northern Hemisphere was probably not vastly different from that of today, though the average temperature was probably a little higher and the richness and variety of plant life a little greater. But all was to change as the great ice-sheets poured down from the north, obliterating the landscape and bringing arctic conditions to much of Europe and North America. Four times the ice advanced and retreated and between each advance the land was reclothed and repopulated. Throughout the third interglacial period, Neanderthal Man spread widely across a Europe rather warmer than that we know today. Leaves and other plant remains indicate the presence of trees that are no longer found anywhere in the Alpine region but which are known from warmer climes.

Thus a remarkably detailed record shows the plant assemblage changing in response to a changing climate: at first only birch trees could tolerate the subarctic climate, but as conditions became steadily milder, so oak, elm, pine and hazel give evidence of a warm, dry phase; later, lime and alder indicate the climate going through a warm oceanic phase; while later still, a beech, hornbeam and alder assemblage suggests a cool maritime climate much like that we experience now.

Against this background of relatively rapid climatic change, with weather patterns also varying dramatically over quite small areas, Man spread and multiplied, leaving behind the nomadic life of the hunter-gatherer and progressing, over a few tens of thousands of years, into the life of a settled agriculturalist.

His choice of settlement sites and routeways was initially subject to a high level of environmental control – his need for shelter, for a reliable water supply, for woodland to provide fuel, plant foods and wild animals to supplement his diet, and open ground, either natural or artificially cleared, on which to grow crops. Already Man was well on the way to dominating his environment. Already he was taking the first steps on the road that eventually would lead him to tackling the problems of creating rain, of diverting the destructive violence of hurricanes and of harnessing the power of the atmosphere and the Sun itself.

But although in recent decades great strides have been made to control the natural elements that create the weather, even with the use of the newest technologies we still have no control over the vagaries of our weather: even today the most sophisticated means of dealing with the peril of an avalanche is to avoid the vicinity altogether and droughts and floods bring disaster to millions of people every year. Man is basically still an animal that is utterly dependent on green plants to trap energy from the Sun, on natural processes that cycle nutrients and on the raging elements of the weather that we cannot hope to control as they are governed by forces infinitely more powerful than anything he possesses.

Climate and Man

Man was originally designed for a tropical environment, for a warm, moist regime with no extremes of heat or cold and no wild fluctuations. His metabolism is programmed to keep his body temperature at 36–37°C (97–99°F), and although extreme heat or cold can be tolerated for varying short periods, according to the build and fitness of the individual, recovery from situations in which the deep "core" temperature has fallen to 26·5°C (80°F) or risen above 43°C (110°F), is virtually impossible.

The human body reacts automatically to environmental temperature changes, adopting a number of measures to keep the body well within its safe limits. When the external temperature drops, the body's metabolic rate is increased, either by adding fuel – eating – or exercising – clapping the hands, stamping the feet; if even more heat needs to be generated, the muscles tense involuntarily and shivering occurs. At lower temperatures the surface blood vessels constrict, reducing heat loss from the body surface and conserving it for the vital organs. Herein lies a danger; for while this vasoconstriction protects the body, it does so at a risk to the extremities, which, having their sensitivity and their warming blood supply reduced, are even more at risk from frostbite. If low temperature is combined with a wind, the cooling effect on the body is vastly increased.

Man is better equipped to tolerate high temperatures than cold temperatures. An estimate of two million sweat glands bring moisture to the body surface, where it evaporates into the atmosphere, effectively cooling the skin surface. This mechanism can remove water at a rate of 2 litres (3·5 pints) per hour and operates safely as long as the body's fluid is replaced. Unfortunately, sweating has been socially outlawed in many Western countries.

Because adaptation is so abundantly demonstrated throughout the animal kingdom it is tempting to look for similar responses in Man. But physical adaptations are the result of extremely slow processes. In evolutionary terms Man is very recent. What set him apart early on in his development was the power of his brain: and here lies the key to his success. Instead of the blunt instrument of a single specific adaptation to one type of environment, Man has infinite adaptability through his behavioural and cultural responses.

He makes the environment fit his own use – whether it is desert or polar wilderness, Himalayan valley or Pacific island. And he does it by adapting the type and amount of the clothing he wears; by varying the design of his dwelling places and the materials of which they are built; by varying the amount and type of food he eats, according to his body's needs, and by adapting his patterns of activity in accordance with prevailing environmental conditions. The further he goes from the benign tropical regime for which he was built, the more he must use his skill, ingenuity and natural perseverance in order to survive the rigours of the environment.

Furthermore, his ability to control the environment now extends far beyond his own body, far beyond his social group. Absolute control is still only a possibility in the distant future, but even now Man can significantly alter local climatic conditions through his drainage schemes, forest clearances, land reclamation programmes and vast irrigation projects; unfortunately such schemes sometimes overreach Man's ability to appreciate their full long-term impact.

EXISTING IN EXTREMES
Through a combination of technological innovations and physiological development, Man has learned to survive in the most extreme climatic conditions on Earth – even those as hostile and unnatural as those beneath the sea.

Millions of sweat glands present in skin allow moisture to evaporate from the body; the heat energy used in the process of evaporation cools the body and so enables people to survive in high temperatures. In fact, this mechanism equips people to withstand hot climates more easily than cold climates. Studies in human physiology show that the colour of people's skin is not necessarily an adaptive response to the world's variety of environments.

The igloo is an architectural marvel in terms of keeping warm; its hemispherical shape presents the smallest possible surface in relation to volume to the environment and it can easily be heated from the centre. The heat causes a vapour-proof glaze to form on the snow-packed walls, which prevents heat-loss by evaporation. Animal skins worn by eskimos provide extremely good protection against the cold and wind because wind does not penetrate the skin and fur is a perfect insulator.

The thatch used in the parasol-type housing of the humid tropics acts as protection against severe sunlight and rain, while at the same time providing ventilation and shade.

Unexpected snow causes chaos in many areas, particularly if the snow melts during the day and refreezes during the night.

Clay polygons were all that were left of the Chew Valley reservoir during the drought of 1976 – the most severe in Britain since rainfall records began. Following the driest 5-year period since the 1850s, the National Water Council maintained that it would take at least two wet winters separated by a normal summer to restore natural water resources to normal.

The changing weather

The effects of climate on Man can be seen in virtually every facet of life. Comfort and efficiency go hand in hand. It has now been established that factory and office workers are more productive, more contented, suffer fewer illnesses and make far fewer costly and sometimes dangerous mistakes if their places of work have temperature and humidity control systems and that accident and error ratings soar in environments in which uncontrolled temperatures rise to levels of physical discomfort.

Weather itself does not cause disease, but many health conditions can be aggravated by particular weather conditions. Prolonged summer heatwaves with very little air movement can bring misery to the millions who suffer from the many forms of pollen allergy commonly grouped together as "hay fever", while excessive heat itself can cause distress to those suffering from respiratory and heart disorders. A particular summer hazard for the residents of some of the world's greatest cities can be the dangerous accumulation of pollutants in the lower atmosphere – trapped by temperature inversion or simply by the absence of any cleansing air circulation at street level. Though steps are being taken in many countries to reduce levels of atmospheric contamination, motor-vehicle exhaust alone can, in hot, still weather, turn the air of a city street into a foul-smelling blue-grey haze.

People who live in tropical countries expect heat all the time, whereas people in continental regions only expect it in summer and so its effects can be coped with. But when the heat is more intense than usual, or lasts far longer than usual, or when a rare hot spell affects a region that is normally cool, the troublesome effects of heat occur. Unexpected hot spells can occur in summer if air has flowed from the tropics or across a hot continent. The heat is intensified if there is high pressure because this brings clear skies, allowing the maximum amount of sunshine penetration. Dry ground also creates an additional heating effect because less heat is taken up for evaporation, leaving more to boost the air temperature.

Freak heatwaves occasionally hit mainland Europe. In 1976 a large anticyclone built up and pulled a stream of hot, dry air into northern Europe from southern Europe; at the same time the normal jet-stream that brings cool air to the region had swung to the north. This situation produced an unusually hot spell: temperatures soared to 32°C (90°F) on 15 successive days and in the accompanying drought crops were ruined and many livestock were lost. A similar occurrence in eastern Europe in 1972 pushed the temperature in Moscow to 36°C (97°F) and even Archangel, near the Arctic Circle, experienced 32°C (90°F). In the central USSR the heatwave set off a series of disastrous forest and peat fires that were uncontrollable for several weeks.

Unexpected cool spells can also have serious consequences, though they are relative to what people are accustomed to and not necessarily due solely to the severity of the temperature drop. To the peoples of Europe, North America and other temperate lands, 15°C (59°F) is a perfectly normal temperature and no hazard or

distress arises until temperatures drop to near freezing, whereas in India hundreds have died of cold in an unexpected cool spell of barely less than 15°C (59°F) – mainly due to their weakness through poor diet, their scanty clothing and the fact that almost all the victims were living out of doors.

The chilly conditions of the temperate winter may create winter sports for the young, but the cold and damp can also bring misery to those with muscular and bronchial complaints. The viruses of colds and other infectious diseases are carried far and wide on exhaled moisture droplets during the cool, damp, overcast weather of winter, while in summer the droplets evaporate quickly, leaving their "passengers" without a vehicle and often also exposed to the killing rays of the Sun.

To the elderly, especially to those living alone and with limited means, there is the added danger of hypothermia – a dangerous condition in which, through inadequate diet and inadequate heating of the home, the core temperature

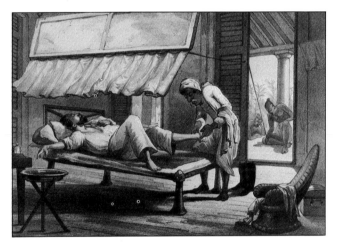

British colonials found the weather in India enervating partly because their diet and clothing were inappropriate. Similarly, Indians are ill-adapted to cool spells.

of the body falls to a fatal level.

With cold, as with heat, the crucial factor is not the absolute temperature but its duration, and the extent to which it departs from the normal range for the area. In Britain, a temperature of −5°C (23°F) with snow and ice may cause chaos: the same conditions would not raise a comment in Canada or Sweden. In 1963, the atmospheric circulation over western Europe became stuck in an abnormal pattern that brought streams of exceptionally cold air across the region. During the severe winter of 1962–63 roads were blocked by snow, livestock perished and vehicle fuel froze.

Sudden changes in temperature are often associated with frontal systems and nowhere is this more common than in the Great Plains region of North America, where weather conditions are largely governed by the interaction of contrasting air masses: hot, moist air from the Mexican Gulf and cold, dry air from Arctic Canada.

Sunlight

Although the intensity of the Sun is felt more strongly near the equator than in polar regions, all places on Earth receive the same total amount of daylight over a year; places near the equator receive 12 hours of sunlight every day all the year round, and in the Arctic and Antarctic, periods of weeks without sunlight in winter are balanced by equal periods of continuous daylight in summer.

Light is only part of the radiation that is received from the Sun. The rest of the spectrum of radiation is invisible and extends to both longer and shorter wavelengths, which include radio waves, infra-red, ultraviolet, X-rays and gamma rays. The longer-wave radiation that affects us is known as infra-red, which is felt as heat, and among the shorter waves that penetrate the Earth's atmosphere are the ultraviolet rays, that produce sunburn. Much of the radiation given out by the Sun never reaches the ground and some is reflected directly back into space by the atmosphere.

The most important loss of radiation is due to reflection from clouds – they reflect about 60 per cent of the light shining on them. This is quite apparent, since cloudy days are much darker than sunny days. Besides being reflected, radiation is scattered and absorbed by dust particles in the Earth's atmosphere. Dust is common in the lower atmosphere, particularly in the neighbourhood of desert areas, which are subject to sandstorms, and areas downwind of industrial regions. This dust and smoke scatters and absorbs some radiation, reducing the strength of direct sunlight. Dust and smoke also give rise to crepuscular rays, the "sunbeams" seen when the Sun shines through gaps in cloud formations; a similar effect can be seen in a room when the Sun shines through a window. The upper atmosphere is normally free of dust, but occasionally a volcanic eruption creates a great cloud of dust that lingers in the upper layers of the atmosphere, scattering and reflecting sunlight; thus it reduces the amount reaching the Earth.

During an eclipse of the Sun, which occurs when the Moon passes between the Sun and the Earth, the source of radiation is cut off entirely. The effects of a total eclipse, which lasts a few minutes over a band of not more than 100 kilometres (62 miles) wide, are strange. Suddenly it becomes dark enough to see the stars and the temperature drops dramatically. Animals respond as though it is night-time and prepare for sleep. A "partial eclipse" is observed outside this small area and the effect of this is not as impressive. If clouds are present, the reduction of light is generally not so acute; if the sky is clear, the scenery has an unusual ghostly look.

Sunlight is composed of many colours. Although this is not usually apparent, one may see it when looking at reflected sunlight in familiar situations. Grass appears green because it reflects green light but uses and absorbs the other colours that compose sunlight. As light passes through a sheet of glass it is bent and the colours are separated, but recombine when they emerge. However, if light is passed through a prism, the rays are bent twice and the colours remain separated when they emerge, forming a spectrum in which the individual colours in sunlight can easily be identified.

Particles in the atmosphere scatter the shorter wavelengths of visible light at the blue end of the spectrum more than the other colours, which results in direct sunlight appearing yellow. The blue light is not lost, it simply reaches us from different directions, which is why the sky appears blue. When the Sun is near the horizon, at sunrise or sunset, its rays shine through a greater thickness of atmosphere, and so are subject to more scattering. Only light of the longest wavelengths at the red end of the spectrum is able to penetrate, resulting in glorious red skies. Conversely, from a high mountain the Sun appears to be more brilliant and the sky a darker blue because most of the particles that scatter the light are in the lower layers of the atmosphere.

Twilight is also due to scattering of light by the atmosphere and occasionally a purple glow is observed in the evening sky. This is believed to be the result of reflection from a layer of dust at a high level in the Earth's atmosphere. From the Moon, which has no atmosphere of its own, and because there are no particles to scatter the sunlight, the Sun appears as a brilliant white disc shining out of a deep black sky.

PEOPLE OF THE SUN

The symbol of the Sun – the warrior Huitzilopochtli – depicted on the pendant (*below*), was the centre of the Aztec religion. According to the Aztecs' cult of the Sun, Huitzilopochtli died every evening to be born anew the following day, when he would begin his struggle against the stars and Moon, driving them away with a shaft of light.

When sunlight or any white light is passed through a prism (*below*) it is separated into its component colours – red, orange, yellow, green, blue and violet. Fortunately we are among the few animals that can experience this whole range of tones and so witness the slowly unfolding colour show of sunrise and sunset.

The Sun's energy sustains all plants and, in turn, all creatures on Earth.

Light and colour

The spoon on the right appears to be broken where it enters the water; this familiar situation is due to the rays of light being bent as they pass from one medium into another medium of different density, such as from air into water or vice versa and from cool, dry air into warm, moist air.

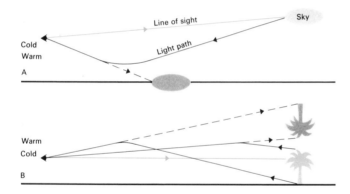

As light travels at different speeds through different materials, light rays are bent when they pass obliquely from one media into another. The most familiar result of this behaviour is the bent appearance that a stick has as it passes from air into water. When light travels through the Earth's atmosphere, it travels at a slightly slower speed than through the vacuum of space, and so light rays entering the atmosphere at an angle are bent slightly. The downward bending of light rays makes the Sun appear to be higher than it really is and keeps it visible for an appreciable time after it has actually sunk below the horizon. The extent of the duration of extra sunlight varies with the location and time of year. A green flash is sometimes seen at the moment that the Sun's disc disappears below the horizon at sunset. It is caused by different colours being bent by different amounts, and since green light is refracted more than red light by the atmosphere, the green component of the Sun's visible spectrum is the last to disappear.

The refraction of sunlight by the atmosphere produces many other interesting effects. Apart from the rainbow (see page 66–67) the best known is probably the solar halo – a circular ring of light the angular distance of which, from the edge of the halo to the centre of the Sun, is 22 degrees. It is caused by the refraction of light by prism-shaped ice crystals. Usually the halo is white, but sometimes the refraction is clear enough for separate colours to be seen. Unlike the rainbow, red instead of blue is on the inside of the circle. Occasionally a second, larger, fainter halo with a radius that subtends an angle of 46 degrees may be seen surrounding the Sun.

Ice crystals in clouds are found in several different forms and they are sometimes scattered at different orientations, but as they fall they tend to align themselves

Mirages are caused by the bending of light as it passes through regions of denser or more rarefied air. The path of the light is bent as it travels from the object to the observer, but our minds are programmed to interpret visual impressions on the assumption that light travels in a straight line.
An inferior mirage (A) occurs when the temperature of the air decreases abruptly with height, and so a distant object appears to be displaced downwards; in a desert a patch of sky may appear like water.
A superior mirage (B) occurs when there is a sharp increase in the temperature of the air with height and an object is displaced upwards; it appears to be floating in air and may often be inverted.

The River Seine is inverted as a superior mirage in the Paris sky.

to be parallel so that their refractions combine to produce a number of visible effects such as arcs and bright spots on the solar halo. A frequent sight is a mock sun, a bright patch of light appearing just outside the halo at the same altitude as the Sun, which is sometimes so bright that it can be mistaken for the Sun. Complex halo phenomena are frequently seen in the Arctic and Antarctic, where ice-crystal clouds are common. Ice crystals can also act as mirrors, reflecting sunlight. One manifestation of this is the sun pillar, a bright column of light extending above or below the Sun, which can sometimes be seen even after the Sun has set. In moonlight these optical effects are much fainter – lunar haloes are particularly noticeable and even lunar rainbows can occasionally be observed.

More unusual consequences of refraction occur when a layer of air close to the ground is much hotter or colder than the air above. These phenomena are always caused by the fact that light travels at different speeds through air of different temperatures – it travels more slowly through cold than through hot air. When the air near to the ground is hotter than the air above it, which is common in desert regions or over a tarmac road on a sunny day, light from the sky passing through the hot layer is bent upwards into the observer's eye, and a patch of sky is seen on the ground which looks like water. This is called a mirage. As one approaches the "water", it disappears or moves on – the familiar experience of many thirsty desert travellers. On the other hand, when a temperature inversion is present and the lowest layer of air is colder than the air above, light from objects below the horizon is bent downwards. As a result, mountains or distant coastlines become visible even though they should be hidden by the curvature of the Earth; such "superior mirages" are most common in polar regions.

When light passes close to a particle such as a water droplet it is diffracted; some of the light bends round the particle. The longer wavelengths, at the red end of the spectrum, bend most. When a thin water-droplet cloud passes in front of the Sun or Moon, diffraction produces a diffuse coloured ring, a corona, with the red on the outside. Unlike haloes, coronas are not fixed in angular size; their diameter depends on the size of the droplets forming the clouds. A typical range is 4 to 10 degrees radius, which corresponds to water droplets of radius 2 to 5 microns. The larger coronas are usually seen only in small patches of colour in the form of iridescence, continually changing greens and purples being particularly noticeable. Iridescence is difficult to photograph because it usually occurs near a bright Sun.

Another result of diffraction is the brockenspectre. This is usually seen on mountains when looking down above a bank of fog or cloud with one's back to the Sun. It appears as an enlarged shadow of the observer with a halo or "glory" surrounding it. The easiest way to see a glory is to travel by air and watch for the shadow of one's aeroplane to be projected on to a layer of cloud below: if conditions are right, it will be "caught in a noose of light" – surrounded by a halo of coloured light.

The brockenspectre, named after the Brocken, a peak in the Harz Mountains of Germany, is a strange sight, but familiar to mountain climbers. The shadow of the climbers is formed against a mist or clouds when the Sun is low in the sky. The great size of the shadow is due to its extent through a depth of several metres, rather than lying in one plane.

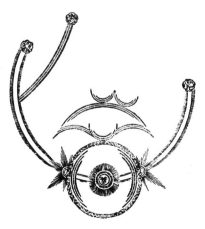

Solar haloes, represented in this early engraving, appear as perfect circles surrounding the Sun. It is surprising that this fairy-like effect occurs as often as it does because the ice-crystals in the cirrostratus clouds that create it have to be extremely regular in shape and size. However, on average a ring around the Sun or Moon occurs about once every four days in middle latitudes and, according to popular belief, such a solar halo foretells rainy weather. This prediction often proves to be correct because cirrostratus clouds are frequently the forerunners of a low-pressure system, which often leads to rain.

The Earth's aura

A layer of ozone found at a height of around 50 kilometres (31 miles) in the upper stratosphere absorbs excessive ultraviolet radiation from the Sun and protects us from severe sunburn. Ozone is simply oxygen in which three atoms are combined in one molecule rather than two atoms as in ordinary oxygen, but its properties are very different from those of oxygen. Ozone forms from the action of sunlight on oxygen, but it slowly decays back to oxygen within the ozone layer. In this layer oxygen and ozone are in a state of "dynamic equilibrium". Some ozone is carried down to lower levels, but it is quickly destroyed by contact with smoke and vegetation, which is fortunate because it causes irritation of the lungs if it is present in considerable quantities in the air.

Ozone concentration varies in a complex way that is related to the seasons, latitude and weather patterns in the troposphere. Studies of these variations give clues about the general circulation of air between the stratosphere and troposphere below.

Recently, concern was expressed that fluorocarbons, the gases used in aerosol spray cans, would rise to the ozone layer and react with it, destroying its protective effect. It is now believed, however, that sunlight, except over polar regions in winter, constantly re-creates ozone, and there is as yet no evidence of a decrease.

Within the stratosphere, which stretches from 10 to 50 kilometres (6 to 31 miles) above the ground, the temperature increases with height, reaching a maximum at the ozone layer. The stratosphere is composed of stable air, since any convection currents rising from the ground cease at the tropopause – the junction between the troposphere and stratosphere. Only a few powerful rising currents of air within cumulonimbus clouds are able to penetrate beyond this boundary. Apart from the few clouds, there is little water in the stratosphere. Aircraft often fly in this layer because it is "above the weather" and there is less turbulence than in the lower tropospheric layers. There is, however, plenty of wind, and the changing patterns of wind and temperature in the stratosphere are an interesting field of study.

One peculiar phenomenon is sudden warming: occasionally in winter the stratosphere over the whole of the Arctic warms by as much as 30°C (54°F) within a few days. Since it occurs in winter it cannot be due to solar radiation. It is believed to involve compression of air from the ozone layer, and it appears to be related to changes in the circulation patterns in the troposphere.

Another aspect of the upper atmosphere that is not associated with solar radiation is airglow. This is a very faint light that is emitted from the sky even on a clear, moonless night. Studies of the spectrum of airglow are difficult to carry out because it is so faint. However, it has been demonstrated that the light is not starlight or even scattered sunlight, but is actually formed in the upper atmosphere. It is believed to be due to molecules that have been split into atoms during the day recombining at night. Evidence from airborne instruments shows that the light is emitted at heights of 80 to 120 kilometres (50 to 75 miles). In contrast, zodiacal light, observed in the evening sky, is due to dust particles scattering sunlight.

Zodiacal light, a softly radiant cone seen on a moonless December night in India in 1874 (*left*). In middle latitudes this bright pyramid of light is best seen after sunset during January, February or March. It is as luminous as the Milky Way and its presence is due to the scattering of sunlight by interstellar dust.

Sunrise seen by Apollo astronauts from an altitude of 230 kilometres (143 miles) on 20 July 1975 (*above*). The horizontal bands of colour are due to the scattering of sunlight by layers of dust in the Earth's atmosphere. Abnormally colourful sunrises and sunsets are caused by dust from comets or volcanoes.

THE AURORA

As the Earth's magnetic field arcs out from the north and south magnetic poles, situated over northern Canada and Antarctica, it traps atomic particles, the protons and electrons that are emitted by the Sun in the solar wind. As the particles descend, between heights of 100 and 300 kilometres (62 and 186 miles) they interact with molecules in the rarefied upper part of the Earth's atmosphere and this produces a beautiful glowing radiation of light – the aurora; it is visible on most clear nights in regions situated within 20 degrees of latitude of the magnetic poles and which are located within the auroral cone.

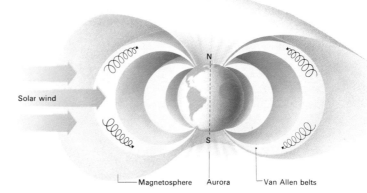

Solar wind

Magnetosphere   Aurora   Van Allen belts

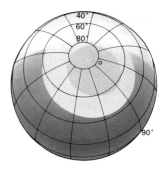

The waving curtain of light (*left*) is just one of the many forms that the aurora may have; it may also be seen as an arc of faint light stretching low across the sky, as a diffuse glow that is hard to distinguish from twilight or it may even comprise brilliant coloured shooting rays that continually change their form.

When the Sun is calm, the aurora can be seen from locations within a latitudinal zone of 65 to 70 degrees north and south. But during high solar activity it can be seen at much lower latitudes than usual.

40°
60°
80°
90°

o Magnetic North Pole

Extent of aurora
Extent of aurora during peak solar activity

Dew

Air always contains invisible water vapour and there is a maximum amount of vapour that air can hold at any particular temperature; warm air can hold more than cold air. If a quantity of air cools, its relative humidity increases until, eventually, the amount of water vapour it contains is equal to the maximum that it can hold at that temperature. The air is then said to be saturated, and that temperature is called the dew point. If the air cools further, some water has to condense and may be deposited as dew. As the ground is continually radiating heat into space, the heat received from the Sun during the daytime is more than enough to balance this loss, and the surface of the Earth therefore becomes warmer. At night, however, the outward radiation results in a steady cooling, and a shallow layer of air near to the ground cools. Eventually if the heat from the Sun continues to be radiated outwards, the air may cool below its dew point, and dew forms on the ground.

Dew consists of tiny drops of water, which are most noticeable on blades of grass and on spiders' webs, where they glisten in the morning sunlight. Dew is particularly liable to form on the roofs of cars and sheds, which, because they are not in contact with warm ground, cool more quickly. The conspicuous presence of a heavy morning dew makes it hard to believe that it is caused by a mere recycling of moisture that is already present in the atmosphere and not by a very heavy downpour of rain during the night.

The water that constitutes dew condenses out of the air, not out of plants – a frequent misconception. Plants do, however, transpire water, and this makes the air around them more humid, so favouring the formation of dew early in the night.

Dew is most commonly formed on calm, cloudless winter nights. If a layer of cloud is present, it reflects some heat back to the ground, reducing the cooling rate. If there is a wind, the air is stirred and the cold air mixes with the warm air above. In both cases the ground temperature falls only slowly, and so will probably not reach dew point before the Sun rises and starts to raise the temperature once more. In summer, the nights may be too short for the temperature to fall sufficiently for dew to form. The amount of water deposited by dew is small compared with that of rain, but occasionally it is sufficient to measure in a rain gauge. Dew is usually evaporated quickly in the early morning by the heat produced as the Sun rises.

If the dew point is below 0°C (32°F) water vapour condenses as ice crystals, forming hoar frost. This white deposit is sometimes thick enough to be mistaken for snow. When the ground temperature falls below freezing point but the air temperature remains above freezing point, only ground frost forms. Both ground and air frosts are of concern to fruit growers and horticulturists because freezing temperatures can damage many plants and fruit crops; grape-vines are among the plants often

The early morning dew drops seen on this spider's web may well indicate fine weather.

Hoar frost (*right*) is deposition of vapour from air, the dew point of which is below freezing.

damaged by a late frost that may strike after the plants have started growing again in the spring.

Condensation inside houses forms in the same way as dew. If the weather is cold, walls and windows cool by conduction, as they are in contact with the cold air outside, and also by radiation to space. When the warm indoor air comes into contact with these surfaces it cools below its dew point, and moisture forms on the walls and windows. The problem is aggravated if the air in the house is already laden with moisture from drying clothes or cooking. The problem can be reduced by ventilation or by insulation, which maintains the inside surfaces at a higher temperature.

In unheated buildings a condensation problem is most likely to occur when a spell of cold weather is followed by warm, humid conditions. If the temperature in the building falls below freezing point, condensation on the windows freezes and takes the form of ice crystals, which form beautiful leaf-like patterns.

JACK FROST
A representation, drawn in 1852, of a jovial rebellion against the long despotism of Jack Frost is depicted below. The spritely elf-like figure is an imaginary character who appears in traditional stories and is supposed to trace the patterns made by frost, thus representing nipping cold.

This legendary figure probably originated in Scandinavia, where, according to Norse mythology, Kari, god of the winds, had a son named Jokul or Frosti – *Jokul* meaning icicle and *Frosti* meaning frost. In Russia, the frost is represented as a white old man, Father Frost, and in German tales as Old Mother Frost.

Fern frost, often known as "Jack Frost's Garden" forms on the inside of window panes during severe weather, making beautiful fern-like patterns.

Clouds

Stratus or "scud" rising from the valley floor (*left*) is produced by moisture-laden airstreams condensing into cloud formations.

Although clouds may be viewed as individual entities their continually changing pattern in the sky can be looked upon as visible evidence of the way the atmosphere is behaving – some atmospheric motions tend to produce cloud and others to disperse it. Also, different combinations of pressure, temperature and humidity inhibit cloud formation, while others may produce a spectacular succession of cloud types and patterns.

Cloud forms when air rises and cools to its dew point, so that some of the water vapour it contains condenses into minute water droplets or ice crystals. These are so small and light that they float in the air, barely having enough weight to fall earthwards. There are two basic or stratiform types of cloud: layer or convective cloud, which is essentially stable and produced when a large mass of air rises, and heap cloud, produced when the atmosphere is unstable, and "bubbles" of warm air rise in convection currents.

The most extensive areas of layer cloud form along fronts and near lows and troughs, where converging airstreams in the lower atmosphere force air to rise. The main types – known as stratus, nimbostratus, altostratus and cirrostratus according to their height and the relative amounts of water and ice they contain – are all rather featureless and tend to produce overcast skies. Nimbostratus (rain cloud) is often seen only as a dark-grey formless mass, all texture or detail being obscured by falling rain or snow. Altostratus is higher and thinner, usually allowing a rather watery sunlight to penetrate, while cirrostratus, the highest, is composed of ice crystals and often produces beautiful optical effects such as sun pillars and solar haloes.

Heap or convective clouds, by contrast, typically have a small base area but considerable vertical development – a direct reflection of the fact that they are formed by pockets of warm unstable air rising often quite rapidly. The most common type is the cumulus cloud, the white fleecy "cotton-wool" cloud of fair summer weather which tends to increase during the day as the ground becomes warmer and then dies away in the evening as the cooling ground ceases to drive the convection cells. Cumulus at sea tends to be less variable because the sea surface temperature remains static through the day. The cloud base is usually flat – indicating the level at which the dew-point temperature is reached, while the "cauliflower" tops show the extent of the rising "bubbles" of warm, moist air. The patches of clear sky between the cumulus clouds are kept clear by the compensating descending air flow of the convection cells.

The more unstable the air, the higher the cumulus cloud will develop, until eventually its top takes on a fibrous appearance, showing that its upper levels have reached the freezing level. This "glaciated" cloud consists of ice crystals and is often pulled out horizontally by the upper level winds to form a characteristic anvil – the unmistakable "trade mark" of a mature cumulonimbus cloud or "thunderhead".

Water vapour does not automatically condense as soon as the air is saturated: in fact, perfectly clean air produced in laboratory conditions can reach a relative humidity of 800 per cent before droplets form spontaneously. In nature this cannot happen. The air is full of tiny particles (aerosols) which act as nuclei and promote condensation as soon as saturation is reached. The cloud droplets so formed are tiny even by comparison with the smallest raindrops: their average diameter is 20 microns (one thousandth of a millimetre or 39 millionths of an inch).

Similarly the air in a cloud may be cooled far below 0°C (32°F) without its water droplets turning to ice crystals. Spontaneous freezing occurs only at −40°C (−40°F) or lower, but the presence of ice nuclei ensures that freezing usually starts at −20°C (−4°F); and once a few ice crystals form, the process accelerates rapidly. The understanding of condensation processes has important implications for rain and hurricane control.

THE FORMATION OF CLOUDS

Clouds form when air is cooled below its dew point and condensation occurs. This process usually begins when a warm patch of the Earth's surface heats the adjacent air by radiation and creates a large bubble of warm air resting on the ground.

As this bubble of air is relatively warm compared to the denser, cold air lying above it, the bubble rises in a similar way to a hot-air balloon. As the air rises, it expands and cools.

Eventually, the rising bubble of air cools to below its dew point and the water vapour it contains condenses out on to the minute particles of dust and salt that are present in air to form water droplets or ice crystals. By this time the bubble of air is too cold and heavy to rise any higher and it remains in the sky as a cloud.

Mountain clouds

Mountain ranges, individual peaks and even high moorland plateaux act as barriers to the wind and exert a strong influence on the type and distribution of cloud that develops. Air will flow around a mountain only if the peak is isolated and the air mass stable and therefore reluctant to rise. More commonly, the air flow is forced to rise over the high ground and as it is forced above the level of its dew point temperature, clouds develop. For this reason many mountains are frequently capped with stratus cloud and even quite low hills may have their summits shrouded in cloud if the air is sufficiently moist.

In many locations throughout the world, for example the English Lake District and Honolulu, Hawaii, cloud caps are an almost permanent feature of the mountain scenery and the height of the cloud base provides a useful indicator of the relative humidity of the air. If the relative humidity value is low, the air is dry and must rise before there is any cloud development.

Sometimes the air near the ground is too dry for cloud to form, but at higher levels – about 5000 metres (16,500 feet) – there may be layers of air with much more moisture in them. As the obstruction of the mountain causes all the atmospheric layers to rise, these moist layers produce clouds high above the mountain. Because of their very distinctive shape, these clouds are called lenticular (lens-shaped) clouds or, alternatively, whaleback clouds, and their smooth, streamlined form shows just where the stream of moist air is being carried up into, and then down again out of, the condensation level. For though the cloud appears as a static object it is constantly being formed at the "upstream" end and dispersed at the "downstream" end. If the atmosphere contains several separate moist layers with dry air between them, each layer may produce a lenticular cloud, resulting in a formation aptly known as a "pile of plates".

Under certain conditions, the air, having been forced

up and then down again in the lee of the obstruction, continues to oscillate in a wave motion which may extend for several kilometres downwind of the mountain. Each time the air rises in a crest that breaks through the condensation level, a small cloud forms; each time the air descends again, the cloud disperses. The result is a chain of lee-wave clouds more or less equally spaced downwind of the mountain. In a very mountainous area each peak may set up a series of waves and the sky may then become a complex pattern of lenticular clouds, constantly changing as the various wave motions interfere with each other.

There are other effects that are produced specifically by high ground. Sometimes a gap is formed in an otherwise overcast sky by air descending on the lee of an obstruction. Such "holes" in the cloud may persist for several hours if the atmosphere is stable and the wind flow steady, and may bring a welcome patch of sunshine to one small area while the surrounding region is uniformly dull and perhaps even wet. Another typical mountain feature takes the form of a long bar of cloud sitting above a mountain ridge. It is formed when the air has risen gradually to the crest and then descends very suddenly down the escarpment. These clouds are sometimes given local names such as the "Helm Bar", produced by a northeast wind blowing across the Pennines in northern England. Similarly, in America the dry wind blowing down the lee slope of the Rockies produces the "Chinook Arch". Table Mountain, the huge flat-topped mountain overlooking Cape Town, is often capped by a layer of very delicate smooth white cloud that appears to hang in delicate folds over the almost sheer rock faces, so earning the name, "the Tablecloth". The cloud is produced by a steady flow of moist, stable air over the mountain and is one of the most distinctive local clouds in the world.

Among the most unusual of all clouds are two very high-altitude formations called mother-of-pearl clouds and noctilucent clouds. Both form in the stratosphere, the mother-of-pearl (or nacreous) clouds at heights of 19 to 30 kilometres (12 to 20 miles) and the noctilucent clouds at heights of around 80 kilometres (50 miles), at which altitude the air is barely one ten-thousandth of its ground-level density. These clouds are extremely thin, with a blue or yellow tinge and are visible for only a short while after sunset or before sunrise when the sky is dark in latitudes higher than 50 degrees; the clouds are lit by the Sun, which is itself below the horizon. The mother-of-pearl clouds are believed to be caused by wave effects initially created by mountains and then transmitted through the atmosphere to high levels of the stratosphere. These wave effects occur when the wind speed is consistent throughout the troposphere; these clouds are frequently sighted in Antarctica.

The Tablecloth (*above*) clinging to the windward slopes and summit of Table Mountain, Cape Town, South Africa, is laid by moist air from the sea cooling to its dew point before reaching the mountain top.

The banner cloud (*right*) attached to Mt Egmont in New Zealand, forms because the mountain does not present a barrier large enough to necessitate air being lifted above it. Instead, a cloud appears behind the peak, blowing in the same direction as the prevailing wind.

The Himalayas (*left*), forming the highest mountain barrier in the world, force air to rise above its windswept peaks, which are therefore frequently shrouded in a veil of cloud.

Cloud types

In 1803 Luke Howard, a London pharmacist, devised a scheme for the classification of cloud types which, like the schemes then being developed by biologists for the classification of animals and plants, used Latin names to identify each type and describe its main distinguishing visual features. The scheme comprised ten basic types, or genera, each having several possible species. Additional qualifying names may be added to describe varieties.

CLOUD GENERA

Cirrus (Ci) Small clouds in the form of white, sometimes silky, patches or bands. Often occur as feathery filaments with their ends swept into hooks by wind shear.

Cirrostratus (Cs) Transparent white veil: smooth and uniform or fibrous. Commonly produces haloes.

Cirrocumulus (Cc) Thin layer, which is either continuous or in patches that are made up of small elements. Commonly forms a "Mackerel sky".

Altostratus (As) Grey, featureless layer cloud that can be fibrous or uniform. The Sun may penetrate weakly, but this type of cloud does not produce optical phenomena.

Altocumulus (Ac) Very variable in form – can be continuous or patchy. As it is usually waved or in rolls, lumps or laminae it is better known as lenticular or crenellate.

Nimbostratus (Nb) A grey, dark, heavy, opaque raincloud.

Stratus (St) Forms a grey uniform layer that may be continuous or patchy and often produces rain, or snow.

Stratocumulus (Sc) Grey or white layer with dark areas. Usually in rolls, undulations and rounded masses but not fibrous. Elements often in a regular pattern.

Cumulus (Cs) Separate dense white clouds with a well-defined form and strong vertical development. Flat base, upper parts brilliant white and cauliflower-like.

Cumulonimbus (Cb) Extreme vertical development of a cumulus cloud. It has a huge tower, is dark at the base and is often associated with precipitation and thunder. Top smooth, occasionally fibrous and pulled out laterally.

CLOUD SPECIES

Fibratus Filaments, without tufts or hooks in *Ci* and *Cs*.

Uncinus Cirrus terminating in hook or tuft.

Spissatus Dense cirrus which often forms top of *Cb*.

Nebulosus In form of thin veil, mainly in *Cs* and *St*.

Stratiformis In an extensive layer mainly in *Ac* and *Sc*.

Lenticularis Well-defined lens or almond in *Cc, Ac, Sc*.

Castellanus Castle-like battlement in *Ci, Cc, Ac, Sc*.

Floccus In small cumuliform tufts with ragged lower part in *Ci, Cc, Ac* and also sometimes in *Sc*.

Fractus In irregular ragged bits in *St, Cu*.

Humilis Cumulus with very little vertical growth.

Mediocris Moderate cumulus with lumpy tops.

Congestus Large, full "cauliflower" cumulus.

Calvus Cb with upper parts just becoming fibrous.

Capillatus Cb with distinct cirrus upper parts.

Thus: *Stratocumulus stratiformis opacus undulatus* is a stratocumulus cloud made up of parallel undulations in a continuous layer which is sufficiently dense to block out the Sun completely.

A plume of hot air from a fire produces a pyrocumulus cloud (*above*), called a "fumulus".

Lenticular clouds are piled above each other (*below*) over Mt McKinley in Alaska.

CONTRAILS AND DISTRAILS

Aircraft exhausts emit a mixture of hot gases containing a large amount of water vapour. As the gases condense behind the aircraft they form a cloud in a straight line called a contrail. The gap between the aircraft and the tip of the contrail occurs because the air takes a few seconds before it cools sufficiently to condense. Paradoxically an aircraft may also disperse a lane of cloud to produce a strip of clear air called a distrail, caused by heat evaporating cloud droplets.

Mamma, meaning breasts, are pouches of water droplets which sometimes hang down from cumulonimbus clouds after or towards the end of a storm. They are believed to be due to subsidence at the base of the cloud causing previously stable air to become unstable.

Cirrostratus clouds (*below*), formed by an early morning temperature inversion at Marlborough Sounds in New Zealand, are white with a wispy hair-like appearance.

Cloud formations

Clouds are not scattered across the sky at random, but in definite formations and arrangements. Even within a single layer of cloud, regular patterns may occur, and these indicate the behaviour of the atmosphere at that level. Commonly the cloud will form a series of parallel bands of oval cloud cells with clear spaces between them, or a series of long, billowing wave forms like the ripples on a seashore. When the upper surface of a shallow layer-cloud cools by radiation, while the lower surface becomes warmer by absorbing heat radiated from the ground, the air in the cloud becomes slightly unstable and small convection cells develop. Rising currents build up the cloud while descending currents tend to disperse it, so giving the cloud a cellular pattern.

Under some conditions, instead of a pattern of oval cloud cells developing with clear air between them, the reverse occurs: a pattern of "open" cells forms in an extensive sheet of cloud, giving the cloud a rather ragged and moth-eaten appearance. This effect may be seen both on a small scale and over areas many kilometres across. Such patterns are seldom seen from the ground, but are

Rounded masses and rolls of altocumulus and altostratus clouds are often thin enough to vaguely reveal the Sun shining through gaps in their delicately mottled formation.

fascinating and impressive when observed from a high-flying aircraft. From above the cloud, it is often possible to see the abrupt edge of a large layer-cloud formation, or see a sudden change from a flat, featureless sheet to a lumpy texture or even to towering protuberances where mechanisms such as ground heating cause a change in the temperature structure of the atmosphere from stable to unstable conditions.

An interesting daytime cloud form, often seen over land, has been given the name "cloud street" which in one case takes the form of a long straight line of cumulus clouds. Each cloud forms in a convection cell over a single "hot spot" on the ground and is then carried away by the prevailing air movement, leaving a new cloud to form in its place. The vertical development of the various types of

cumulus gives a good measure of the degree of instability in the air. Rather flat, pancake-like clouds indicate stability and a likelihood of fine weather, while growing turrets reveal vigorous convection and a probability of showers. Once the tops take on a fibrous appearance, glaciation has started and the cloud is developing into a cumulonimbus. Heavy precipitation, thunder and lightning are then likely. Castellanus clouds, rising like castle battlements, usually from a common base, show growing instability developing from within the atmospheric layers rather than from ground heating. They too are often a precursor of heavy rain or thunderstorms.

Land and sea have contrasting effects on cloud formation. If the land is warmer than the sea surface, cloud will form inland, while the skies out to sea remain cloudless. In this situation large cumulus clouds often develop over islands and this point was not missed by early marine explorers, including the Polynesian navigators, whose skills showed an extraordinary understanding of oceanic and atmospheric phenomena – the sight of a cloud helped them to discover an island long before it came into view. Conversely, clouds that only occur out at sea are being formed in a stream of cool air blowing from the land out over a relatively warm sea. The lower layers of the cool airstream are warmed and gradually become more and more unstable; eventually convection starts and cloud formation then occurs.

Wind invariably changes in direction and speed with height, and therefore heap or convective clouds are often distorted in their upper levels. In temperate latitudes, such clouds are generally associated with westerly winds, which tend to increase with height. The cloud tops consequently lean forwards. By contrast the trade winds typically decrease with height and so cumulus clouds found in latitudes that are dominated by the trade winds have a characteristic backwards lean. Cumulonimbus clouds extend right up to the top of the troposphere and the tell-tale anvil formation is the result of high-level winds blowing the fibrous cirrus cloud top away from the main cumulus tower. When the equatorial rain belt is particularly active, with dozens of huge cumulonimbus clouds developing every day, the upper atmosphere becomes full of cirrus cloud blown from the anvils.

Over the past 20 years, meteorologists have benefited enormously from satellite technology and the marvellously informative photographs these orbiting observation posts can offer. Individual clouds cannot be seen, but patterns of open and closed cells show clearly, as do the enormous spiralling cloud systems of the temperate-latitude low-pressure systems and the stark white linear features of cold fronts. In the tropics, apart from the occasional hurricane, cyclonic cloud spirals do not occur, but a number of characteristic cloud patterns have been identified, including inverted V-shapes, cell clusters and comma-shaped formations. These "cloud clusters" were unknown before the development of satellite imagery and even now their mechanisms of formation and development are far from being fully understood.

CLOUD SEEDING

Rain is formed naturally when ice crystals are present in clouds, but Man has found a trigger mechanism that produces rain artificially, giving real hope to people in drought-stricken areas. In rain making, natural processes are simulated by introducing dry ice (frozen carbon dioxide) into clouds. A more economic alternative to dry ice is silver iodide crystals, which physically resemble ice and so have recently been introduced to use as nuclei for crystallization. The crystals set up a chain reaction that rapidly turns the whole cloud into snow and eventually into rain. Although Man has always dreamed of controlling the weather, widespread cloud seeding is an impracticality – it is difficult to control how much rain is produced. Also people in areas adjacent to clouds that have been seeded can claim that their rain has been stolen.

A cumulus cloud is shown before seeding (*above right*) and (*below right*) with rain falling from it after a seeding experiment using silver iodide, near Wassa in New South Wales, Australia.

A cumulonimbus storm cell seen from a northeasterly direction in Montana, USA, on 21 July 1967.

Fog

Fog is made up of tiny droplets of liquid water. It forms when air is cooled below its dew point so that some of the invisible water vapour it contains condenses to form water droplets. Fog is really a type of cloud and differs from it only in the way it is formed; cloud is formed when air rises and is cooled, whereas fog is formed when air cools near the ground surface. The phenomenon known as hill fog is in fact low cloud, and forms when air is cooled as it rises to pass over high ground. It is seen to be fog only because the ground rises up into the cloud.

Radiation fog is the most important kind of fog. It forms over land as air cools and occurs most often on clear nights when there is a slight breeze. It frequently forms over damp surfaces such as ponds and marshes, or over ground that is still wet from recent rain. It does not form over the sea or large lakes because a large body of water normally contains more than enough heat to prevent the air in contact with it from cooling sufficiently for its saturation point to be reached. As cold air is heavier than warm air, fog forms more readily in valleys than on slopes or on hilltops. Following a clear night the weather in a valley may remain foggy, damp and cold well into the morning, but if one walks up the hillside, quite suddenly the fog disappears, and is replaced by brilliant sunshine. Looking back one can see the hills and mountains rising like islands from a huge lake.

Fog is most likely to form on clear, cloudless nights. If a layer of cloud is present, it reflects the heat back to the ground and prevents the temperature from falling low enough to reach dew point. Similarly, strong winds also prevent fog formation because the turbulence produced prevents a deep layer of cold air from forming. At the other extreme, if air is completely still, only a very thin layer becomes cold enough for condensation to occur,

and a layer of ground fog is likely to form. It can be seen early in the morning as a shallow layer of air, a metre or so above the ground – any cattle standing in it seem to be floating because their legs are hidden by the fog.

Like most types of fog, freezing fog is composed of liquid water droplets, but the droplets are in a super-cooled state, only forming when the temperature falls below $0°C$ ($32°F$) and freezing as soon as they come into contact with a cold surface. Fog that is actually composed of ice crystals is rather rare and occurs only at extremely low temperatures. Although fog can be extremely dangerous because it reduces visibility so drastically, the variety of factors that combine to produce a fog on any particular night are so delicately balanced that it is always difficult to forecast. A fog forecast can only specify the general area where fog will form.

When warm air flows over an area of cold sea, sea fog is formed. It often occurs in summer along the Californian coast of North America, where cold sea currents well up from below the sea surface along a narrow strip parallel to the coast. Near Newfoundland, sea fog forms when warm airstreams blow north over cold iceberg-filled water that flows southwards from the Arctic. Similarly, on the east coast of Britain, fog forms when easterly winds blow over the cold North Sea, especially in spring.

In contrast, steam fog is formed by cold air coming into contact with warm water. It is most common in coastal Arctic regions, where there are ice-cold air-streams from snow-covered land blowing into an area of sea the temperature of which is above freezing point. Being wispy and patchy in appearance it is often called "Arctic sea-smoke". The same phenomenon is also seen over a warm lake on a cold night, or as "steam" over roads when the Sun shines after a shower.

Morning mist or fog is frequent in the Courmayeur Valley in France (*left*) because the moist air cools by radiation during the long winter nights.

A shallow layer of swirling steam fog is produced over Yellowstone River in America (*right*) when cold air passes over the relatively warm water.

Below freezing point, fog droplets remain liquid if they are suspended in air, but they freeze as soon as they come in contact with any object, such as this apple tree (*below*).

Smog

Early morning mist forms over damp, low-lying fields when the air cools by radiation during long winter nights and the cold air drains into the hollows.

Visibility, the distance that one can see through the atmosphere, is greatly reduced by particles of smoke, dust or water. A fine mist of water droplets, for instance, can reduce visibility from the 40 or so kilometres (25 or so miles) that one can see through clear, dry air to between 1 and 2 kilometres (0·6 and 1·2 miles). Although fog and mist differ only in intensity, if there is dust in the atmosphere, mist can form on a day when the humidity is much lower than that required for fog formation. This is because the fine particles in the atmosphere form nuclei for the water droplets to condense on.

The term haze is normally used to describe a suspension of solid particles in air. They consist of either dust or fine sand that has been lifted into the air by turbulent winds. The tiny haze particles can be carried a long way before they are washed out of the atmosphere and on occasions sands from the Sahara are carried far into northern Europe, where they are deposited as a fine red dust. When carried by the trade winds, dust from the Sahara can even reach the Caribbean Islands.

Man-made smoke is an even more common cause of haze and in many industrial areas visibilities greater than 30 kilometres (19 miles) are rare. Hazes can also be created by large-scale forest fires and burning stubble. The smoke plumes produced in this way have a yellowish appearance, and using satellite photography they can easily be distinguished from rainclouds by their distinctive colour. Haze caused by salt is found along coasts or on islands where strong winds blow in from the ocean. Besides reducing visibility, salt hazes mask colours so that

AIR POLLUTION
When car exhaust fumes and industrial waste, such as sulphur dioxide, are mixed in air and exposed to sunlight, they undergo a photochemical reaction that leads to the formation of a type of smog which not only reduces visibility but also causes plant damage and eye irritation. These conditions affect a large proportion of California (*below*), and are also felt in most other industrialized areas.

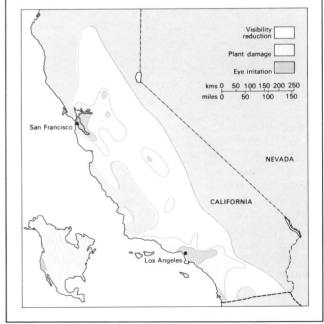

Smog, the twentieth-century equivalent of the "pea-souper", smothers San Francisco, allowing only the tip of the bridge to protrude.

Fogs occurred more frequently than ever before in major cities during the nineteenth century and made life most uncomfortable (*above*).

everything appears less vivid.

Smog, a combination of smoke and fog, persists for longer than fog, is extremely unpleasant and has a number of harmful effects. As with mist, water droplets form around solid particles in the atmosphere and as a result smog forms more easily than ordinary fog and is slower to clear. In winter and autumn, particularly when there are frequent temperature inversions, smog can persist for several days. The formation of smog is encouraged by restricting local ventilation and it is ironic that areas of the world in which the air supply is most limited are often the areas in which Man has chosen to build his cities.

Until the 1960s London, in Britain, was notorious for its dense "pea-soupers". They were sometimes so thick that nothing could be seen beyond the length of an arm. As a result of the particularly dense "pea-souper" smog of December 1952, which lasted for five days, some 4000 people died of either bronchitis or pneumonia. In Belgium in December 1930, 63 people died because masses of poisonous gases pouring out of factories in the Meuse Valley were trapped beneath an atmospheric inversion lying over the narrow valley. It caused ten times the normal death rate – many of the fatalities being attributed to fluoride poisoning.

During the 1950s and 1960s strenuous efforts were made to reduce the amount of smog. Banning smoky fuels from urban areas and restricting emissions from factory chimneys has had some success in reducing the number of solid particles in the atmosphere. Nevertheless many toxic gases such as sulphur dioxide are still routinely pumped into the atmosphere as factory waste and the amount of atmospheric carbon dioxide and carbon monoxide from motor-car exhaust fumes is steadily increasing, particularly in industrial areas.

Photochemical smog is essentially a man-made phenomenon. It is created completely independently of the atmospheric humidity level, being initiated by the action of sunlight on fumes from car exhausts, and consists of a mixture of nitrogen dioxide, ozone and a chemical known as PAN (peroxyacyl nitrate). A combination of these gases causes eye irritation, coughing and fatigue and also damages crops. Some of the pollutants contained in PAN, such as ozone, can be airborne for considerable distances. For example, ozone damage in tobacco crops has been observed as far afield as the Connecticut Valley, due to pollutants transported in the air from the Boston–New York urban corridor.

Photochemical smog occurs in large cities during spells of hot, sunny weather. Globally it is most intense in the North American city of Los Angeles, which has the perfect conditions for the formation of smog: millions of cars, clear skies and plenty of sunshine. During the summer months cold winds tend to blow inland from the sea and produce a temperature inversion over the city that prevents the fumes from rising, effectively trapping the smog against the surrounding mountain range. The Los Angeles smog has become a serious problem and several proposals, some being rather fanciful or completely unpractical, have been suggested to alleviate it; however, as yet there is no feasible solution.

Rain

Each raindrop is composed of about a million cloud droplets. These minute cloud particles, averaging only 0·02 millimetre (0·0008 inch) in diameter are so light that they float in the air until they become large enough and heavy enough to overcome the resistance of the air and fall out of the cloud as raindrops. Despite occasional reports of rain falling from a clear sky, rain always depends on the presence of cloud, usually of the cumulonimbus or nimbostratus type.

The process of rain formation is more complex than might be expected and has baffled scientists for many years. However, two basic mechanisms are now broadly accepted. The first was proposed in 1933 by a Swedish meteorologist, Tor Bergeron, and later developed by the German physicist Findeisen. The theory is based on the observation that many clouds extend into the levels of the atmosphere at which the temperature is in the range $-20°C$ to $-40°C$ ($-4°F$ to $-40°F$) and that clouds at these levels are made up of a mixture of ice crystals, supercooled water droplets and water vapour. But at these temperatures, air has a very peculiar property: if it is saturated with respect to water then it is supersaturated with respect to ice. This means that, as far as the ice crystals are concerned, there is too much vapour in the air. So some of the vapour freezes on to the ice, and the crystals grow larger. But this process reduces the amount of water vapour in the air, making it now unsaturated with respect to water. Some of the droplets therefore evaporate to redress the balance.

By this process there is a continuous transfer of moisture from water through vapour to ice, and the ice crystals grow rapidly. Eventually they become large enough to fall as snow and as they descend they pass down through the $0°C$ ($32°F$) level, where they melt and continue their descent as raindrops.

The "ice-crystal" process can account for most of the temperate latitude rain, but in the tropics rain often falls from warm clouds containing no ice crystals and so a second mechanism – the "coalescence process" – was proposed by the American physicist Irving Langmuir.

In temperate countries, in particular, umbrellas of every shape, size and colour seem to blossom from nowhere at the first sign of rain. However, since warm air contains more moisture than cold air, more rain is produced from a given amount of upward-moving air in the tropics than in high latitudes.

A home-made umbrella-cum-tent (*below*) provides first-class protection against heavy tropical rain.

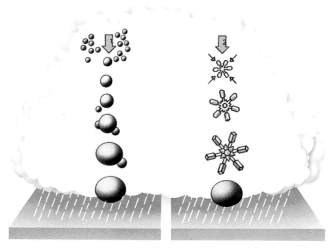

Raindrops form within clouds either by small water droplets colliding and coalescing with one another (1) or by large ice crystals melting into drops as they are warmed (2).

Cloud droplets are mostly very light and remain suspended in the air, but a few have sufficient weight to start falling slowly through the cloud. As they do so they collide with other droplets, coalescing to form bigger drops. The deeper the cloud, the bigger the drops grow and the faster they fall, although there is an upper limit, at about 5 millimetres (0·2 inch) diameter, at which the drops become deformed and break up again. Very shallow clouds produce only drizzle – that is, rain comprising very small droplets of up to 1 millimetre (0·04 inch) diameter. Deeper clouds produce raindrops usually of about 3 millimetres (0·12 inch) diameter. Drizzle should not be confused with light rain: drizzle consists of very small droplets, but can be quite dense, and in places where warm moist winds rise over mountains, constant drizzle may produce more than 10 millimetres (0·4 inch) of precipitation in a day.

The type of rain produced reflects the circumstances in which precipitation is initiated. A large mass of air rising at a warm front will develop layered clouds and produce steady rain. By contrast, air forced to rise quickly at a cold front will produce heavy squall-like showers from cumulonimbus clouds. Any situation of convergence, whether associated with a low-pressure centre or not, will lead to air being forced to rise, and hence to rainfall. Similarly, where moist winds from an oceanic region move inland and are forced to rise over high ground, precipitation will be a common feature of the local climate, while the area in the lee of the hills will be noticeably drier.

In Chinese mythology, the dragon is a beneficent creature. It is a symbol of life-giving rain (and also acted as the national symbol and the badge of the royal family).

Rain records

Using a rain gauge (*above*) to measure rainfall at the Paris Observatory, France, 1881.

"Singin' in the rain" (*below*) – the classic scene from the film of the same name.

Rain does not fall evenly either in space or in time. On any particular rainy day the amount of water actually reaching the ground can vary considerably, even within a relatively small area, and particularly in hilly terrain; one locality might suffer a torrential downpour while a neighbouring village remains quite dry. Even in flat, open terrain, the natural movement of the cloud system across the land, and the constant development and decay of the individual cells within the cloud mass, can cause large variations in rainfall from place to place.

Rainfall is measured in terms of the depth of water that would have covered the ground if none of it ran off or percolated into the soil. In temperate regions an "average" rainy day might produce between 5 and 30 millimetres (0·2 to 1·2 inches) of rain.

In order to maintain records of precipitation, the rain is collected in a special rain gauge. There are several types, but the simplest consists of a funnel either 125 millimetres (5 inches) or 200 millimetres (8 inches) in diameter connected via a narrow tube to a graduated reservoir, designed so that water collected in it cannot evaporate away. The funnel has vertical interior walls, to avoid water splashing out, and has a steeply bevelled or sometimes horizontal outer lip to prevent water running into the funnel from outside its catchment area. Among the more elaborate gauges in use is the tipping-bucket type, in which the accumulating rain in the reservoir causes a float to rise, so operating a pen, which makes a permanent and continuous record on a paper chart clipped to a rotating clock-driven drum. Each time the container becomes full it automatically tips and empties, so maintaining the continuity of the trace.

To obtain reliable measurements, a rain gauge must be sited well away from trees and buildings, which provide shelter and distort air flow and so may reduce the amount of water reaching the instrument. Also, the gauge should not be placed in too exposed a site, because in strong winds the eddies formed by the gauge itself may blow raindrops away from the funnel mouth and so distort the readings. Not surprisingly it is virtually impossible to obtain precise records of rainfall. Nevertheless, when rainfall records are totalled over a month, and averaged over several gauges in an area, the result is a statistically acceptable mean which has many very practical uses.

Rainfall is of paramount importance to Man since it provides virtually all the water we use – for human consumption, for our agricultural practices and for our industrial processes. Fortunately, although rain falls in an irregular manner, it then percolates into the ground, which acts like a giant sponge in evening out the supply. But as population increases, the growth of huge urban complexes and activities such as irrigation make it necessary to create additional water storage and supply facilities. In most countries dams have been built across major rivers in order to retain, for months, a significant proportion of the water which would otherwise run off the land and into the sea in a matter of days or weeks. In some parts of the world, Southern California for example,

ALL MANNER OF SHOWERS

Whirlpools and strong air currents that give rise to rain clouds can sweep aloft a whole variety of objects which are subsequently deposited some distance away with alarming, but often humorous, consequences. There are recent, reliable, records from many parts of the world of showers of spiders, fish, frogs and maggots, but the most common of these strange occurrences is that of showers of coloured rain: these are the result of airborne sand or dust particles being trapped in the forming raindrops. The early nineteenth-century cartoon of a violent downpour (*below*) verifies the old saying "raining cats, dogs and pitchforks".

Showers of oddities were depicted in Conrad Lycosthenes' work *Prodigiorum ac ostentorum chronicon*, published in Basel in 1557. The first shows a rain of toads recorded in 1345, the second a shower of fishes which occurred in Saxony in 989, and the last a most unusual fall of crosses, reported in Sicily in 746.

where natural rainfall cannot satisfy demand, water is piped from sources some hundreds of kilometres away; and in a number of very arid coastal areas the desalination of sea water has proved to be a viable, if expensive, alternative water supply.

In areas where rainfall is restricted to one season, or is generally very sparse throughout the year, people adjust their demands accordingly and there is a general awareness of the need for supplies to be conserved. In other parts of the world, Europe and the northern United States in particular, rainfall is usually so plentiful that there is little if any attempt to use this resource in moderation. Consequently the effects of drought can strike very hard at these heavily populated urbanized areas. In most of Europe rainfall was far below normal almost every month from May 1975 to August 1976. During the last three months of this drought, reservoirs dried up, crops failed on an unprecedented scale, cattle had to be slaughtered because of the lack of grass or drinking water and domestic supplies of water were strictly rationed. It was a sharp reminder to millions of people of just how vital a commodity water really is.

While the European water shortage of 1975–76 caused widespread discomfort, and financial losses to some areas

of agriculture, its effect was in no way comparable with the killer droughts that afflict some parts of the world. In northern Australia, and parts of southern Africa, South America, Central America and Asia, drought, or partial drought, is a fact of life. But perhaps nowhere have the effects of drought been witnessed in such stark reality as in parts of north-central Africa in recent years. Here, in the Sahel region and across the Sudan, Ethiopia and Somalia, drought has devastated human populations on a scale unimagined in the temperate Western World.

In many drought-prone societies the rain-making ceremony has a special significance, offering at least a shred of hope. Perhaps technology will some day be able to provide more certain results. In the right conditions rain can now be created artificially – but the process is expensive and still far from reliable; as a scheme for modifying the weather to suit mankind, it has a long and colourful history. Although nobody has as yet established proven techniques for making clouds that would otherwise pass on their way unchanged and deposit their burden of moisture over one particular area, there is no doubt that clouds can be encouraged to produce rain by the presence of microscopic particles, which act as seeds on to which droplets of moisture or ice can grow.

Rainbows

The rainbow, considered by many to be the most beautiful of all atmospheric optical phenomena, has inspired poets and songwriters of all cultures through the ages. In many cultures it is revered as a divine symbol, representing a bridge between the Earth and the heavens or a link between the real and the spirit worlds. The Pueblo Indians of the southwestern United States believed that rainbows were the means by which their ancestors originally came into this world from the "worlds below".

According to the Bible, in the book of Genesis, the rainbow was created by God as a reminder of His covenant not to send another flood to inundate the Earth: "I do set my bow in the cloud, and it shall be for a token of a covenant between me and the earth. And it shall come to pass, when I bring a cloud over the earth, that the bow shall be seen in the cloud: and I will remember my covenant, which *is* between me and you and every living creature of all flesh; and the waters shall no more become a flood to destroy all flesh."

The rainbow is also commonly held to be a pathway to good fortune, a magical sign pointing the way to the mythical crock of gold at its foot. If one can only reach the rainbow's end, all will be well. A safe enough claim, as one might expect of a saying that has endured for centuries. For as fast as an observer approaches a rainbow, so does it retreat before him. The reason of course is that the rainbow does not exist as a physical entity: it is an optical effect, created as an image in the eye of the beholder at a particular time and place. Even two people standing side by side do not "see" the same rainbow – though they may well give identical descriptions of the visual impressions they are experiencing.

When light passes through a medium of varying density, or from one medium to another of different density (for example from warm air into cold, or from air to water, or water to glass), the speed of the ray of light is altered and the ray is bent, or "refracted". In certain conditions this results in the white light ray splitting into bands of colour – red, orange, yellow, green, blue, indigo and violet. A rainbow is the result of one such set of circumstances. The observer, standing with his back to the Sun and facing a shower of rain, sees the arc of colour formed by light passing through individual raindrops where it is refracted, split up and reflected to his eye. The common, or "primary" arc, red on the outside and violet on the inside, forms in raindrops that are at an angle of about 42 degrees from an imaginary line drawn from the Sun, through the eye of the observer, to a point on the ground ahead of the observer – a point that is also the centre of the arc. If the Sun is close to the horizon, the bow will form a semicircle; the higher the Sun is in the sky, the flatter the arc will be, and if the Sun is higher than 42 degrees above the horizon, no rainbow will be seen. Thus rainbows are seen most frequently in the early morning and late afternoon.

The curvature of the Earth naturally restricts the observed rainbow to a semicircle at most, but aircraft passengers, flying between the Sun and a rain shower,

are sometimes fortunate enough to see the rainbow as a full circle – a rare sight.

A secondary rainbow can sometimes be seen outside and above the primary rainbow. It is invariably fainter, the colour sequence is reversed, and the subtended angle is about 52 degrees. This arc is formed by refraction and a double reflection of the light ray inside the raindrop. Occasionally even more subsidiary rainbows, called "supernumeraries", may be visible, and on a few rare occasions observers have seen as many as four supernumeraries on the primary arc and three or four on the secondary. (Other optical effects caused by the reflection and refraction of light by water droplets and ice prisms are described on pages 44–47.)

Certain places are noted for the frequency of their rainbows and one such place is Honolulu. Northeast of the city lies a range of mountains that causes almost constant heavy drizzle, while the skies to the southwest are clear and the afternoon sun shines brightly, producing brilliant rainbows over the hills. Sometimes, near sunrise or sunset, the sky is dominated by red light and the rainbow cannot manifest its full range, but appears instead as a dramatic red arch. The most spectacular rainbows occur when sunlight is refracted by large raindrops; when the drops are small, the colour separation in the rainbow is poor.

A rainbow seen from the ground takes the form of a semicircle in the sky (*above*), while one observed from an aircraft here appears superimposed on the sea (*left*).

Light hitting a raindrop passes straight through, except at the edges, where the surface of the raindrop makes an acute angle with the direction of the light from the Sun and acts like a prism, splitting the sunlight (white light) into its constituent colours. An observer standing between the Sun and a rain shower sees these colours reflected from the backs of the raindrops. From each drop he sees only that colour which is reflected at precisely the right angle to enter his eye and therefore from a rain shower sees a series of colours each reflected back from different raindrops.

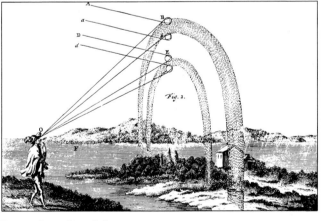

Formation of a rainbow (*above*) from *Mathematical Elements of Natural Philosophy Confirmed by Experiments*, 1747.

If, during a rainbow, the observer were suspended in mid-air, the light that he would see reflected back from the shower would emanate from the whole sky and would thus form a complete circle.

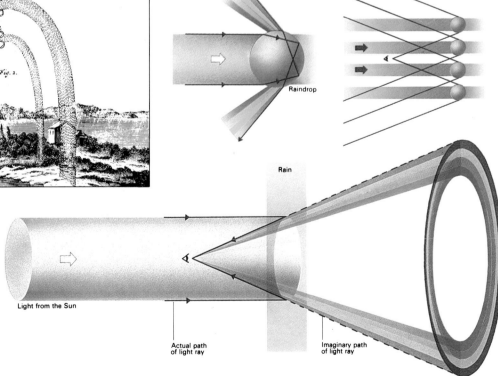

Floods

Most floods are, of course, caused by too much rainfall in too short a time. But several other factors – the lie of the land, the nature of the land surface, the amount of water already in the ground and whether or not the ground is frozen – determine the severity of a flood.

Among the most severe are "flash floods", which can occur when an intense thunderstorm pours a deluge of rain on a relatively small area in a very short space of time. Flash floods are rare events, but they can happen anywhere, even in the driest deserts. Calama, in Chile, reported to have had no rain in more than 400 years, suffered a torrential rainstorm on 10 February 1972 which caused catastrophic floods and hundreds of landslides.

Rivers and drains can cope with the normal, but often not the exceptional, event. Even in cities where heavy storms are common, and the drains are built to take the run-off, the occasional superstorm will prove too much. The drains just overflow and the rush of water causes widespread damage, even loss of life. On 14 August 1975, London experienced its heaviest rainstorm ever when 170 millimetres (6·7 inches) of rain fell in about three hours. Cars floated down streets, sewers burst, basements filled with water and damage to property was widespread. Yet a few kilometres away only 10 millimetres (0·4 inch) of rain was recorded. A similar storm affected the town of Laingsburg on the edge of the Karroo Desert on 25 January 1981. More than 250 millimetres (9·8

THE GREAT FLOOD
The inundation with which we associate Noah's Ark was probably one of many that wreaked havoc in the Tigris–Euphrates region of present-day Iraq during the fourth millennium BC. Evidence that there had been at least one major flood came from archaeological excavations at Ur in the 1930s: between layers of soil laden with mud, brick, ashes and pottery was a thick layer of water-laid mud.

Lynmouth, in Devon, England, was devastated by a major flood on 15 August 1952. Following torrential rains on nearby Exmoor, streams leading into the town's main river were overflowing and laden with rocks and boulders, some weighing several tonnes, which ploughed through bridges, roads and houses in their path.

Rickshaws ferry people through the flooded streets of Dacca, Bangladesh, in August 1974. This part of the world is probably one of the most susceptible to major floods.

Venice, in northern Italy, was awash after the River Arno had burst its banks on 4 November 1966. This was the result of a month of almost continuous rain.

inches) fell in less than 12 hours, transforming the dried-up bed of the Buffalo River into a raging torrent that sent a wave of mud through the town, engulfing nearly three-quarters of the settlement.

The effects of a flash flood are made far worse by hilly terrain, in which the floodwaters are channelled into narrow gulleys and valleys, often with devastating results. One such storm hit Big Thompson Canyon, in Colorado, on 31 July 1976. An intense storm poured 250 millimetres (9.8 inches) of rain, more than half the average for a normal year, on to the area in just a few hours. All the water surged into the canyon, sweeping away roads, buildings, cars and livestock. A thousand people were lifted out by helicopter: rescuers later recovered 139 bodies from the mud and wreckage.

More widespread flooding is usually caused by large, slow-moving low-pressure systems. Tropical storms are the most copious rain producers, but even temperate low-pressure systems can sometimes produce long periods of continuous heavy rain sufficient to cause flooding. In September 1968 a low-pressure system remained stationary in the English Channel while a continuous stream of warm moist air flowed round it, rising and dropping its moisture on southeast England. Some places received up to 200 millimetres (7.8 inches) in three days – not much when compared with a flash flood, but the ground was already saturated after a wet summer and the heavy rains covered three counties. Much of the water ran into the fast-flowing River Mole which overflowed, turning streets into rivers and depositing thick mud throughout densely populated areas south of London.

In November 1966 a combination of circumstances caused terrible flooding in Florence when the Arno burst its banks and destroyed, or seriously damaged, hundreds of paintings, books, sculptures and other works of art. The floods resulted from heavy rains over much of northern Italy, strong warm winds that caused melting of snows in the Dolomite mountains and the channelling effect of the narrow mountain valleys. The steep mountain rivers carried huge amounts of debris, including large boulders, and this destructive load was hurled at the lowland towns with disastrous results. Not only Florence but much of Italy and neighbouring countries suffered flooding at that time, indicating that a large-scale atmospheric system had been responsible.

But one of Britain's most widespread floods was caused not by rain but by melting snow, in March 1947. Rivers burst their banks, thousands of homes were damaged by flooding, huge areas of farmland were inundated and thousands of animals were drowned.

Floods cause an enormous amount of misery, destruction and hardship every year, even in areas of the world where they occur fairly regularly and constitute a "normal" feature of the wet season. Although most people think of floods in meteorological terms – the result of too much rain in a short period of time – floods are technically classified as hydrological phenomena, associated with the movement of water on land.

Snow

Snow crystals form in layer clouds at temperatures between $-20°$ and $-40°C$ $(-4°$ and $-40°F)$. First, tiny ice crystals form on dust nuclei in the atmosphere. The air in the cloud is supersaturated with respect to ice, so vapour immediately condenses on to the crystal, increasing its size. At the same time, water droplets in the cloud evaporate in an attempt to regain equilibrium, so providing a continuous supply of vapour for further growth of the ice crystal.

Several different forms of crystal occur naturally. High cirrus clouds are composed mainly of prisms about 0·5 millimetre (0·02 inch) long, with cavities; cirrostratus bears mainly short, solid prisms; altostratus has a mixture of prisms and thin hexagonal plates; and clouds at lower levels have crystals of a variety of shapes and sizes.

Laboratory experiments carried out to investigate how the crystals grow have shown that the form of the crystal depends on the temperature and degree of saturation of the cloud, and that very slight changes can have a marked effect on crystal form. Ice crystals are relatively heavy and tend to fall at about 50 centimetres per second (19·5 inches per second), often growing as they do so. If they fall out of the cloud into dry air they may evaporate. If they fall below the $0°C$ $(32°F)$ level they melt into rain, and if they reach the ground intact they are called snow. Thus snow can take several physical forms: stars, plates, prisms or needles. Needle crystals require moist air for their formation, whereas plate crystals can grow slowly when the air is dry but rapidly when the air is moist; columnar crystals form in dry air and the dendritic, star-shaped ones always require a moderately moist environment. These exquisite shapes are a result of complex sequences of evaporation, condensation and deposition in the micro-environment around each crystal.

Usually, however, snow does not fall as single crystals but as composite snowflakes formed when crystals become wet, collide, then freeze together again. This happens most markedly at fairly "high" temperatures – around freezing point. At lower temperatures aggregation does not occur since the crystals themselves are dry. The biggest snowflakes, up to 6 centimetres (nearly 2·4 inches) across and made up of hundreds of individual crystals, form between zero and $2°C$ $(32°$ and $36°F)$. If temperatures rise any higher, the flake melts to form rain or the half-melted snow called "sleet" in Britain.

The fact that the heaviest snow occurs when temperatures are around $0°C$ $(32°F)$ makes the forecasting of snow very difficult. A slight change in temperature can make the difference between a heavy snowfall and a downpour of rain. Indeed, in many cases precipitation starts as rain with a temperature of $3°$ to $4°C$ $(37°$ to $39°F)$, but as the rain evaporates into the unsaturated air below the cloud it takes up latent heat, so cooling the air sufficiently for the precipitation to reach the ground as sleet. Conversely, snow may fall almost to ground level before melting and being recorded as rain. The fact that

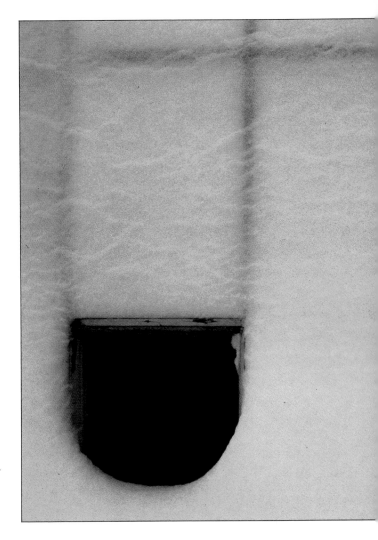

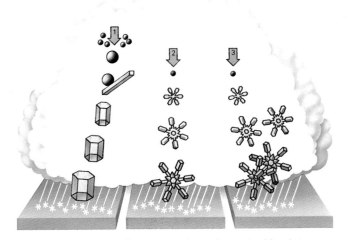

The shape and size of snow crystals are determined by their height, temperature below $0°C$ $(32°F)$ and the degree of saturation of the cloud; prisms form at low temperatures (*1*), flakes at high (*2, 3*).

Ideal skiing conditions (*above*) are those in which the snow is light, dry and uncompacted – referred to by skiers as "powder snow". Commonly, however, such fresh snow soon thaws, only to freeze again, forming heavy "granular snow".

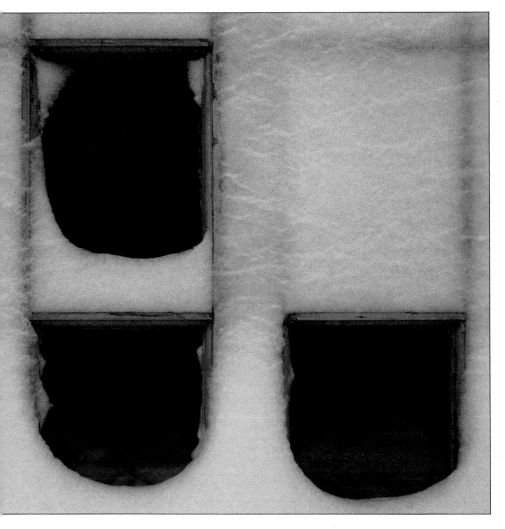

Dry snow has penetrated broken window panes, literally bringing a snowstorm indoors.

this happens is exemplified by the case of rain falling in the streets of New York while the security guards on the top of the Empire State Building were throwing snowballs at each other.

All precipitation in polar latitudes, most in temperate latitudes and some in the tropics is initially snow, but melts to rain as it falls through warmer levels in the atmosphere. For the snow to survive and reach the ground, the temperature must nowhere be higher than about 2°C (36°F). Soft hail (also called sleet in the US) can reach the ground at temperatures as high as 6°C (43°F) because the pellets fall faster than snowflakes. But, apart from the temperature factor, the conditions for snow to fall are exactly the same as for rain: the fundamental requirement is an upward movement of air produced by an area of low pressure, the convergence of airstreams or by the physical barrier of a mountain range. Warm air holds more moisture than cold, so the heaviest snows tend to occur when the temperature is close to freezing rather than at extremely low temperatures. It is some-

times said to be "too cold for snow", but this is never strictly true. However, like most sayings it does reflect a characteristic situation. The lowest temperatures at any locality are usually felt on clear nights, and if snow is imminent then clouds will invariably move in first and the temperature will rise in consequence.

Snow is most common in areas that have the lowest winter temperatures, generally in the interior parts of the great continents. In maritime regions, snow is less common, but when it does fall it can be very heavy due to the huge quantities of water carried inland by the warm oceanic air masses. Certain localities, such as the area south and east of the Great Lakes in North America, are particularly prone to heavy snowfall; here, dry continental air from the northwest picks up moisture and heat as it passes over the lakes and becomes very unstable. Then, on reaching the shore, it is forced to rise by a range of low hills or when it becomes supersaturated after passing over lakes, and the entire moisture load is dumped as a heavy fall of snow.

Blizzards

A snowstorm can bring chaos to road traffic and make a great many outdoor activities extremely difficult, particularly for farmers and other people who depend upon good weather. A blizzard, however, is a much more violent phenomenon combining very strong wind, low temperature and fine powdery snow, which reduces visibility to zero. The very fine blowing snow has even proved itself to be as deadly as any choking dust. Some people who have been killed in blizzards have died from suffocation, their lungs being choked with fine snow.

Snowstorms and blizzards are common in Canada and the northern United States. In the winter of 1977–78, 18 major storms were recorded in Illinois, causing 62 deaths and more than 2000 injuries. And in March 1888, New York City was buried by a sixty-hour blizzard and was completely cut off for two days from all contact with the rest of the world. One of Britain's worst blizzards hit southwest England in 1891, when, following a mild February, a low-pressure system moved in from Biscay, deepening rapidly. Warm air laden with moisture from the Atlantic rose up over cold air blowing in an easterly gale across southern England, and dropped its moisture as snow. Enormous drifts blocked all roads and railway lines, trees were blown down and thousands of animals perished.

In mountainous country, snowstorms and blizzards can create conditions just as severe as those in the Arctic and there have been many cases in which inexperience of mountain weather has led to hill-walking and climbing parties being stranded, sometimes with tragic results. The confusion caused by the wind and blowing snow is increased by "white-out" conditions when the Earth and sky are indistinguishable and the walker loses all sense of orientation.

The snowiest place in the world for which records are kept is the small resort of Paradise in the Mt Rainier National Park in the northwestern United States. In the winter of 1971–72 a total of 31 metres (102 feet) of snowfall was recorded. The walls of the resort hotel have to be supported every autumn with huge internal beams to prevent the building being crushed during the winter.

Snow falling at around 0°C (32°F), in calm or light wind conditions, is soft and feathery because of the air trapped in it and very white due to the high proportion of incident light it reflects. Piled high on fences, roofs and branches, it can make a beautiful sight, especially when the Sun is shining. By contrast, snow falling in very cold weather is dry, more powdery and less prone to sticking to ledges. If the snow is blown about, the crystals fragment, giving a more compact mass. The cover is also likely to be less even, with only a thin covering on open fields, where the wind is strong, but with huge hard-packed drifts forming in the lee of obstructions and in hollows such as railway cuttings.

In continental areas, where thick snow and low temperatures are common, snow is cleared from roads with huge machines that act like enormous vacuum cleaners. But in maritime regions heavy snow, though less common, is far more disruptive. Authorities are often blamed for being ill-equipped, but the problem is the snow itself: it tends to be wet, and wet snow cannot be blown clear. Compacted drifts have to be laboriously dug out by snowploughs or mechanical shovels.

Several factors affect the length of time the snow lies on the ground. As soon as the temperature rises above 0°C (32°F), melting will occur, and this is greatly speeded up by warm winds or rain. However, too rapid melting while the underlying ground is still frozen can create a serious flood hazard. Alternatively, snow may disappear by sublimation, that is by evaporating directly from solid to vapour without ever existing as liquid. This may occur in a long, dry, cold spell.

As soon as snow has fallen its character starts to change. If the air temperature is above freezing point or if there is heat from the Sun, the top surface of the snow melts a little; when the temperature then falls below freezing at night, the water freezes again, and the snow develops a hard but brittle shell. If the snow persists it becomes very compressed and may also become stained with algae and discoloured with atmospheric dust. In many arctic and mountain areas large patches of snow may persist through the summer. If the snow partly melts, and meltwater then percolates through to fill interior air spaces, eventually the one-time snow pocket becomes ice.

Clearing snow from a runway at Aberdeen airport, Scotland, using a giant blower unit. Because of the unpredictability of the weather, city authorities the world over are invariably caught unawares by snowfalls. The result is chaos.

On 20 January 1978, in New York more than 350 millimetres (14 inches) of snow fell in 24 hours. The blizzard paralysed the city, with land, sea and air traffic being forced to a halt. In Downtown Manhattan, for example (*right*), cars were simply abandoned; either they were unable to be driven through the deep snow or their engines were frozen.

FORMATION OF AN AVALANCHE

An avalanche results from the creation of overwhelming stresses in a particularly weak layer of snow. Within snow on the ground there tends to be layers of varying compactness – here a layer of loose snow is sandwiched between more compact layers; this makes the former susceptible to great internal stresses. A snowfall adds extra weight to the top layer such that its downward pressure is increased (1). Should, in consequence, stresses within the weak layer overcome its inherent strength, a fracture occurs (2). Triggered by the weight of a skier, perhaps, the fracture extends sideways and downwards, and suddenly a huge slab of snow breaks away and hurtles towards the base of the slope; a sharp, step-like fracture is left behind (3). As the slab falls under the force of gravity it tends to fragment into blocks.

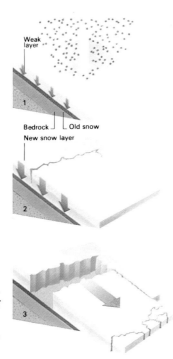

Weak layer

Bedrock ⌐ Old snow
New snow layer

The avalanche shown in motion (*left*) was initiated by a skier disturbing the delicate balance of snow on the mountainside; the picture is a composite of four that were taken within a few seconds of each other, as can be seen by the progress of the skier. The aftermath of the event is shown below.

No matter where in the world snow may fall, Man usually finds some way of using it for his own ends. At one extreme it has meant adapting his entire lifestyle to a snow-bound wilderness, while at the other it has provided the basis of a huge leisure industry serving the large, and extensively urban, populations of Europe and North America with ski resorts.

Of the many possible sporting activities, skiing is by far the most important. Originating in Norway as a purely practical means of individual transportation it has, over the past century, spread almost worldwide. In addition to the main ski centres in the mountain ranges of the Alps and Rockies there are flourishing centres in Scotland, Australia, New Zealand – almost anywhere with snowfall. Even Hawaii has a small ski industry on Mauna Kea Mountain, which receives a cap of snow in most winters. To many of these areas, skiing is a major industry: when the snow failed in Colorado in 1977, local airlines, hotels and other services suffered very heavy financial losses.

But snow in mountain areas brings its own inherent danger – the avalanche. The biggest occur in the Andes, Himalayas and mountains of Alaska, but by far the greatest danger to human life and property is in the Alps, where the whole region is densely populated, not least the vulnerable valley floors. Avalanches occur on slopes that are generally steeper then 22 degrees and may be triggered by a rise in temperature, a powerful gust of wind, or even a loud noise. Even a lone skier venturing across a slope on which the snow is ready to slip can start the whole mass moving; once started, nothing will prevent the snow surging down the mountainside and into the valley.

An avalanche can bury a village in seconds – its power can smash aside trees and buildings as though they were made of matchwood. There are very few preventative measures that can be taken, though early-warning systems have achieved a high degree of success in saving lives. Controlled explosions are used in some areas to start small avalanches where snow-fields are becoming unstable, thus preventing a possibly catastrophic slide later. Planting forest barriers and erecting deflection structures is largely ineffective – a large avalanche will sweep them aside and, worse, will carry the debris downslope like battering rams.

A further hazard in mountain country is the cornice, a wave-like overhanging mass of compacted snow, formed where the wind blows over a crest and eddies back. Such structures are notoriously dangerous to climbers as they can give way at any time. They are consequently another potential cause of avalanches. Cornices are not only found in mountains: in 1836 a massive cornice developed on a cliff edge in Sussex, England. Eventually it collapsed, crashing down close to a row of houses. The snow mass exploded on impact, due to compression of the air pockets within it, and houses were lifted off the ground and wrecked, killing eight people altogether.

Flakes and crystals

Single snow crystals can assume a wide variety of exquisite forms (*below*), but they are rarely seen because the snowflakes that reach the ground are usually clumps of fragmented crystals.

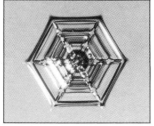
Hexagonal plate

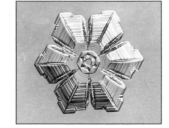
Sector plate

Dendrite

Needle

Bullet

Tsuzumi

The most common form of frozen precipitation is the snowflake – a composite structure of many tiny hexagonal ice crystals that are frozen together. Some crystals are like feathery stars, others are more plate-like in structure, but no two are ever alike.

Wilson Bentley (1865–1931), a Vermont farmer, was fascinated by snow crystals and made a lifelong study of them. He took photographs of more than 5000 snowflakes, using a microscope, and published a collection of 2500 of the structures. He was a careful and perceptive investigator. During the summer months he measured the sizes of raindrops and in 1904 suggested that rain could form in either of two ways – one of them from snowflakes. Although this view is widely accepted today, Bentley, alas, was ignored by scientists of his own day.

The combination of low temperature and atmospheric precipitation can produce a variety of results. One of these is "soft hail", which is also known as "snow pellets" or "graupel" and consists of opaque white grains of ice between 2 and 5 millimetres (0·08 and 0·19 inch) in diameter which fall quite fast and bounce high off the ground. Soft hail is a common form of precipitation from cumulonimbus clouds developing in unstable polar airstreams during winter and spring. It forms from the collision of ice crystals and supercooled water droplets.

Another form is known as "snow grains" – much smaller than snow pellets, generally less than 1 millimetre (0·04 inch) in diameter and usually flat or elongated. They consist of small ice needles or snow crystals that have been coated with rime. They are the frozen equivalent of drizzle and are usually associated with shallow stratus cloud or wet freezing fog.

At very low temperatures, some of the water droplets in a fog may freeze and the ice crystals then grow at the expense of the remaining drops, which evaporate. The result is an ice-crystal fog: cirrus cloud at ground level. Because of the absence of water droplets, the effect may not resemble fog at all. The tiny ice crystals fall very slowly, glittering in the sunshine, giving rise to the name "diamond dust". These "ice needles" may produce other optical phenomena such as sun dogs and sun pillars. They usually occur only in stable conditions, at temperatures that are well below freezing, but they may occasionally fall from low stratus clouds if temperatures are less than $-4°C$ (25°F).

Yet another variation on the theme are "ice pellets". As opposed to snow pellets, these are lumps of transparent, hard ice, often irregular in shape and up to 5 millimetres (0·19 inch) in diameter. They are in fact frozen raindrops, formed when rain from a warm air mass falls through a deep layer of air of below freezing point. These conditions are common in the northeastern United States, where ice pellets are known as "sleet". (In Britain, the term "sleet" denotes partly melted snow.)

When rain or drizzle falls through freezing cold air it does not necessarily freeze but may instead reach ground level as a supercooled liquid. If the ground itself is also below freezing, the rain freezes instantly on to everything it touches, coating roads, grass, trees, cars, overhead cables and everything else with a layer of clear, smooth ice. This form of precipitation – "freezing rain", "glaze", "glazed frost" or "ice storm" – can produce such deadly road conditions that outdoor movement is virtually brought to a halt.

The ice resulting from freezing rain is sometimes called black ice. This term also includes the ice that forms when wet roads freeze at night; it is not literally black, but transparent and invisible. It occurs most frequently after a cold spell, when warm moist air flows in over a stagnant mass of very cold air. Usually the freezing rain lasts for only a few hours before a thaw sets in. Occasionally, however, the cold air persists. In January 1940, England suffered a three-day ice storm in which roads were like skating rinks, doors froze solid and the weight of the glaze brought down telephone wires, posts and trees throughout the country. Birds and small animals were killed in their thousands and there were records of birds being killed in flight by the sub-zero rain. The only recorded case of a glaze persisting longer than a week is in Connecticut, when glaze fell in late December 1969 and remained on trees for six weeks.

Trawlermen are familiar with the problems of gales

and wild seas, but the combination of these with sub-zero temperatures and flying sea-spray brings one of the deadliest hazards – icing of the superstructure and rigging. In February 1968 a fishing fleet was caught off the coast of Iceland in hurricane-force winds and temperatures of −11°C (12°F). Crews worked non-stop, hacking at the thick ice encasing every part of the ships exposed to the spray to prevent them becoming top-heavy. During three weeks of this atrocious weather, several ships lost the grim struggle, overturned and sank, with a loss of nearly 60 lives. Many techniques have been tried to alleviate the effects of ice storms, including heated elements and pneumatic collars, which expand to crack the ice shell as it forms, but icing remains one of the gravest threats to shipping in northern waters.

In Arctic regions, many glaciers reach the sea. There, they "calve" – large blocks of ice break off and are carried away with the current, forming icebergs, which are a serious hazard to shipping, particularly in the Newfoundland area. As the underwater part of an iceberg melts, the berg may become top-heavy and suddenly tip on its side to find a new equilibrium, which is why it is dangerous for a ship to be in the vicinity. Unnoticed icebergs have caused the sinking of many ships, including the famous "unsinkable" liner *Titanic* in 1912.

A fire engine (*above*) coated in glazed frost. Rain falling from an advancing, warm, upper cloud into a stagnant air mass near the ground, which is at temperatures below 0°C (32°F), freezes on contact with all cold surfaces with potentially disastrous consequences.

Tabular icebergs (*below*) are flat-topped; they are the result of the breaking up of huge ice sheets such as those on Antarctica. More irregular-shaped icebergs are formed when wind and water open up crevices in a glacier that has reached the sea.

Hailstones (*above*) can batter crops, flowers and fruits to a pulp, with dire consequences for farmers.

A violent hailstorm (*below*) in Saxony, Germany, in AD 837, killed several people.

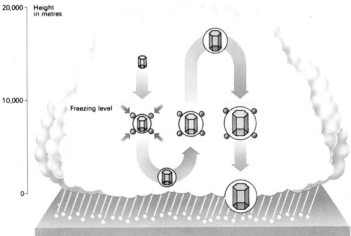

20,000 — Height in metres

10,000

Freezing level

0

Hailstones are frozen raindrops which have been tossed up and down by the violent vertical air currents in a cumulonumbus storm cloud, growing as droplets freeze on to them until they are heavy enough to fall to the ground. On their journey through the cloud the raindrops alternately melt and freeze, and a cross-section of a hailstone reveals layers of clear and frosty ice. A hailstone may stay suspended in a cloud for several minutes.

Frosty layer

Clear layer

Hail

True hail, as distinct from "soft hail", which is really a form of snow, consists of spherical lumps of ice ranging in size from about 5 millimetres (0·2 inch) in diameter, upwards. There is another variety called "small hail", which consists of a nucleus of soft hail encased in a thin crust of clear ice. This variety may fall from small cumulonimbus clouds, but true hail forms only in cumulonimbus clouds in which the upcurrents are strong enough to carry the weight of the stones as they grow. Such clouds must be very vigorous and contain a substantial amount of water – conditions that require relatively warm weather with strong surface heating to generate violent uplift. Consequently, true hail is a phenomenon associated with the towering clouds of a mature thunderstorm, and hail typically falls as heavy, but localized, showers within the area of a thunderstorm.

Hailstones originate as pellets of soft hail or as frozen raindrops which rise and fall on the violent air currents in the stormcloud, growing by accretion as cloud droplets freeze on to them. The layered structure often visible in hailstones reveals the up-and-down movement, which continues until a point is reached when the updraught can no longer support the stone and it falls out of the cloud. The layers also reflect the different type of deposition at each level. At very low temperatures the droplets freeze rapidly, trapping lots of tiny air bubbles, which make the ice white. At higher temperatures the freezing takes place more slowly, forming clear ice. Large hailstones often have an onion-like structure, being roughly spherical with alternate layers of white and clear ice. This means that the hailstones must have passed up and down through layers at different temperatures. To keep a stone suspended for the ten minutes or so necessary to produce a large hailstone, updraughts in excess of 30 metres per second (98 feet per second) are required.

Although normally spherical, or nearly so, hailstones can occur in quite bizarre shapes, which are probably due to several stones colliding within the cloud and becoming frozen together. One such stone fell on Sydney, Australia, in 1971 – it had four "horns" 2 centimetres (0·8 inch) long growing from a spherical lump of clear ice. There have even been reports of living creatures such as frogs falling to Earth encased in hailstones, presumably having been swept into the air initially by the powerful updraughts of a passing tornado.

Hail is rare in polar regions because the cold air only contains vapour, and it is the release of latent heat as large amounts of vapour condense that generates the violent upcurrents necessary for the build-up of hailstones. Large hail is also rare in the tropics. This is because one of the requirements for hailstone growth is that wind direction should change markedly with height, so that whenever a hailstone is thrown clear of the cloud it is likely to be swept back in at another level to continue growing in the vertical currents. Although there are abundant cumulonimbus clouds in the tropics, they rarely have this wind structure. Furthermore, in tropical latitudes, any hailstones that do form are likely to melt in the warm air long before reaching the ground.

The central plains of North America, where the most severe thunderstorms and tornadoes occur, are also the areas most frequently hit by hail and, not surprisingly, the areas in which the largest stones have been recorded. Record weight is currently 766 grams (27 ounces) for a stone which fell at Coffeyville in Kansas in 1970. The stone was 44 centimetres (17·2 inches) in circumference

Fossilized prints of hailstones are well preserved in a layer of shale dating from 160 million years ago; a fossilized ammonite is also visible in the rock (*centre top*).

and formed from an aggregation of about 20 smaller stones. Over the years there have been several reports of gelatinous, or slimy, material falling from the sky. Often the events have been associated with meteor sightings and this has given rise to the name "star slime".

In 1909 a man walking through Lowell, Massachusetts, saw a brilliant meteor flash to Earth. On investigation it was found to be a jelly-like mass on the ground with an almost intolerably offensive smell. Another sample, which fell near Dallas, Texas, in 1979, was found to contain uranium and lead, and this analysis was thought to support a possible extraterrestrial origin. On the other hand a naturalist who examined samples of this jelly-like material concluded that they were secretions from frogs or toads, perhaps disgorged by birds that had eaten the creatures. There is also a form of alga, called nostoc, which forms gelatinous masses. Thus a terrestrial origin is also quite possible. Biological material of this type could be picked up in the powerful updraughts of a tornado, and the accompanying reports of meteors might in fact be explained as sightings of ball lightning.

Perhaps the most unpleasant example was the green slime that fell on Washington in 1978, coating cars and buildings, killing plants and causing sickness in animals. Pesticide and discharged jet fuel were proposed as possible culprits, but, as yet, nobody knows the real cause of offensive slime.

Hail damage

The area of America from Texas to Montana, and from the foothills of the Rockies to the Mississippi River, is known as "Hail Alley", and in this belt farmers find substantial outlay on hail insurance an absolute necessity. Total hail damage each year in the United States costs over $500 million. "Hail Alley" extends northwards into Canada, and in parts of Alberta hail is so prevalent that any given square kilometre can expect to be hit once every two years. Hail can also present a hazard to aircraft.

The hazards of hail have naturally prompted Man to seek ways of preventing it, and in many primitive cultures, warriors will shoot arrows into stormclouds to frighten away the evil spirits. Christians in the Middle Ages believed that the ringing of church bells was an effective deterrent, but unfortunately the bellringers' lives were thereby put at some risk since hail usually falls during thunderstorms, and in the days before lightning conductors the church tower was hardly the safest place to be during a storm.

Folklore has it that cloudbursts often followed the great battles in the days when bombardments were by cannon using crude, smoky gunpowder. The reports may be overdramatized, the showers may have been purely coincidental – and yet it is just possible that the pall of smoke hanging over the battlefield might have effectively seeded potential rainclouds. There is, in our modern, technological world, a direct echo of this ancient link between cannon and cloud seeding. In the USSR, where great prairies of grain are at risk from hailstones that can flatten an entire crop within minutes, one feature of many communes is an anti-aircraft battery – not for use against aircraft but to fire special shells into the clouds. The shells are designed to burst, releasing chemical agents into the clouds to seed them. The more particles there are the better, since the same amount of cloud moisture is then distributed between many more, but smaller, droplets of rain or ice crystals, rather than fewer, potentially destructive, large hailstones. Farmers in the USSR claim considerable success with the technique and use a variety of rockets as well as shells in their war against the weather.

In parts of Italy the orange crop is protected from hail damage by a framework of scaffolding erected around each tree: then, at the first sign of an approaching storm, a roof of rush matting is laid over the top. If hail does fall, it beats harmlessly on the roof and then, as it melts, drips through to water the tree.

Quite apart from the "normal", roughly spherical, layered type of hail, old journals and modern record books alike contain all manner of reports of strange phenomena. For example in July 1979, in East Anglia, Britain, there was a fall of "ice flakes" about 3 millimetres (0·1 inch) thick and up to 30 millimetres (1·2 inches) across during a summer thunderstorm, and a few days later, in the same area, there were reports of hailstones shaped like double-ended peardrops.

More serious are the rare isolated cases of very large lumps of ice falling from the sky. In June 1829 one such "ice meteor" weighing 2 kilograms (4·4 pounds) fell at

Hailstones are usually no larger than 10 millimetres (0·39 inches) in diameter, but these huge stones, some as large as golf balls, fell in the Mid-West of the USA in July 1975, devastating a large area of cropland.

"Hail Alley" (*right*), in the southern USA, is a vast area of agricultural land which is regularly subjected to severe hailstorms. Here, however, unlike in the USSR, little has been done to explore methods of crop protection.

Cordoba in Spain; in June 1971 a block of 900 grams (2 pounds) whistled past the head of a man working in a garden in Rouen, France; and in January 1972 a cubic metre (35·3 cubic feet) block of solid ice crashed near a house in Surrey, England. These are not hailstones: they are far too big, and unlike hailstones, which always fall in showers of millions, these ice meteors are solitary objects. An extraterrestrial origin has been offered as one explanation; another strong possibility is that some may come from aircraft. Waste water accidentally falling from an aircraft appears unlikely, but it is possible that airframe icing might build up to a considerable thickness and then break away in large lumps. However, this cannot be a complete answer because ice meteor reports go back long before the advent of powered flight.

It has been suggested that they could be some form of super-hailstones – but if so the mechanism of their formation is as yet unknown. One example was analysed and found to be layered in structure, composed of cloud water, and clearly formed part of a larger block weighing up to 2 kilograms (4·4 pounds). There was a thunderstorm a few kilometres away and ten minutes earlier a single brilliant lightning flash had been reported.

One explanation is that a hailstone nucleus might become trapped in a tornado-like vortex in the cloud and grow very rapidly by accretion while being supported by the unusually strong upcurrents. Another suggestion is that a lightning stroke might produce a jet of electrically charged water droplets, projected violently upwards to freeze together into a large mass of ice. However, a recent American study has shown that in one-third of all known cases there have been no clouds of any size within 1000 kilometres (620 miles) of the meteor landing. Until a better solution is discovered, the airframe icing theory must remain the most generally acceptable theory.

CANONNADE PACIFIQUE

Pour préserver de la grêle leurs fruits et leurs fleurs les horticulteurs de Bagnolet tirent le canon sur les nuages

Firing shells containing silver iodide crystals into hail clouds proved to be a successful way of reducing the size of hailstones; moisture in the cloud accretes on the tiny crystals rather than on the larger, frozen raindrops. In the past, explosive shells were fired into hail clouds on the assumption that the pressure waves would either cause large hailstones to fragment or would speed up the freezing of raindrops to such an extent that the hailstones would be filled with air and become light. Efforts to reduce the damage from hail still continue.

Thunderstorms

One of the most familiar and characteristic features of temperate summer weather is the occurrence of long, hot spells punctuated by the drama of a thunderstorm.

Typically, after several days of calm, sunny, cloudless but increasingly hazy weather, one day dawns noticeably warmer and more humid than the rest; late in the morning through the haze, a bank of cumulus clouds builds up much higher than usual. As the day goes on, the clouds billow upwards into towering columns, brilliant white above but ominously leaden grey at their bases. As the storm clouds approach, the sky becomes dark, the wind drops, the air feels even warmer and more oppressive, and the distant rumble of thunder is heard.

The boiling bank of dark grey cloud forming the leading edge of the storm surges overhead. A few very large drops of rain hit the ground and suddenly there is a blinding flash and the loud crack of thunder as lightning strikes close by. Within minutes the heavens seem to open as the stormclouds release torrential rain, often accompanied by hailstones, and this downpour lasts for up to half an hour. Lightning and thunder continue to flash and bang all around and the wild effect of the storm is increased by cold, gusting, wild winds that sometimes blow violently at great speeds.

Almost as quickly as it began, the storm eases: the rain ceases, the sky becomes brighter and the sound of thunder recedes into the distance. The Sun comes out and the air feels fresh and cool as the retreating thundercloud, with its great turrets and massive anvil, shines brilliantly white in the clear air.

The essential conditions for the development of thunderstorms are that there should be warm, moist air in the lower atmosphere and cold, dense air at higher levels. Under these conditions there is nothing to prevent a bubble of warm air at ground level from rising, and – once it has started rising – from rising faster and faster.

Thunderstorms occur most frequently on hot summer afternoons when ground-level air is subject to a high degree of heating and convection currents are forming. But a hot day is not the only factor necessary to produce a thunderstorm. If there is an anticyclone nearby, the air above will be stable and convection cells will tend to die out, producing only small "fair weather" cumulus clouds instead of the great vertical towers of a stormcloud. On the other hand, if cold air is moving over the warm lower-level air, the atmosphere becomes extremely unstable and may even try to overturn the layers – a condition of very strong instability in which violent storms occur. If, in addition, there is a convergence of airstreams of different properties at ground level, forcing the air masses to rise, then storms will be widespread.

The most common situation for thunderstorm development is along a cold front moving in after a long hot spell; storms do not necessarily occur in hot weather: they can occur on any cold front, or near the centre of a low pressure system, or even in winter when the air is cool. The important factor is the relative temperature of the upper and lower layers, and that the inherent instability should extend to a great height. Winter storms are, however, generally much less intense than those that occur during hot spells in the summer season. Many places in equatorial regions experience thunderstorms every day during the rainy season, while some places record thunder on more than 200 days every year.

Today we are so familiar with electricity that it is hard to realize that barely 250 years ago it was virtually unknown except in its spectacular natural occurrences, the lightning flash. Yet nature's sparks still make Man's best efforts look puny. The electrical discharge of a lightning strike carries a current of many thousands of

amperes, for a tiny fraction of a second, raising the temperature of the air through which it passes to incandescent white heat. Since the light from the flash travels almost instantaneously, the flash is seen before the thunder is heard and the time interval between them gives a measure of the distance of the flash from you: about 3 seconds per kilometre (5 seconds per mile).

The power of lightning can split a tree apart, virtually demolish a building or kill outright a man or beast unfortunate enough to be struck. But its effects are often unpredictable: people struck by lightning may only suffer from shock in some cases. On rare occasions being struck by lightning has even proved to be beneficial to health. In contrast to effects following an electric shock, the heart of a lightning victim usually resumes beating with a normal rhythm after artificial resuscitation. Also, degenerative processes, due to no blood reaching the brain seem to be delayed and the patient will often recover without permanent damage.

The formation of the huge electrical charges in a thundercloud, although as yet not fully understood, is certainly associated with rain, hail and the presence of powerful upcurrents of air within the cloud. Sometimes lightning may develop in high-level clouds, and the precipitation from them evaporates before reaching the ground. All in all, it has been estimated that about 1800 thunderstorms are active over the face of the Earth at any given time.

Thor, the Norse god of thunder (*above*), was supposed to be a red-bearded man of tremendous strength, his greatest attribute being his ability to forge thunderbolts.

A spectacular bolt of lightning (*left*), the most powerful electrical phenomenon in nature.

Sparks in the sky

The seething turbulence inside a big cumulonimbus thunderhead makes the cloud behave like a gigantic electrostatic generator. Positive and negative charges are concentrated in different parts of the cloud, where they build up enormous potential differences, and when these reach the critical field strength of about half a million volts per metre the charges are released in the spectacular spark discharges we know as lightning flashes.

Experiments made in the 1930s first revealed the way in which the electrical charges are distributed. Scientists released balloons into the thunderclouds, each balloon trailing a long wire and carrying instruments to measure and record both the current flowing in the wire and the prevailing atmospheric pressure. At a height of 8 kilometres (5 miles) the instrument package was released to fall back to earth by parachute. When these recordings were analysed it was found that the upper part of the thundercloud, where the temperature is below $-20°C$ $(-4°F)$, is positively charged, while the lower part, where the temperature is generally near or just below freezing, is negatively charged. There are often small areas of positive charge near the base of the cloud and in the mid-levels as well, such concentrations generally being associated with heavy precipitation.

The problem of determining how the charges come to be separated in the first place proved more difficult – and is still far from being solved. Many mechanisms seem to be involved, including collisions between solid and liquid water particles in the cloud and changes of state of water between solid, liquid and vapour. The most important mechanism, however, seems to be as follows. Pellets of soft hail form in the upper parts of the growing cumulus tower and, because of the ever-present "fine weather" electric field of 120 volts per metre, they become positively charged on their lower surfaces and negatively

charged on their upper surfaces. As they fall, the pellets collide with raindrops and snow crystals being carried upwards by the powerful convection currents. The drops bounce off the descending hail pellets, taking with them some of the positive charge as they continue upwards. In this way, positively charged droplets are carried into the upper reaches of the cloud.

As the charges build up in different regions of the cloud, equal and opposite charges are induced on the ground beneath the cloud. In clear, dry air a field strength

Lightning occurs when a large positive charge builds up in the frozen upper layers of a cloud and a large negative charge, along with a smaller positive area, forms in the lower portion of the cloud, where the initial leader stroke originates (1). As the cloud base is negatively charged, it is attracted towards the normally positive earth and eventually a lightning stroke forms a conductive path through the air (2). The return stroke is a positive discharge from the ground to the cloud, and is seen as lightning (3). The enormous surge of power from the return stroke – as much as 100 million volts – travelling up the conductive path results in a sonic bang known as thunder (4).

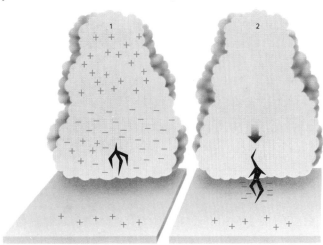

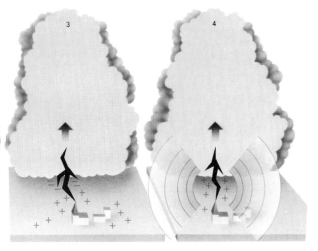

Time-exposure photographs (*left*) show how vertical fork lightning makes a conducting channel for the return stroke from the ground to the cloud. The air temperature rises by thousands of degrees centigrade during this split second creating the right conditions for a visible flash.

of about three million volts per metre is required before a discharge can occur, but in clouds the critical level is around half a million volts, and this is easily achieved in the highly charged conditions of a mature thundercloud. When the limiting level is reached, the scene is set for a lightning flash and although we normally experience the event as a single blinding flash, high-speed photography has revealed a far more complex and fascinating sequence of events.

First a "leader stroke" zigzags towards the ground at about 100 kilometres (60 miles) a second as it seeks the path of least resistance. In its wake it leaves a trail of ionized air that will provide a ready path for the main stroke to follow. Many of its branches will die out, but one arrives close to earth, where it is met by a bright streamer of light from the nearest point on the ground – often a nearby pointed object, a tree or spire, where the potential gradient is greater than elsewhere. Having established a complete conducting path an immense surge of energy rushes up from the ground at about one-tenth the speed of light. An electric current of 10,000 amperes is carried in a core of air only a few millimetres across: the air instantly becomes intensely hot, glowing with a blinding incandescence at up to 30,000°C (54,032°F), while its violent expansion surges outwards at the speed of sound in the shock wave we hear as thunder.

Following the main positive surge up to the cloud, a negative charge rushes down the path from cloud to ground. There is a pause of about one-twentieth of a second while the charges build up again and then more strokes flash up and down the ionized path – often three or four strokes, sometimes many more, in a multiple discharge lasting for a quarter of a second or more.

Ribbon lightning occurs when the single conducting stroke is moved bodily sideways by strong winds. Here it explosively strikes the sea surface.

Ball lightning

The devastating effect of a lightning strike is among the most spectacular of nature's phenomena. Gases, liquids and solids lying in the path of the huge spark are heated, in a minute fraction of a second, through tens of thousands of degrees. The result is explosive. Sometimes deadly. The amount of damage depends on the current passing through the object – and how good a conductor that object happens to be.

The most vivid lightning strokes are those between cloud and ground. These are the strikes that cause the most damage – the type we often call "forked" lightning. But five of every six discharges never hit the ground at all: they flash between one part of a cloud and another. They are just as forked as the cloud-to-ground flashes, though less intense, but they are often hidden from direct view by the cloud itself and so are seen as a flickering light high in the clouds, often called "sheet" lightning. The difference between forked and sheet lightning is not their form but the way in which they are observed: cloud-to-ground flashes would, if hidden from direct view, be called sheet lightning.

Cloud-to-cloud flashes can themselves produce an impressive display – especially if they occur at very high altitude, accompanied by little or no thunder or rain, as sometimes happens in summer hot spells or in tropical regions. Series of flashes have been seen to progress more than 100 kilometres (60 miles) from end to end of a bank of clouds: some individual flashes up to 15 kilometres (9·3 miles) long, some linking cloud banks, others ending in mid-air.

The rather unusual "beaded" lightning persists for some seconds, but then appears to break up into a string of luminous fragments which gradually fade. The effect is seen only during very heavy rain, indicating that it is primarily an optical effect: parts of the zigzagging flash are seen end-on and appear brighter than the other parts, most of which are obscured by the density of the rain.

Even when there are no thunderstorms, the atmosphere has an electric field gradient of about 120 to 150 volts per metre vertically, negative on the ground and positive in the air, yet we appear to be completely insensitive to its existence. However, in the vicinity of a storm the field is greatly increased and a number of very curious phenomena may be witnessed.

When voltage potentials in the region of 100,000 volts per metre develop, the field around a pointed object is even stronger and a "brush" discharge can occur. One such discharge, "St Elmo's Fire", occurs as a bluish-green or white light that appears to cling like a halo to a ship's masthead and rigging, or to the wing-tips of an aircraft. In one twelfth-century report, "St Elmo's Fire" appearing at the masthead of a warship was thought to be a vision of the Virgin Mary.

A more unusual brush discharge was reported in 1897 in Dakota, where, during a storm, the ends of the twigs on a tree all sported pea-sized electric sparks. When a man took hold of a twig, the spark transferred to his thumb: when he let go, the spark reappeared on the twig, but he felt no shock. Sometimes falling raindrops may themselves carry a charge. In Cordoba, Spain, in 1892, just after a flash of lightning, large drops of rain started to fall and each one, on hitting the ground, emitted a spark and a faint crack.

A perfect illustration of the way in which the potential gradient between the Earth and the atmosphere quickly builds up to a critical level and then discharges in a flash of lightning occurred in July 1980, when a group of men fishing from a boat off Whitby, in Yorkshire, suddenly

The "fire" that sometimes appears at ships' masts (*below*) was named after St Elmo, a fourth-century Bishop from Gaeta, Italy.

The lightning that flashes from the ground to the base of a cloud is most clearly visible when it is not obstructed by other clouds (*right*).

felt their hair standing on end. It was a perfect day, the sea as flat as a mirror. Without further warning a flash of lightning struck the sea close to the boat and immediately their hair fell flat.

Perhaps most curious of all lightning phenomena is that known as "ball" lightning – usually reported as a luminous spherical or pear-shaped body with a blurred outline, floating about with a slow and erratic motion. It normally causes no harm, either from electric shock or from burning, but one of its main characteristics is its unpredictability: it may fade and disappear silently, vanish suddenly like a bubble on touching some solid object, or disappear in a violent explosion, though the latter is fortunately rare.

For a very long time scientists did not believe in the existence of ball lightning, and it is probably true that many early reports of "fireballs" causing extensive damage were really examples of ordinary lightning strikes. However, there are now many well-documented cases and determined efforts are being made to unravel the mystery of the ball-lightning phenomenon. One theory is that the ball consists of plasma – a substance neither solid, liquid nor gas – and recent experimenters in America believe that they produced, for a brief time, a floating plasma ball.

THE KUGELBLITZ

Reports of ball lightning, sometimes known by its German name of *kugelblitz*, have been made throughout history, often by people who have been previously unaware of its existence. Although it has never been reproduced in the laboratory, continued interest in this strange luminous sphere has led scientists to apply theories of its formation to control thermonuclear reactions.

The drawing (*above*) records the ball lightning that was seen by several people in a barn in Salagnac, France in 1845.

A photograph which claims to show a *kugelblitz* (*above*), conforms to other reports of the phenomena – it either hangs suspended in the air or floats eerily through it, as seen here, until it fades or explodes.

Storm cells

The majority of thunderstorms are made up of a number of individual cells, each of which has its own air circulation and its own cycle of activity. There is an initial growth phase during which the cumulus tower builds up rapidly, ice crystals start forming and electrical charges are generated by the turbulence of the air currents. A mature stage follows during which thunder and lightning are at their most intense and precipitation from the cloud base, in the form of rain or hail, becomes torrential. The final, decay, stage sees precipitation gradually die away, the upcurrents cease and the cumulus part of the cloud-mass disappear to leave only the very high anvil composed entirely of ice crystals.

Each stage in the cycle lasts for about 20 minutes, and within each fully developed storm cell lies the mechanism for starting off the next. The powerful cold downdraughts from a mature cell spread out across the ground and cut off part of the supply of warm moist air that is the "fuel" for the cell: that warm air, however, must go somewhere and, displaced by the downdraught, it is forced upward somewhere else nearby – so starting off the development of the next storm cell.

A mature cell is usually about 8 kilometres (5 miles) wide and 10 kilometres (6·2 miles) high. Some thunderstorms, particularly the isolated storms that occur in an unstable polar airstream, consist of a single cell only and often do not persist for more than an hour. In most storms, however, cells develop in rapid succession and generally two or three will be active at any given time. Hence, as the storm itself moves across country, and

individual cells mature and fade, the intensity of a storm may appear to wax and wane over a period of perhaps several hours. The multi-celled composition of a storm is also clearly illustrated when, as commonly happens, lightning can be seen flashing from two or more different directions at once, or when a storm appears to have passed by and then suddenly a new squall appears from an unexpected direction.

Since thunderstorms generate their own winds, the wind direction one may feel at any particular time will be no guide to the direction of the storm's movement. Ahead of the storm, the general wind that is driving the storm across country is largely balanced by the convergent winds drawing air into the base of the towering storm clouds, resulting in the familiar "calm before the storm". Except in the rare event of a tornado developing, the air flow into the storm does not produce any noticeable wind. The downdraught of the mature cell, however, creates a strong, gusting squall as it fans out from the base of the storm – sometimes extending for several kilometres, especially on the "downwind" or "leading" side of the storm.

The arrival of the squall is often accompanied by a sudden rise in the barometer reading as the cold air is comparatively dense and exerts greater pressure. If there is a steady supply of warm, humid air, and the cold downdraught can be steered away to one side, there is nothing to prevent a single cell from persisting for hours and becoming very intense. This happens occasionally in most countries but quite frequently in the central plains of

An umbrella connected to earth by a metallic lead was believed to provide personal protection against lightning.

Cumulonimbus are usually thunderstorm clouds (*left*), because the conditions necessary for their development are the same as those required for storms.

STORM SURVIVAL

Since the lightning flash is initiated from above, it tends to strike the highest pointed object available, be it a tree, a tall building or a lone walker in an exposed place; lightning is directly responsible for more deaths each year than any other weather phenomena. Therefore, if one is in a storm it is important to avoid being the tallest object or near to the tallest object in the vicinity. However, if caught out in the open it is best to crouch down low with feet together so that the current cannot go up one leg and down the other. The most dangerous lightning flash is one which strikes the head and passes through the heart *en route* to the earth.

Lightning passing through a golf flag has created a star-shaped scorch mark on this green (*below*).

North America, where conditions are often ideal. Warm air flows in at the base, rises and flows out of the top of the towering cloud mass while cold air flows in at the middle levels and streams out at ground level at the rear of the storm. This type of persistent and violent storm cell depends on the presence of air at the right temperature and humidity at lower and middle levels and also on a marked change in wind direction with height. It is in just such conditions that the storm may produce a tornado – that slender vortex of devastating wind that can wreak havoc on anything in its path.

Occasionally in temperate latitudes a "super-storm" will establish itself in a stable position, remaining in one place for several hours while it pours a deluge of rain on one unfortunate area while neighbouring regions, as little as 20 kilometres (12 miles) away, remain quite dry. One such storm battered London on 14 August 1975. The torrential downpours from such storms can have tragic results when flash floods cause rivers to burst their banks and city drainage systems cannot cope with the volume. Crops are ruined, buildings damaged and lives are sometimes lost as cars become caught up by the swirling floodwaters.

However, because lightning not only emits light but also emits other types of radiation, including radio waves, thunderstorms can be accurately tracked and located by using suitably designed radio receivers which are some distance from each other. The "atmospherics" produced in this way are often heard as crackles that interfere with normal radio broadcasting.

Lightning damage to buildings can be disastrous (*left*) and expensive, but the surrounding land may benefit from its effects because lightning is a natural producer of fertilizer. The lightning discharge in air produces ozone, ammonia and oxides of nitrogen, which react with rain water to form a soluble fertilizer.

Winds

Whether a wind feels pleasant or unpleasant depends not only on its strength but also on its temperature and humidity. In the hot, humid climates of equatorial regions, almost any wind is welcomed, and among the most pleasant winds in the world are the trade winds that blow over the oceans and coastal land areas of the tropics. These winds are characteristically very steady; they blow day after day at speeds rarely in excess of 15 metres per second (33 mph) and bring relief from the oppressive heat and humidity of these regions. It is the trade winds that are largely responsible for the very pleasant climatic conditions that prevail in places such as Hawaii, coastal Queensland and the Caribbean.

In terms of the general pattern of global winds, the westerlies of the Northern Hemisphere temperate zone superficially appear to be similar to the trade winds. However, the westerlies are much less regular than their tropical neighbours. Although the average, or "prevailing", wind is westerly, and of moderate strength, there is often a change in strength and direction as low-pressure systems pass through. Sometimes calm weather or even easterly winds will prevail, after which the westerly winds return with renewed strength.

Since temperatures in the temperate regions are generally lower than in the tropics, the westerlies are more likely to be unpleasant than pleasant. The westerlies of the Southern Hemisphere are very different. Far from being variable, they blow almost constantly, and furiously, giving rise to the names "Roaring Forties", "Furious Fifties" and "Shrieking Sixties", according to the latitude at which they blow.

Winds in the temperate zone can blow from any direction at any time of year. Some regions of the world, however, have monsoons – winds that blow consistently from one direction for much of the winter and from another direction during the summer. Monsoons mainly affect regions in the tropics, and by far the most marked monsoons occur in India.

In winter, when the Asian continent is cooler than the Indian Ocean, cool northeasterly winds blow across India and neighbouring countries bringing dry, generally pleasant weather, though the wind does have a marked drying effect on the land. In April and May the northeast monsoon dies away: winds become very light and give little relief from the brilliant sunshine and air temperatures which soar to over 35°C (95°F). Then a remarkable change

The Portuguese windmill (*left*), used for grinding grain, has a typical Mediterranean design – giant sails supported on a horizontal axle by a large round tower. Wind was the traditional source of inexhaustible power prior to the Industrial Revolution, but since then many windmills, particularly in Europe, have fallen into disuse. Recently the idea of using wind power to generate electricity has been given much attention, but most sites are unsuitable because the wind is too fickle – it must attain a speed of more than 8 metres per second (18 mph) to be of any use; where the wind blows strongly for long periods, however, new experimental windmills are being built.

occurs. Within just a few days the pattern completely changes. Southwesterly winds sweep in from the Indian Ocean bringing a welcome drop in temperature and heavy downpours of rain. This southwest monsoon, which lasts from June to September, is much the more important of the two monsoons, because it brings with it virtually all the rain that much of India receives in any year. Hence the term "monsoon" is often used to suggest torrential rainfall, when it really means a seasonal wind.

Air flow over the ocean is generally smooth and steady, but over land the flow of air is greatly impeded by friction and by turbulence caused by surface irregularities such as vegetation, hills or man-made structures. The drag effect makes the surface winds generally lighter over land than at sea. At 500 metres (1650 feet) the wind is invariably steadier and stronger and this effect is noticeable even at the top of a high building. The generally lighter ground-level winds are much more prone to gusting caused by the turbulence of the air flow; occasionally faster-moving air from higher levels is pulled into the ground-level flow. In modern cities the channelling effect of buildings, particularly those on a regular grid pattern, is marked, while eddy currents in the lee of tall buildings have, at times, created gusting winds of near gale force – much to the distress of residents and the embarrassment of the architects concerned.

Circulating the globe about 10 kilometres (6 miles) above the surface are sinuous bands of strong winds – jet-streams. They are very narrow, only a few hundred kilometres across, but may extend more than half-way round the Earth, and within them the wind velocity may be anything from a brisk 30 metres per second (67 mph) to as much as 150 metres per second (335 mph). The existence of these high-level winds was not even suspected until the Second World War, when pilots of high-flying aircraft discovered great discrepancies between eastbound and westbound flight times.

There is a major jet-stream in each hemisphere at approximately 50 degrees latitude, blowing from west to east but writhing about to form a series of loops whose size and position are constantly changing. These high-level winds control the development and movement of lows and highs in the lower atmosphere.

Other westerly jet-streams are found over the sub-tropical regions, but these have little direct effect on surface weather. The sole easterly jet-stream blows at a high level over the Indian Ocean and Africa during the northern summer, carrying away the huge volumes of air that have risen during the monsoon, releasing their torrential rains over India. Although the velocity of these tunnels of rapidly moving air is several times greater than hurricane-force winds, they cannot be directly compared with winds that occur on the Earth's surface because the air in the tropopause, where jet-streams are found, is far thinner and the energy that the wind carries is correspondingly less.

Gusts and breezes

Trees, such as this pine (*right*), indicates the direction of the persistent winds that blow down from Mt Egmont across Taranaki in New Zealand's North Island.

The eight winds, first recognized by Aristotle (384–322 BC), are depicted as a sculptured frieze on the Athenian octagonal "Tower of the Winds". Each wind is represented by a mythological figure personifying the characteristic weather associated with it. Thus the cold blustery north wind is represented by Boreas, an old man, warmly clothed and blowing his conch shell (*below*). The easterly wind is represented by the scantily dressed Apeliotes (*bottom*).

In the culture of ancient Greece, the winds from all eight points of the compass had individual names and in Athens the "Tower of the Winds", built in about 100 BC, had on each of its eight faces a design depicting a god dressed in a manner appropriate to his particular wind. (The Tower of the Winds is used as the official emblem of the British Royal Meteorological Society.) However, today it is generally believed that most of the winds we experience are not created by gods but are due to the global circulation of the atmosphere and by the anticyclones and low-pressure systems superimposed on it. But the topography of the land can greatly modify the pattern of air flow over quite large areas and can even create entirely separate local circulation systems.

Vast continental mountain ranges like the Rockies and the Himalayas not only block the wind but exert a major control on the entire circulation. Smaller ranges like those of Scotland, Norway and New Zealand tend to force the air flow to rise over them, with the result that the windward side of the range receives a good deal of orographic rainfall while the leeward side is markedly drier.

If the air has released much of its moisture on rising then it will warm up more rapidly as it descends because it contains less water requiring to be turned back into vapour. Thus on the lee side of mountains the air flow is both drier and warmer than on the windward side. Such winds have a great effect on weather conditions, and in turn on Man's activities, and in many parts of the world they are given special names – Zonda in Argentina,

Severe local westerly winds rushing down from the Pennine hills destroyed three 114-metre (375-foot) high cooling towers at Ferrybridge, Yorkshire, on 1 November 1965.

Austru in Romania and Nor'wester in the Canterbury Plains of New Zealand. Associated sudden temperature rises are common, and occasionally dramatic, the fastest on record being a rise from −20°C (−4°F) to 7°C (45°F) in just two minutes at a location in South Dakota, USA.

The Chinook wind, that blows in the eastern foothills of the Rockies, the name being derived from the local Indian tribe, is generally welcomed in winter by cattlemen because of its ability to remove snow cover very quickly. Spells of chinook too early in the year can, however, have drawbacks: plants may germinate too soon and animals may start to shed winter coats, with disastrous consequences if there is a sudden return to very cold weather.

The same general welcome is not extended to the localized Föhn wind in Europe. It is widely blamed for headaches, heart attacks, depression and suicides; its effects are equally marked on people working indoors as those out in the open. Attempts to relate the health hazards associated with the Föhn wind to humidity, electrical phenomena or harmful gases in the air have been quite unsuccessful and it is now thought that perhaps the rapid changes in temperature and humidity may physiologically upset some people. The warmth of the Föhn wind is not due to the origin of the air but to compression when descending the mountain slopes of the European Alps.

Lee-slope winds can be particularly violent at times. At Boulder, Colorado, the wind sometimes pours down the slopes of the Rockies like a waterfall, producing tremendous winds gusting at more than 50 metres per second (112 mph) and causing damage comparable with that left in the wake of a tornado. But while such windstorms occur perhaps twice every year in Colorado, elsewhere they are justly regarded as freak events.

In a freak windstorm on 16 February 1962, the city of Sheffield in England suffered exceptional wind damage when a lee-slope wind was trapped by a layer of warm air overlying the colder surface layer and acting like a lid. The warm air not only prevented the cooler air from rising over the hills and then sinking back smoothly but also caused the rising air to "bounce" against the "lid" and rebound back to ground level, compressing the air flow from a deep layer of atmosphere into an abnormally shallow ground layer. Lee-slope winds are important in many aspects of land use – from the avoidance of dangerous cross-winds on exposed motorway sections to the reduction of tree damage in forestry plantations.

Where a mountain peak stands in isolation, the air flow is able to part and flow around, rather than over, the obstruction. This is particularly likely to occur when the air mass is very stable and therefore reluctant to rise. Places on the sides of mountains, and especially in passes between mountain peaks, may therefore experience stronger winds than the peaks themselves. At the Pali Lookout, a famous mountain pass near Honolulu, an observer can throw his hat over the cliff and the wind will immediately throw it back.

Localized wind circulation may also develop where adjacent parts of the surface are heated at different rates, the most familiar wind of this type being the sea breeze. On a sunny day the land warms much more rapidly than the sea and a circulatory system develops with warm air rising over the land, moving offshore and descending over the sea to flow back towards the shore as a cooling sea breeze. Such gentle onshore air movements greatly modify coastal climates and are a particular boon in places like Perth, Western Australia, where, in summer, the heat can soon become oppressive if "The Doctor" – the local sea breeze – fails to develop around midday.

The advancing edge of the sea breeze can move inland by as much as 300 kilometres (180 miles) before it dies out in the evening. The return flow seawards is generally less than 1 kilometre (0·6 mile) above the surface and if bush fires are burning, this movement is clearly indicated by the abrupt change in direction of the rising smoke. At night, the circulation reverses and a cool land breeze blows over the coastline and out to sea.

Sea breezes have their counterparts in mountain regions also where the surface of a mountain will heat up more quickly than the adjacent air mass over the valley. Air therefore rises over the slopes and sinks over the valley. The daily cycle is reflected in the clouds, which build up towards late morning, perhaps bringing showers, and then disperse again by the evening. At night, cold air in contact with the flanks of the mountain sinks into the valley bottom, where it collects as a pool, often having a very marked effect on temperature but seldom causing an air flow strong enough to be felt as a wind.

Wind force

The most obvious characteristic of any wind is its strength. A very light wind is sometimes, though increasingly rarely, called a zephyr, while a slightly stronger wind would be called a breeze. The word wind is used until such times as the more dramatic gale or even hurricane become necessary. In general use these terms are imprecise – a gale is any wind which causes people difficulty in staying upright, blows loose objects about and breaks twigs and small branches off trees. In meteorology, however, the term has a very definite meaning: a wind of 17·4 to 24 metres per second (39 to 54 mph).

Another important wind element is the direction from which the wind is blowing; the direction and the physical nature of the surfaces over which it has travelled account for the characteristic features of any wind. For example, a hot, dry wind, the Santa Ana, blows off the Mojave Desert through the mountain passes to the coast of Southern California. This wind, most common in autumn and winter, occurs when the Pacific anticyclone extends northeast of its usual position. It is greatly feared, because any natural fires that break out during this period are fanned into infernos by this exceptionally hot, dry wind. Similarly, in southeast Australia the northeast wind in summer, the Brickfielder that blows in directly from the desert, is notorious for being hot and dusty.

In direct contrast, the Mistral is a cold north or northwesterly wind that funnels down the Rhöne Valley in France. Cold northerly winds are familiar throughout most of Europe, but on the usually balmy shores of the Mediterranean Sea this strong, cold wind can have a quite startling effect. The Mediterranean region is also in the path of the Scirocco – an oppressively hot, dry wind that blows north out of the Sahara Desert, scorching the coastal belt of North Africa and then crossing the Mediterranean Sea to reach the southern shores of Europe as a warm, humid wind which tends to produce languor and inertia in the people of those regions.

The Harmattan blows south from the Sahara across the countries of West Africa, extending to the Gulf of Guinea in winter. It brings welcome relief from the usual humid heat of the tropics, but also brings dust storms and air that is so dry that it withers any vegetation in its path. The Haboob is a powerful hot wind that produces sandstorms in the Sudan, while in Egypt the Khamsin has the same effect, sweeping in from the south loaded with dust. One of the more pleasant winds of the Mediterranean region is the wind known as the Levanter – a moist easterly wind that blows along the length of this land-locked sea bringing mild, moist air to Gibraltar and the neighbouring mainland.

The interior regions of large continental landmasses are source areas for many cold winds, among them the Pampero, a very cold southwesterly wind which blows across the Argentinian pampas. The eastern United States experiences similar cold, dry winds blowing down from Canada and equivalent strong northeasterly winter winds blow across Russia and central Asia.

Along the southern coast of Australia, advancing cold fronts tend not to produce much rain but cause the temperature to fall very suddenly – by 10 to 20°C (18 to 36°F) in just a few minutes as a cool wind known as the Southerly Buster blows in.

If a wind is forced to blow over a large expanse of ice and snow, a katabatic wind is produced – a surging downflow of extremely cold air – the type that is responsible for many of the violent raging winds for which the coast of Antarctica is notorious: these blow continuously, day after day, month after month, at speeds that average 80 kilometres an hour (50 mph). Similar winds, known locally by names such as the Chief, the Old Man or the Purga, that carry a swirl of snow and ice crystals blow out of the Arctic, making outdoor conditions unbearable for the natives of Siberia.

The pleasant trade winds that dominate the weather of the Hawaiian islands are occasionally interrupted for a few days by a spell of warm, unusually humid winds from the Kona or leeward side of the islands. These Kona winds are often accompanied by widespread and very heavy rains.

Katabatic winds (*above*) bring cold weather as they blow across the ice of the Antarctic.

Seasonal winds, the monsoons, bring giant rain clouds (*below*) to Thailand.

THE BEAUFORT SCALE

For thousands of years, prior to the advent of steam power, mariners were totally dependent on ocean currents and the global wind system and so it is hardly surprising that the first attempt to standardize the reporting of winds was made by a sailor, Admiral Beaufort, who devised a scale of wind force in 1805. It originally referred to the amount of canvas a sailing vessel could carry in specific wind conditions, but later the scale was adapted to relate to the visible effect of wind on the sea. With the addition of definitions for use on land, the Beaufort Scale, ranging from 0 to 12, is still in use.

Calm conditions, at force 0, prevail when the sea appears smooth (*above*).

Breezy conditions, at force 5 (*above*), are portrayed by moderate waves.

Gale conditions, at force 8 (*below*), are indicated by high waves and foam.

Using the wind

WIND-POWERED SHIPS

In response to rocketing oil prices, ship designers are reverting to the sailing ship to harness the wind and thus exploit a free energy source. New ideas include fitting fore-and-aft-type rigs or aerofoils, which are cheap to build and used widely in aircraft design. Vertical axis windmills are in the early stages of development, but there are difficulties in designing them so that they can survive at sea. A method of propelling ships using kites which can fly high up, where the winds are strong and stable, is also being developed. The world's first commercial energy-saving sailing ship, the *Shinaltoku Maru*, was launched on 1 August 1980. This revolutionary Japanese vessel (*below*) is a converted tanker with two novel folding square sails which supplement the main engine. The two computer-controlled sails reduce fuel consumption and require no extra crew.

The most common means of measuring wind speed is by use of the cup anemometer, an instrument composed of a small electrical generator in a weatherproof housing driven by a rotor made up of three semi-conical cups mounted on a vertical spindle. The faster the cups are driven by the wind, the greater the generator output, and this is calibrated to read out directly on to a continuous paper trace.

The alternative pressure-tube anemometer works on the same principle as the air-speed indicator on an aircraft: a wind-vane keeps the open end of a tube facing into the wind and the pressure is transmitted down the tube to be converted into a continuous print-out of wind speed. Wind direction, indicated by a weather vane, is also recorded continuously in all meteorological stations.

For those lacking such sophisticated equipment, a rough idea of wind direction can be gained by holding a moistened finger aloft. The upwind side will feel colder due to increased rate of evaporation. However, any estimates of wind direction, and speed, made at ground level are likely to be inaccurate due to the disruptive effects of nearby trees, buildings or hills. In order to achieve some standardization, all meteorological stations aim to place their wind-recording equipment at least 10 metres (33 feet) above level, open terrain.

It is often inconvenient to use expensive instruments on remote sites and a common method of assessing the wind in such conditions is to put up a flag and see how quickly it becomes tattered. This is not a very precise way of measuring wind speed, but it is a surprisingly good indicator of general wind exposure – an important factor

Wave power, which is directly dependent on the wind, is being investigated (*right*) in an effort to find an alternative source of energy. The contouring raft in this wave-tank experiment is based on an idea by Sir Christopher Cockerell, the inventor of the modern hovercraft.

in siting plantations in exposed hill country.

For many centuries ships were totally dependent on the wind, their principal source of power and also, at times, their greatest danger. Mariners were consequently skilled in reading the wind conditions and in sailing at almost any angle to the wind in order to maintain headway. Gales were a danger, proving to be the death of countless frail craft, but almost as hazardous were calm conditions in which a ship may be "becalmed". Today's huge vessels are not quite so dependent on winds, although there are occasional disasters in freak storm conditions. Conditions are still important, as ships can save significant fuel costs if they sail with a following wind. Thus most shipping lines use the services of meteorological agencies, which provide forecasts and recommend those routes which, at any given time, make best use of the prevailing wind patterns. These forecasts emphasize wind direction and force, giving information in terms of compass points and Beaufort scale; galewarnings are issued independently.

For small pleasure craft, wind is as critical a factor as at any time in the past. Part of the skill in participating in any large competition lies in the sailor's ability to read and act upon every minute fluctuation in wind speed and direction in order to extract the last ounce of energy from the wind. And since 1972, many countries have included a meteorologist in their Olympic yachting team for precisely that reason. But however skilled the sailor, and however well briefed he or she is, small vessels are always at the mercy of unpredictable weather. Tragedy struck in the Fastnet yacht race in August 1979 when a storm of unusual severity for summer swept across the area of the race bringing winds of hurricane force which left 23 boats sunk or abandoned and 15 lives lost.

One of the main effects of wind patterns on shipping, however, is the indirect effect of the wind on water. Wind is the main generating force of the ocean currents, driving the great oceanic currents like the Gulf Stream in the North Atlantic and the Kuro Shio in the North Pacific, and also, through a complex interaction of the Earth's rotation, the shape of the ocean basins and the physics of fluid motion, driving the complex pattern of secondary currents, eddies and coastal upwellings. The latter in particular are of significance for Man, being the feeding grounds for some of the world's greatest concentrations of fish and also because of their controlling effect on some coastal climatic regions. It is inshore upwelling of cold water off the Californian coast in summer that gives San Francisco and other towns on this coast their cool summer climate and frequent incidence of fog.

The winds also generate the surface waves of the oceans: the stronger the winds the bigger the waves. The gales that blow around low-pressure systems generate waves of all wavelengths and in the immediate locality the sea is wild and confused, sometimes a real danger even to large modern ships. Waves that have travelled across hundreds, perhaps thousands, of kilometres of open ocean without interference arrive as huge breakers on some favourably positioned shores, and these are the swell

Hang gliders are intimately familiar with the nature of wind fluctuations and soar by taking advantage of rising thermal currents, which can seldom be detected on the ground.

waves so avidly sought by the surfing enthusiasts. The Hawaiian Islands receive swell on their northern shores in winter from the North Pacific low-pressure systems, and on their southern shores in summer from low-pressure systems in the Southern Hemisphere temperate zone.

Perhaps the most dramatic impact of the wind is the damage it can do to major structures, and in this respect it is the repeated hammer blows of a gusting wind that do the real damage rather than the sustained pressure of a constant high wind.

Therefore, when designing a bridge or building, the architect must estimate, accurately, the highest sustained winds and highest gusts that the structure may be expected to experience and design the structure accordingly. In this respect the "wind tunnel" is an invaluable aid. Scale models of the structure and the surrounding terrain can be tested in airstreams of varying strength to reveal the effect of the wind on the "upwind" structures and also the way in which the airstream is modified after hitting the first obstruction. However these tests are not infallible as man-made structures do get blown down: the suspension bridge over the Tacoma Narrows in Washington State, USA, developed such violent oscillations whenever a strong wind blew that the bridge was nicknamed "Galloping Gertie" and eventually broke up during a severe storm.

Airstreams

A low-pressure system is a large rotating system of interacting air masses, generally between 500 and 2000 kilometres (300 and 1200 miles) across, so named because it is a region of low atmospheric pressure. Its barometric characteristic gives it the name "low", while the circulation of its winds provides yet another alternative, "cyclone". Although the name cyclone is usually reserved for intense tropical low-pressure systems, the adjective cyclonic is used for any feature associated with such a system, be it temperate, tropical or subtropical.

A "deep" low-pressure system is one in which the central pressure is very low. An "intense" low-pressure system, on the other hand, is one in which the isobars are tightly packed together and which therefore has very strong associated winds. While most deep low-pressure systems are also intense, occasional shallow low-pressure systems may also be intense and produce localized gale-force winds.

The low-pressure heart of a low-pressure system is associated with rising, unstable air, fed by convergent air flow at ground level, and this combination naturally produces cloud and rain. But rain does not occur throughout the system. Rain, hail or snow is mainly concentrated along bands, which may be fronts – boundaries between air masses of different characteristics – or troughs, where convergence is strongest. Young deepening low-pressure systems are the most copious rain producers, while in a mature cyclone the rain is usually showery, even in the central portion.

The deepest low-pressure systems are found in latitudes between 50° to 65° north and south, where the systems migrate from west to east. In the Southern Hemisphere there is a continuous procession of low-pressure systems around the globe, but in the Northern Hemisphere, their incidence is far more variable: sometimes they follow one after another for weeks; at other times there are long breaks, or the lows swing far to the north or south of their normal track. Their detailed behaviour is governed by the much larger-scale upper air wind patterns.

No two low-pressure systems bring exactly the same weather conditions, though the sequence of events is generally predictable. The temperatures experienced depend on the temperature of the air masses involved and the amount of rain depends on the temperature and moisture content of the warmer air mass as it rises over the cooler mass. Continental lows tend to produce less rain because the air masses involved are drier; however, in central USA for example low-pressure systems can bring violent squalls and heavy rain when warm, moisture-laden air from the Gulf of Mexico meets cold Arctic air flowing down from the Canadian interior. When the two types of airstream meet, they do not mix, but fronts are formed at their boundaries.

Quite commonly a smaller low, called a secondary, forms underneath the jet-stream on the equatorial side of a large low-pressure system. These secondaries can bring heavy rain, but they are fast-moving and their influence is generally short-lived. Old low-pressure systems, by contrast, tend to bring cloudy weather with light winds and sporadic heavy showers for two or three days at a time.

In winter, the marked temperature contrast between the very cold air over North America and the warmer, moist air over the Gulf Stream provides a breeding-ground for low-pressure systems. Usually they deepen as they move northeast over the Atlantic on their way to the British Isles and Europe, but sometimes they hug the coast on a more northerly track then move inland across the coast to bring gales, snow, freezing rain or showers of ice pellets to east coast cities such as Boston. A similar situation exists off the coast of Japan. In the Southern Hemisphere the source areas are well south of the inhabited zone and only the edge of the low-pressure zone is felt in Australia and New Zealand.

A distinct boundary forms between warm air and cold air converging towards the centre of a low-pressure system, and is followed by cirrostratus and altostratus clouds.

Low-pressure systems usually develop close to the polar front jet-stream, where the temperature gradient is strongest, and then move along it. But the jet-streams are not static: they meander, and in consequence the tracks of the low-pressure systems also change. Occasionally a branch of a jet-stream will swing far to the south and in this situation a "cut-off" low may become stranded around 30° to 40°N, bringing an unwelcome spell of unsettled weather either to California or the Mediterranean region. Cut-off lows are more common in the Northern Hemisphere than the Southern, where their most frequent occurrences is in the Tasman Sea.

The small polar lows, the small low-pressure systems that form in a polar maritime northerly airstream over the ocean, often bring snow and are common culprits of unexpected snowfalls.

The latitude band 25–35 degrees is normally frequented by anticyclones, or high-pressure systems, but occasional subtropical lows form there. The conditions in which

A view of a cyclonic storm system located 1920 kilometres (1200 miles) due north of Hawaii that was taken on 11 March 1969 by the Apollo 9 space craft on its 124th orbit around the Earth.

The airstreams that feed continental low-pressure systems in summer are hot and dry and create terrific dust storms, such as those experienced by the Tuareg tribe travelling across the Sahara desert (*below*); cumulus clouds of dust are lifted to great heights in the thermal air currents.

they form are not fully understood, although some certainly develop from cut-off lows that have drifted towards the equator. On the eastern flank of a sub-tropical low a stream of very warm moist air flows polewards, rising to produce widespread heavy rain, sometimes with thunderstorms or even a tornado embedded in it. In November 1978, Honolulu received a deluge of 30 centimetres (11·7 inches) of rain in five days from one of these storms – the "Kona" storms of Hawaii.

Even the tropics suffer from low-pressure systems, and they are particularly serious if they develop sufficiently to become hurricanes. Within five degrees of the equator, low-pressure systems do not form, but quite frequent heavy rain is nevertheless produced by areas of convergence. Such areas, unlike those in temperate regions, do not become organized into weather systems but remain as ill-defined areas of heavy precipitation and thunderstorm activity, usually lasting for less than 24 hours and almost impossible to forecast.

Holland's dykes, which protect reclaimed land lying at or below sea level, were flattened by water rushing down the North Sea during the storm surge of 1953. It was nine months before the sea walls were fully repaired.

THE THREAT OF FLOOD
Dangerous flood conditions in the River Thames estuary are created when a trough of low pressure moves southwards from the North Sea, causing the sea level to rise into a "hump". A storm surge occurs if this mass of water, travelling from the deep ocean, reaches the relatively shallow southern part of the North Sea and moves into the bottleneck between southeast England and the Low Countries. To exclude storm surges from the estuary, the Thames Barrier has been designed. Its four main gates, in the process of construction (*left*), are the largest of their kind in the world. In the event, the Storm Tide Warning Service at Bracknell will alert the barrier control centre, where engineers will decide whether closure is necessary and if so the optimum time to act. The gates will then be swung into their defensive positions, sealing off the river.

Storm surges

Many people were drowned in the floods in Holland on
1 February 1953 when a storm surge, generated by a deep and
fast-moving low-pressure system, travelled down the North Sea.

No two low-pressure systems bring exactly the same
weather and temperatures involved depend on the air
masses that are drawn into their circulation. However,
most low-pressure systems do bring thick clouds, rain or
snow, and this weather affects a large area. Variations do
occur on hills and mountains, where precipitation may be
heavier and is most likely to be snow and the winds are
stronger, whereas the sheltered valleys may only receive
a little rain. An oncoming low is indicated by a drop in
the barometric reading, thick cloud and an increase in
wind speed, and as the low-pressure system approaches,
the first drops of rain may be felt. The influence of a low-
pressure system extends outwards, farther on the equatorial
side than on the polar side due to the trailing fronts.

However, the most persistent bad weather is experienced on the polar side of a low-pressure system, particularly the northeasterly side. Here a ground-level observer
is within the colder air mass, while directly over his head
the rising warm air is releasing its moisture as rain or snow.
It is in this sector of a vigorous low-pressure system that
the risk of exceptionally heavy rain and consequent
flooding is greatest.

Low-pressure systems can cause "storm surges", which
occur when freak stormy conditions suddenly raise the
level of the sea with the result that low-lying coastal areas
are inundated. The level of the sea normally fluctuates: the
familiar tides rise and fall twice each day, and at times of
full or new Moon the tidal oscillations are greater than

usual. However, prevailing atmospheric pressure can
also affect the sea level. When the pressure is low, sea level
rises and vice versa. Strong winds can cause water to "pile
up" ahead of them and if the wind happens to be directed
towards a narrow sea passage or estuary the consequences
can be disastrous.

A low that affected the whole of Europe and caused a
storm surge in the North Sea on 3 January 1976 developed
to the west of Scotland and deepened rapidly as it moved
across the North Sea and then across Denmark and into
northern Poland. It brought severe gales to every
country in its path and winds gusted at more than 45
metres per second (101 mph). Fortunately on this
occasion the sea defences held.

However, in 1953 the coastal populations of Britain
and the Low Countries were not so lucky. A deep low-
pressure system developed in the northern tip of Scotland
then swung southeast into the North Sea, followed by a
severe northerly gale. Mean wind speed reached 40 metres
per second (89 mph) in Orkney, thousands of trees were
flattened in Scotland and a ferry-boat was capsized
between Scotland and Northern Ireland. But worst of all
was the storm surge that drove down the North Sea.
Huge areas of eastern England were flooded and 307
people were drowned. In Holland the toll was even more
horrific: dykes collapsed under the force of the water,
200,000 hectares (494,000 acres) of reclaimed land were
inundated by the sea, and 1800 people lost their lives.

Similarly, the author Daniel Defoe vividly recorded
another storm created by an intense low that moved
across Britain on 26 November 1703, with southwesterly winds on its southern flank reaching speeds in
excess of 45 metres per second (101 mph). It was named
the Great Storm because there had never been one like it
before and there has never been a similar series of low-
pressure systems following one another across the
Atlantic on the same scale since. According to Defoe "the
air was full of meteors and vaprous flames" as the
hurricane-force winds tore across the country, demolishing everything in their way. Hundreds of ships were lost,
tiles were ripped off roofs, thousands of trees were up-
rooted and 400 windmills were reported to have been
blown over. The Eddystone lighthouse disappeared
without trace, and a storm surge of water up the Severn
estuary drowned thousands of cattle and sheep.

Although tropical and subtropical regions are not
affected by low-pressure systems to the same extent as
temperate latitudes, there, too, storm surges can have a
serious impact. The Bay of Bengal is one such vulnerable
area, narrowing sharply towards its northern extremity
and surrounded in the north by low-lying coastal flood-
plains, including the vast Ganges delta. Here the danger is
made even more acute by the huge concentration of
people. When a cyclone or tropical low moves into the
area, there simply is nowhere for people to take refuge.
In November 1970 a severe cyclone and its associated
storm surge killed close to one million people in this area
in one of the worst natural disasters ever recorded.

Typhoon, the name given to hurricanes in the China seas, is thought to be derived from the Chinese *tai fung*, meaning "wind which strikes", but it is also possible that the word originated from the Greek monster Typhoeus, the father of storm winds.

Hurricanes grow over warm tropical water that has a surface temperature of more than 27°C (80°F), their main development regions being in the western Atlantic, Pacific and Indian oceans.

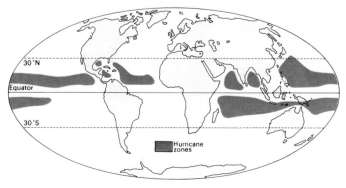

The fury of hurricane Ellen is captured in this dramatic satellite photograph (*right*), taken on 20 September 1973 by the Skylab 3 mission as the vortex of the mature hurricane passed over the Atlantic.

Hurricanes

The hurricane, typhoon or tropical cyclone is the most spectacular individual component of the terrestrial weather machine – an enormous spiralling weather system containing winds of furious intensity and great banks of stormclouds that produce the heaviest rains known on Earth. Yet, paradoxically, at the very heart of the hurricane is a small area – the "eye" of the storm – in which the winds are light, the skies are clear and the air is warm. There is, as yet, no complete understanding of exactly how these mammoth storms are born, but they are basically the same type of weather system as the "lows" that sweep across Europe from the Atlantic, or into the western seaboard of the United States from the Pacific.

Hurricanes, however, are cyclones on a grand scale. These huge storm systems have two basic requirements: warmth and moisture. Consequently they develop only within the tropics – between latitudes 5° and 20° north and south of the equator and in regions where the sea temperature is more than 27°C (80°F). Almost invariably they move in a westerly direction at first and then swing away from the equator, either striking land with devastating results or continuing out over the oceanic expanse until they encounter cool surface waters and die out naturally. A storm born in the western Atlantic, at 15°N, might therefore cause havoc in the Windward or Leeward Islands, then swing north through the Greater Antilles, eventually tearing into the American mainland across either the Gulf or Atlantic coasts. In this part of the world the storms are called by their most familiar name, "hurricane", derived from a Caribbean Indian word.

Atmospheric and oceanic conditions favour hurricane development most frequently in the summer and autumn months. The region of greatest storm frequency is the northwestern Pacific, where the storms are called "typhoons" – a name of Chinese origin, whereas storms which occur in the Bay of Bengal, the southwest Indian Ocean around Madagascar and Mauritius, and the seas north of Australia are called "cyclones". The terms "tropical cyclone" and "tropical revolving storm" are used by meteorologists for all such systems. Weaker cloud-and-rain systems within the tropics are called "tropical storms" if the maximum wind speed is in the range 17 to 31 metres per second (38 to 69 mph), "tropical depressions" if wind speeds are less than 17 metres per second (38 mph) and "tropical disturbances" if there are no strong winds and no circulation of wind and clouds around a central area. Such minor disturbances are very common in the tropics and some do develop into full-force hurricanes.

No two hurricanes are exactly alike, but a typical mature storm might be 600 kilometres (375 miles) in diameter with its circulating winds spiralling in towards the centre at speeds of up to 50 metres per second (112 mph). The size of the eye can vary in diameter from as little as 6 kilometres (3.7 miles) to 40 kilometres (25 miles). The atmospheric pressure at the centre is sometimes below 950 millibars, although the deepest "low" ever recorded was a remarkable 870 millibars, at the centre of Typhoon "Tip", which roared past the island of Guam in October 1979. The diameter of that storm was 2220 kilometres (1400 miles) and its highest wind speeds reached 85 metres per second (190 mph). This is the kind of wind that can drive a plank of wood right through the trunk of a palm tree and blow straws end-on through sheets of corrugated iron.

No less impressive is the rainfall produced by a mature hurricane. Between 80 and 150 millimetres (3 to 6 inches) is quite common, although when wind speeds exceed 25 metres per second (56 mph) the standard rain gauge is hardly capable of accurate measurement: most of the precipitation is blown straight past, but the gauge does at least provide an absolute minimum reading. In 1896 Mauritius received 1200 millimetres (47 inches) in just four days and in 1911, Baguio in the Philippines received 1170 millimetres (46 inches) in a single day and 2200 millimetres (56 inches) in a four-day period. Some of these extreme amounts are due to forced uplift, where winds approached high ground, but even low terrain can provide its share of spectacular statistics. A storm in Texas in September 1921 unloaded 587 millimetres (23 inches) of rain in a day, while a hurricane that hit Puerto Rico in 1928 dropped 750 millimetres (30 inches) over the mountains and it was estimated that the total mass of water dropped on the island was $2 \cdot 6 \times 10^9$ tonnes (2,600,000,000 tonnes).

All this water represents energy, because the water was originally carried into the air as vapour and when the vapour condenses again into liquid it releases what is known as its latent heat. This heat is the fuel on which the storm depends. The rate of heat-energy release inside the hurricane cloud-mass is staggering: some 10×10^{12} kilowatt-hours per day – roughly equivalent to 1000 times the total electrical power generated in the United States. With this kind of energy driving them it is not difficult to understand the catastrophic effects that these storms can have on the land and communities that happen to be in their paths.

A single storm can change the geography of an island forever by tearing apart a reef that may have stood for thousands of years. The complete cash-crop of an island can be destroyed in a few hours by winds that do not simply shake the fruit from the tree but literally rip up the entire plantation, and only massive aid programmes can offer any hope of re-establishing the crop for future years. Fortunately storms of such extreme violence are not common. However, the ubiquitous palm tree, which may have to withstand several hurricanes during its life, has evolved the ability to bend before all but the most powerful gusts. The same is true of many other tropical species, whereas a temperate-latitude forest, unadapted to such forceful winds, would be almost totally wiped out if struck by the winds of a typical hurricane.

The birth of a hurricane

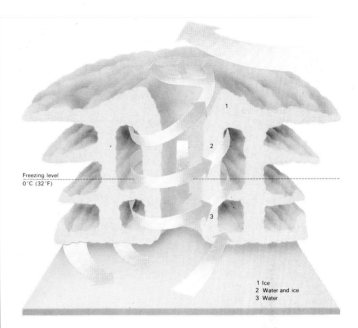

Freezing level
0°C (32°F)

1 Ice
2 Water and ice
3 Water

The rising column of hot, moist air within a hurricane condenses to produce heavy rain at the base. The storm is fed by air spiralling in at low levels and being sucked upwards by high-level winds. Cold air descends in the eye.

Wind and atmospheric pressure vary much less in the tropics than in the temperate latitudes. There is nothing, for example, to compare with the constant succession of frontal systems which form such a characteristic feature of the North Atlantic frontal zone – the birthplace of much of northwest Europe's weather. However, frequent small disturbances do occur, accompanied by concentrations of cloud and falls of rain. The disturbances are sometimes called "easterly waves" and, as the name implies, they tend to travel from east to west, embedded in the trade winds. Most remain weak and die out within a few days, but a few become unstable and start to develop in size and complexity.

The conditions for the transformation from a minor disturbance to a potentially huge and powerful system are not fully understood, but certainly involve interactions between winds in the upper and lower layers of the troposphere. Normally in the tropics there is little interaction: the upper winds are generally light, with weak patterns of convergence and divergence. But, when an area of upper-level divergence passes over the top of a newly formed disturbance it has the effect of a suction pump – drawing away the rising air and so causing the convergence at sea level to become stronger. Even this will not bring about the birth of a hurricane because very often the upper and lower circulation patterns soon become disconnected again.

For an incipient hurricane to develop it needs a supply of fuel, and this is provided when water vapour condenses and releases its latent heat into the surrounding air. The air starts to rise and becomes warmer. As it warms, it rises faster. This in turn pulls in more moisture-laden air

at sea level, which rises and releases yet more heat. Once this chain reaction is established, the energy machine is in motion and may well continue to develop into a full-scale hurricane with violent inward-spiralling winds, producing huge cumulus clouds and torrential rain, with a column of gently descending warm air at the core. If the rising air does not contain sufficient moisture, or if it is too cool in the first place, the chain reaction will never develop. For this reason hurricanes can form only over warm oceans in the tropics, where the sea temperature is always more than 27°C (80°F). For the same reasons they tend to die out over land and when they drift too far from the tropical zone. Furthermore, hurricanes cannot develop in the very narrow band lying approximately five degrees either side of the equator. Here, the Coriolis force is zero, or nearly so. There is nothing to impart that initial rotation to any incipient system and so, whenever a region of low pressure develops, surrounding air simply pours in to fill it. Away from the equator, any air flow converging on a "low" is deflected by the Coriolis force so that a spiral structure is immediately established.

A hurricane contains a very efficient mechanism for maintaining itself. Moisture-laden air spirals in towards the centre and then rises to form a ring-like wall of towering cumulus clouds, which release an almost constant deluge of rain. The associated release of heat encourages the air to rise still farther and faster. This main zone of cloud, rain and violent wind forms a narrow band about 20 kilometres (12·5 miles) wide about 30 kilometres (19 miles) out from the centre. Farther out, tall clouds are more isolated, rain is showery and winds less violent. In the upper troposphere the water droplets

Inside the eye of Hurricane Betsy (*below*) the United States Air Force hurricane hunter aeroplane is surrounded by a towering circular wall of clouds that seems to curve up and out like a funnel. The pilot steered through turbulent banks of clouds and rain before his aeroplane suddenly dropped 33 metres (108 feet) into the calm of the eye itself.

in the clouds turn into ice crystals, forming cirrus clouds, which are thrown outwards by the spin of the storm system to form diverging spirals. In satellite photographs it is the outward-spiralling upper-level clouds that give the storm its characteristic "spiral nebula" shape; the inward-spiralling ground-level winds are hidden.

The central eye of the storm is usually free of cloud and contains a column of gently descending warm air. At ground level there is only a small rise in temperature, but in the middle troposphere, at about the 500 millibar level (usually at a height of about 5·5 kilometres/3·4 miles), the temperature within the eye may be 18°C (64°F) warmer than at the same level on the outer margin of the hurricane. This warm core is an essential part of the hurricane structure because, since warm air is less dense than cold, it exerts less pressure: the core therefore maintains the low-pressure heart of the storm, which in turn maintains the inflow of air to the base of the storm.

To be inside the eye of a hurricane is a strange experience. The wind is gentle, the sky overhead is either clear or dotted with small clouds, and the air is warm, humid and oppressive. As the eye moves over you the wind drops with amazing rapidity from violent gale to almost calm. You are completely surrounded by a wall of cloud and the roar of the wind can often be heard from several kilometres away. It is a welcome respite from the fury of the storm – but a brief one. Within a few minutes the eye will have passed over and the winds return with a deafening roar, this time from the opposite direction. Buildings and trees that survived the leading edge of the storm are not yet safe, and anyone straying far from shelter is certainly courting danger.

Hurricane detection

Although hurricanes have a reputation for being unpredictable, their movements do, on the whole, conform to a recognizable pattern. Usually they travel westward at between 15 and 30 kilometres per hour (roughly 10 to 20 mph) in association with the middle-level atmospheric winds. (In the immediate vicinity of a hurricane, the upper- and lower-level winds are of course generated by the storm itself.) The general westward drift of the hurricane is usually accompanied by a steady migration away from the equator – in a clockwise direction in the Northern Hemisphere and anticlockwise in the Southern Hemisphere. Hurricanes die away as they move far enough away from the equator, where there is no moist warm air to power them.

Gradually the hurricane moves out of the range of the mid-level easterly winds and into a zone of light winds, eventually coming under the influence of the temperate zone upper westerlies. Northern Hemisphere hurricanes therefore tend to recurve to the north and then northeast, while Southern Hemisphere storms recurve to the south and then southeast. And it is during this recurvature phase that the hurricane's behaviour is likely to be at its most erratic. Small changes in the wind pattern, or the occurrence of patches of cool surface water, can cause changes in the storm's development or movement, sometimes causing it to veer off course or even perform a complete loop. For example, Hurricane Flora meandered over eastern Cuba for five days in 1963 and Hurricane Betsy was initially heading towards the Bahamas and then turned towards the Florida strait, finally crashing into Louisiana in September 1965.

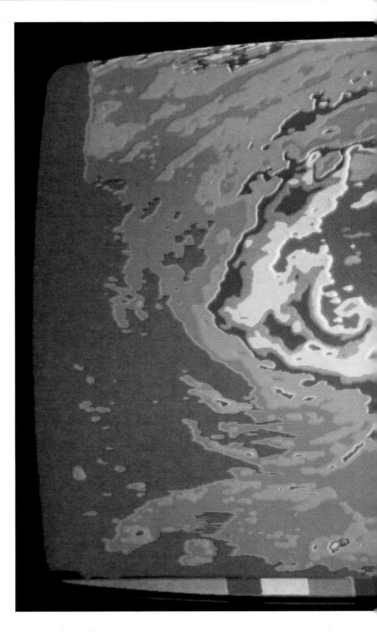

The tracks of Hurricane Frederic were traced over a period of three days in 1979 (*below*) by the United States National Environmental Satellite Service, allowing the initial atmospheric disturbance to be picked up as it formed over the ocean (A) and the course of the storm to be accurately followed (B and C.)

A computer-enhanced satellite photograph of Hurricane David (*right*), taken on 3 September 1979, enabled the storm to be identified before it reached any land areas. The eye shows up on the radar screen as a luminous crescent that appears red and is cooler than the surrounding streaky purple rain bands.

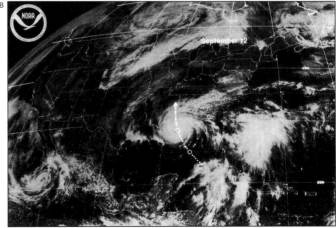

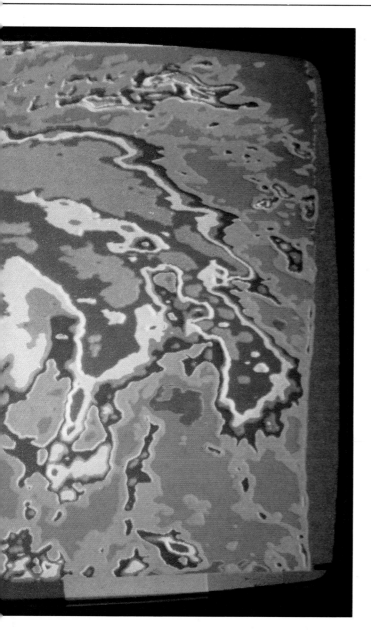

One major problem for those tracking and forecasting the storm's behaviour is that the storm itself is very small when seen against the vastness of the ocean. A deviation of just a few degrees, or a direction change a few hours earlier than expected, can make the difference between a storm tearing through a coastal city or blowing itself out in sparsely populated countryside.

As a hurricane moves into temperate latitudes its character changes and it gradually becomes modified into an ordinary temperate-latitude cyclone. However, if it should encounter a moist, active trough of low pressure in the westerlies it may, after almost dying out, acquire a new lease of life. Some hurricanes, after recurving, sweep northeast across the Atlantic in September and October and bring heavy rain to the British Isles, although by then the winds have lost most of their strength.

Many hurricanes decay while still in the tropics, either through moving over cooler surface waters and becoming starved of energy, or, more commonly, through moving into an unfavourable wind pattern. For example, hurricanes born off the west coast of Mexico often move north or northwest and in so doing they enter a region in which the lower-level winds are northeasterly trades, while the upper winds are southwesterlies. In this situation the upper winds drag the top of the storm in one direction and the lower winds drag the base of the storm in another. The structure of the hurricane cannot be maintained and the storm dies.

The character of a hurricane is also profoundly altered as soon as it strikes land. The air flowing in at the base is no longer so moist and the storm therefore loses its energy source and starts to fill. The eye disappears and the winds abate. Rainfall, on the other hand, tends to increase because friction with the ground, being greater than friction with the sea surface, causes the winds to slow and to turn more towards the storm centre. This increased convergence causes greater uplift and consequently heavy rainfall over a wide area. Many inland areas receive substantial amounts of rain from such storms and in Australia they are called "rain depressions". One hurricane deposited enough rain on Baquio in the Philippines to cover the entire island in 1 metre (3 feet) of water.

The move from ocean to land may indeed be the beginning of the end for the hurricane, but it is at this point that its full impact is felt. The hurricane hits the coast at full strength and its violent winds can wreak total devastation on the land and communities in its path. Homes may be flattened, agricultural and industrial installations wrecked and crops beaten to the ground. Public services are put out of action and emergency services are stretched to the limit as they attempt to cope with the gale-damage and human casualties of the initial assault; flooding and landslide hazards often follow a hurricane as the area is subject to a deluge of rain; also, lack of power, communications and transportation facilities inevitably occur when cables are brought down, bridges are damaged and roads are blocked by fallen trees and landslips.

Taming hurricanes

It may seem vain for men to aspire to modify the behaviour of a system as powerful as a hurricane, but the theoretical solution does exist – and the rewards are potentially enormous. The annual cost of hurricane damage is considerable: in 1979, Hurricane Frederic crossed the American coastline and wreaked havoc to the tune of $250 billion (250,000 million in the UK). On average throughout the 1960s, hurricane damage cost the United States alone $500 million each year, and in the late 1970s several hurricanes such as Frederic each ran up a damage bill in excess of $1 billion (or 1000 million in UK).

Unfortunately, although the general course of hurricanes is clear from the circulation of the atmosphere, the detailed course of an individual hurricane is hard to predict. Recently, the hurricane forecaster's art has been improved by a team of researchers from the US National Oceanic and Atmospheric Administration (NOAA). Since 1979, teams aboard instrumented aircraft have been instructed to fly inside hurricanes that were approaching land, and pilots instructed to feed data back to modellers and forecasters at NOAA's laboratories in Miami. With the aid of this "on line" information, the resulting forecasts of the paths of several recent hurricanes have been remarkably accurate. But although reliable forecasts do alleviate some of the havoc caused by hurricanes, allowing areas at risk to be evacuated, a good forecast cannot prevent the hurricane.

Experts calculate that a 10 per cent reduction in the strength of the winds in the eye of the hurricane would

The aftermath of Hurricane Celia – the single hurricane that destroyed millions of Texan homes in August 1970 and caused $454 million worth of damage.

PROJECT STORMFURY
Satellite data is processed by electronic computer systems at the National Hurricane Center in Miami and the Joint Typhoon Warning Center in Guam so that when a prospective tropical cyclone becomes apparent the Stormfury hurricane seeding team is alerted. To be eligible for a seeding experiment, the hurricane must be within 1100 kilometres (684 miles) of Stormfury's operating base at Puerto Rico, and be likely to stay in range for at least 12 hours. It must have no more than a 10 per cent probability of approaching within 90 kilometres (56 miles) of a populated land area within 24 hours after seeding. The project's research aircraft (*right*) are uniquely equipped with advanced atmospheric sensors and radar, which provides a continuous three-dimensional image of the hurricane.

produce a 30 per cent reduction in the amount of damage caused. This represents a colossal amount of money, even in the context of the United States annual budget. Every autumn, during the hurricane season, a team of experimenters – "hurricane research scientists" – wait for a suitable hurricane on which to test their newly devised preventative measures. The experiment is code-named "Project Stormfury", and although no suitable candidate for the test has appeared in the past few years, the Stormfury team is ready to move as soon as one does.

The main difficulty at present is that the theory and the techniques of hurricane prevention remain unproven. Also, there are potential political repercussions of perhaps tampering with a hurricane that might then go on to cause serious damage and even loss of life. Hurricane modification experts now have the frustration of waiting for a storm that, besides being big enough to be truly representative, also has to come close enough to land to be tackled and yet stay far enough out to sea to prevent any risk to populated areas. Storms that meet such stringent requirements do not appear every year and so the Stormfury team has had to watch helplessly as Frederic in 1979 and Allen in 1980 created millions of dollars' worth of damage that might perhaps have been avoided if they had been allowed to "seed" the hurricanes. Cloud seeding is at the heart of the proposed technique of hurricane modification.

The key to the strength of a hurricane depends on the size of the eye. The bigger the eye, the lower the maximum windspeeds and therefore the less damage the hurricane will cause. If the wall of clouds surrounding the eye of the hurricane – the eye wall – were seeded, more rain would be produced which would release more heat energy and make the hurricane more destructive. But if a new eye wall could be created outside the original one, the old eye might expand to the new wall – with a consequent reduction in wind speeds. The plan is therefore to seed clouds outside the eye wall in an attempt to make them dump their moisture, release heat into the atmosphere, and in so doing create a new zone of rising air, leaving the original eye wall to die away, starved of its life-giving supply of incoming moist air.

The seeding operation involves the most accurate flying, under exceedingly difficult conditions; the aircraft unloading pyrotechnics which burn as they fall through the clouds, releasing a smoke trail rich in silver iodide, which acts as a nucleus on which water droplets can form. Each step in the technique has been tested. The programme must now await a full-scale "live" test.

Seeding is not likely to become a routine precaution for a good many years yet, but the groundwork has now been done. Project Stormfury might be accelerated if other countries that are also affected by hurricanes could co-operate and its area could be extended to give access to Pacific hurricanes and to the Southern Hemisphere. But economics prohibit this development, although the programme, when complete, might bring enormous savings in money, property and in human life.

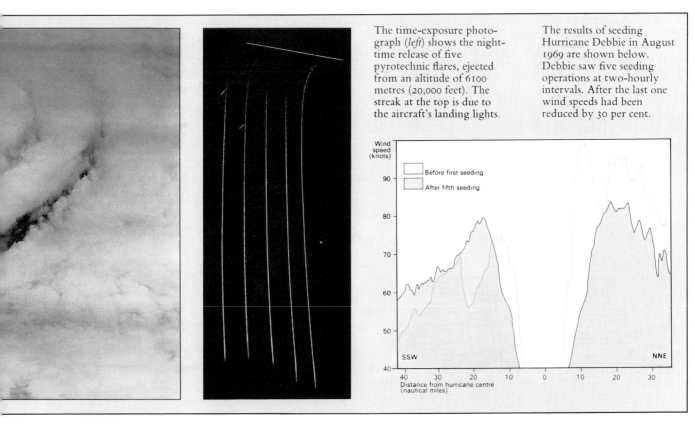

The time-exposure photograph (*left*) shows the night-time release of five pyrotechnic flares, ejected from an altitude of 6100 metres (20,000 feet). The streak at the top is due to the aircraft's landing lights.

The results of seeding Hurricane Debbie in August 1969 are shown below. Debbie saw five seeding operations at two-hourly intervals. After the last one wind speeds had been reduced by 30 per cent.

Wind speed (knots)

☐ Before first seeding

☐ After fifth seeding

Distance from hurricane centre (nautical miles)

Tornadoes

In terms of concentrated, destructive violence, no other atmospheric storm compares with the tornado. Like a hurricane, the tornado consists of a mass of unstable air, rotating furiously and rising rapidly around the centre of an area with low atmospheric pressure. But there the similarity ends. Whereas a hurricane is generally of the order of 500 kilometres (310 miles) in diameter, a large tornado is likely to be little more than 500 metres (550 yards) across, while a small one may not exceed 50 metres (55 yards). However, while the overall damage caused by a hurricane is vast and widespread, its intensity does not match the narrow track of total devastation that marks the path of a tornado.

The maximum speed of the wind in a tornado is not known for certain because whenever one of the storms has passed close to an anemometer, the instrument has either been wrecked or blown away. However, speeds of up to 68 metres per second (152 mph) have been recorded, though analysis of the movement of wisps of cloud, from photographs taken of tornadoes, suggests that speeds of 75 to 100 metres per second (167 to 224 mph) are reached. These speeds are far higher than those characteristic of hurricanes. Also, around the edges of a tornado, tiny subsidiary whirls continually form and dissipate and these must produce local gusts that are even more violent.

Wind alone, however, is not the only damaging force at work in the tornado. The pressure at the centre of the storm is extremely low (again it has not been measured accurately), so that as the storm passes over a particular spot there is a sudden and dramatic fall in pressure. When this happens over a building, the result is that the pressure inside the structure is suddenly far greater than that outside and the building literally explodes. A further hazard is the presence of violent updraughts, which are often strong enough to lift livestock and people and carry them considerable distances, and occasionally violent enough to lift items as heavy as trucks and railway engines off the ground. It is hardly surprising that deaths and severe injuries are common among those unfortunate enough to be caught in the path of a tornado. Grains of sand and small stones may be blown with the force of bullets, so that they penetrate deep into exposed flesh; pieces of straw may be embedded like darts in wooden fence-posts and walls, while even a car or building may offer little protection against large timbers and metal roofing sheets hurled, spinning and bouncing, through a town.

The sight and sound of the tornado seem to underline its awesome threat. Most are seen as a forbidding black cone hanging down to ground level from an equally black cloud-mass – looming out of the semidarkness and often accompanied or preceded by thunder, lightning and a heavy burst of rain or hail. The arrival of a tornado has been graphically described as sounding like an express train hurtling through a tunnel; like an entire fleet of jet aircraft, or like the bellowing of a million mad bulls. The name itself is derived from the Spanish word for thunder – an apt association of both the sound and the thunderstorms that so often accompany a tornado.

By far the most severe storms occur in the Great Plains region of the United States – particularly in "Tornado Alley", the belt of country running from Texas through Kansas to Illinois and on into Canada. They can occur at any time of the year, but are most frequent from April to September. The destruction caused by these storms is almost beyond belief and those who live and work in Tornado Alley treat tornadoes with the utmost respect. A high proportion of houses are equipped with tornado cellars, the only real means of protection, and at the approach of a storm everyone takes refuge. The United States experiences about 700 tornadoes each year, but even with cellars, advance warning broadcasts and every possible vigilance, the storms claim an average of 100 lives per year.

Because the track of a tornado is so narrow it is not at all rare to find that buildings along one side of a street are completely wrecked, while those opposite have suffered little worse than a few broken windows. Yet despite its awesome destructive power, the tornado can at times behave in a strangely gentle manner. On one well-documented occasion, the walls of a shop were split wide open and a baby girl was carried out through the gap and over the intervening buildings to land, quite unhurt, in a garden several streets away. In another instance a woman was quietly milking cows in a barn when the entire building was picked up and carried away leaving her and the cows completely unscathed. Mirrors have been found several miles from their source, not even cracked. It is thought that this apparent gentleness occurs when an object falls towards the ground through an updraught, which is just strong enough to cushion a descent without actually preventing the downward movement.

Scattered buildings and farm machinery (*below*) have been damaged not only by the direct impact of a tornado but also by twisting forces and unequal wind speeds within it.

The destructive power of our delicately balanced and temperamental atmosphere can muster up a "twister" anywhere in the world – the diameter of this one (*left*), in Kenya, is only a few metres, but they can be as wide as 1·6 kilometres (1 mile).

Pressure differences within the tornado that swept through Flint, Michigan, in May 1956 caused the extraordinary bending of glass windows (*below*); curtains were sucked through and trapped when the glass was suddenly allowed to spring back into position.

Tornado formations

Although tornadoes form in many parts of the world, because of the mechanics involved in inducing them, nowhere are they as frequent, or as violent, as on the Great Plains of North America. A recent study of the location and frequency of tornadoes in the United States revealed some long-term changes that have not yet been fully explained.

Apparently, the frequency of the occurrence of tornadoes since 1916 has increased dramatically. One explanation of this increase is the greater efficiency of reporting tornadoes because of the denser distribution of population. However, by analysing case histories since 1916, it was also found that tornadoes followed a roughly circular clockwise pattern of occurrence, completing a circuit in a 45-year cycle.

A current explanation of this is that the cycle may be connected to sunspot activity which oscillates over a period of slightly over 11 years; as four sunspot cycles are equivalent to the 45-year tornado cycle, efforts are being made to establish whether the relationship is a purely coincidental one or a meaningful one. Also, the way in which sunspot activity could actually influence the location of tornadoes is being investigated in attempts to understand the origin of these killer storms.

An essential feature of the storm is its spin, and while it might be expected that a very special set of conditions would be necessary for air to rotate with such violence, this is not the case. All that is needed is a very strong up-current of air that is maintained for several minutes. Air rushes in at ground level and stage one is complete. Surface air masses have some natural spin generated by the movement of the Earth, but when air converges, the spin is concentrated into a tightening spiral, and the speed of movement increases enormously. Tornadoes nearly always spin cyclonically – that is, anticlockwise in the Northern Hemisphere and clockwise in the Southern. Occasionally tornadoes occur in pairs and in that situation one of them rotates anticyclonically, though the mechanism of this phenomenon is not yet understood.

Strong upcurrents occur wherever there is sufficient instability in the atmosphere. They may be triggered by surface heating, which causes bubbles of hot air to start rising, or by convergence of ground-level air, which causes large-scale uplift. If the lower layer is moist as well as warm, the water vapour condenses, releasing latent heat, which makes the air even more buoyant and causes it to rise faster. And if the higher-level air is dry as well as cold, the rising air becomes even more unstable and the upcurrents are accelerated again.

Under normal circumstances, cold, dry air will not persist for any length of time above warm, moist air. This can only happen when the wind directions at the two levels are very different so that a stream of cold, dry air is made to flow across a stream of warm, moist air. Whereas this situation is rare in most parts of the world it is quite common in central North America. Here the north-south barrier of the mountain ranges makes it relatively easy for warm, moist air from the Mexican Gulf to flow

A death-defying desire to record the awesome sight of a tornado overcame cameraman Maurice Levy in April 1957. From his unique time-lapse pictures (*below*), wind speeds within the twister could be accurately estimated.

The low-slung funnel tapering from the main cloud base of a tornado that swept across North Dakota on 20 June 1957 (*right*). The writhing funnel may retract from the ground during its travel across the countryside.

northwards, giving the region its hot, sticky summer days and mild winter spells. But in the higher atmosphere, above the level of the mountains, the prevailing winds are from the west and these, after dropping much of their moisture on the west coast of the continent, sweep down from the Rockies as cold, dry winds relative to the low-level Gulf air. Where the air masses meet, one above the other, conditions are perfect for violent instability, storms and tornadoes.

Temperature inversions may prevent an immediate onset of storm development by acting like a "lid", but if daytime heating is strong enough, or if an approaching cold front causes lower-level air to converge and start rising, then the whole system may be tipped out of control and severe storms are the inevitable result. The further development of the storms, and why some produce tornadoes, is the subject of much research. One important feature is the development of a small low-pressure area, the "tornado cyclone", which initially concentrates the storm activity into a small area with a

diameter of a few tens of kilometres. These miniature storms persist for about an hour, rotating very rapidly and spinning off embryonic tornadoes.

The speed of movement of tornadoes across country is variable, but their direction is generally fairly predictable – the normal track is northeasterly. Much more variable, however, is the contact between the storm funnel and the ground. Frequently the storm will lift clear of the ground, skipping perhaps several kilometres and doing no damage, only to "touch down" again with undiminished fury. So clearly defined are the edges of the wind-bands that there have been cases in which a storm, lifting clear of the ground, has skimmed along just above the ground – tearing off the upper storeys of buildings while causing no direct damage at all to the lower parts of the buildings or to walls, trees and vehicles in the streets below. An observer of one such incident described it as being ". . . like someone went down the street with a giant chain-saw", which vividly illustrates the mode of action of many tornadoes.

Tornadoes begin and end their lives as funnel clouds – the characteristic conical cloud formation projecting below the cloud base but at this stage not reaching the ground. Funnel clouds themselves present no danger: indeed many never develop into tornadoes at all. Their presence, however, is ample warning that conditions are right for tornado development, and even if a tornado fails to develop there will almost certainly be a storm with thunder, lightning and heavy rain or hail. When a tornado is about to die it often becomes extended into a long, slender "rope" cloud – no longer in touch with the ground but hanging from the cloud base and trailing nearly horizontally, moving sinuously for a while before finally dissipating completely.

The exact reasons for the origin of a tornado are still something of a mystery, but the most important conditions appear to be a very steep lapse rate with corresponding atmospheric instability. Most damage is caused by the extremely rapid fall of pressure associated with it which causes buildings to explode.

Tornado warnings

Tornadoes often occur in swarms, and one of the worst tornado disasters in American history was caused by just such a storm complex. The date was 11 April 1965 and the disaster was named "The Palm Sunday Outbreak".

This particular storm was caused by warm, moisture-laden air streaming northeast over the upper Mississippi Valley ahead of a fast-moving low-pressure system while a mass of relatively dry, cool air was moving in from the west. Thunderstorms started to form at the boundary between the two air masses – a common enough feature of the region's summer weather – but at the same time a strong westerly jet-stream began blowing at a speed of up to 80 metres per second (179 mph) over the area. These conditions were perfect for tornado development and at 11 am a warning was issued. Between 12.45 and 9.45 pm, 37 separate tornadoes formed in an area covering much of six states. One of the tornadoes demolished two churches, a town hall, a store and a number of houses in Pittsfield,

A twin funnel tornado observed on 11 April 1965 in Indiana was probably caused by closely spaced updraughts and downdraughts in the spring-time thunderclouds.

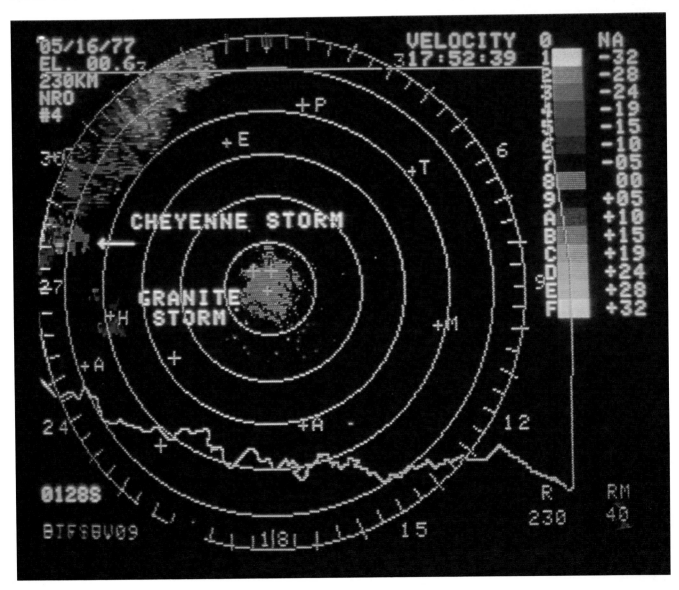

Ohio, all within half a minute; another wrecked 100 homes and the shopping centre of a small town and a third threw an Iowa farmhouse 18 metres (60 feet) into the air before crashing it to the ground. In all, 271 people were killed within the nine-hour onslaught.

Tornadoes are often spawned by tropical hurricanes or deep temperate-latitude low-pressure systems, and the resulting winds, with the tornado superimposed on a general gale, are tremendous. When Hurricane Carla hit the southern USA in 1961, 46 people died – but 11 of the deaths were caused by tornadoes produced by the hurricane. Almost invariably, tornadoes formed in this way are produced in the right forward quadrant of the main storm and, rather surprisingly, rarely from the zone of hurricane-force winds, but from the gale-force wind zone farther from the centre. As yet, meteorologists have been unable to ascertain whether tornado development occurs predominantly in this outer region or whether tornadoes formed nearer the centre are simply masked by the prevailing violent winds.

Although we now understand fairly well the general conditions that favour the development of tornadoes, there is still a great deal to be learned about the details of the processes involved. The development and constant improvement of the tornado warning service is naturally a high research priority in the Great Plains region of America. It is quite impossible to forecast the exact time and location of a tornado strike, but the general conditions for the formation of the storms are now familiar. General warnings can therefore be broadcast and then updated with more specific alerts as the storms are identified. Also, the Torro tornado intensity scale, which ranges from 0 to 12, is used to give an indication of the extent and severity of any expected damage.

Radar has proved itself an invaluable aid because a tornado produces a characteristic image on the radar screen – a pronounced hook shape reflecting the tight spiral of the cloud formation of the storm. These hook echoes represent the heavy rain or hail that often occurs along the flank of severe storms and may have diameters of several kilometres; tornadoes typically emerge from the near southern edge of the hook-shaped regions of these storms. However, unfortunately not all tornado-breeding storms have this characteristic feature and radar signals cannot be used as a totally reliable indication of approaching tornadoes, but the sight of such an echo in a thunderstorm usually leads to a tornado warning.

Direct study is very difficult, for obvious reasons, though proposals have been made to fire instrumented rockets through the storms or to drag an instrumented vehicle across the storm path. In the Midwest, on days when tornadoes are expected, teams of trained observers go in search of the storms, aided by radar tracking stations. A special type of radar, known as Doppler radar, can measure the wind speeds in a tornado from a safe distance, and observations made using this new technique suggest that a tornado is initiated in the lower middle levels of a thunderstorm and subsequently grows upwards and downwards. High-flying aircraft have observed crater-like depressions in the tops of thunderclouds when tornadoes have been sweeping across the ground below. The possibility that this offers of detecting embryonic tornadoes long before there are any warning signs at the cloud base has important implications for improvements in forecasting them.

Laboratory experiments using circulating masses of water to represent the air masses, and a variety of computerized mathematical modelling techniques, have been used in an attempt to simulate tornado mechanics. So far, the results suggest that the critical factor is the rate of uplift: if it is too fast or too slow the vortex will not form. But the research process is slow and there is certainly no immediate prospect of controlling these violent windstorms. In the meantime the emphasis must be on accurate early warning systems and forecasts; and the well-tried tornado cellar.

Colour-doppler radar is used in tornado analysis. Reds and blues show movements towards and away from the centre of the screen. Grey areas are either stationary or are moving perpendicularly towards the radar dish.

A doppler radar antenna (*above*) is able to detect the horizontal motion of raindrops or hailstones within a thunderstorm and can pick out conditions that are capable of producing a tornado 20 minutes before it forms.

Tornado sightings

The basic conditions for the formation of a tornado can occur almost anywhere in the world, but the explosively violent combination of atmospheric conditions so common in central North America rarely happens elsewhere. If a high-level air mass is overtaking a body of air with different properties at the surface, then conditions are favourable for tornado formation. Summer heating often acts as a trigger, but tornadoes can occur at almost any time of day or any time of the year. In temperate latitudes, tornadoes often occur in swarms which seem to be associated with fast-moving winter storms.

Like the hurricane, the tornado is believed to have a calm "eye", though direct observation is almost impossible. The most unusual case on record of a man actually finding himself inside the eye of a tornado occurred on 22 June 1928, when a Kansas farmer, Will Keller, saw a storm approaching and ran to his shelter. Looking back he saw the funnel rise from the ground, and realizing that he was temporarily in no danger he waited and watched, fascinated, as the ragged open end of the funnel moved right over him. . . . "Steadily the tornado came on, the end gradually rising above the ground. I could have stood there only a few seconds, but so impressed was I with what was going on that it seemed a long time. At last the great shaggy end of the funnel hung directly overhead. Everything was as still as death. There was a strong gassy odour, and it seemed that I could not breathe. There was a screaming, hissing sound coming directly from the end of the funnel. I looked up and to my astonishment I saw right up into the heart of the tornado. There was a circular opening in the centre of the funnel, about fifty or one hundred feet in diameter, and extending straight upwards for a distance of at least one half-mile, as best I could judge under the circumstances. The walls of this opening were of rotating clouds and the whole was made brilliantly visible by constant flashes of lightning which zigzagged from side to side. Had it not been for the lightning I could not have seen the opening, not any distance up into it anyway.

"Around the lower rim of the great vortex small tornadoes were constantly forming and breaking away. These looked like tails as they writhed their way round the end of the funnel. It was these that made the hissing noise. . . .

"The opening was entirely hollow except for something which I could not exactly make out, but suppose

Twisters are common in the wastelands of West Africa, but their presence is often not recorded because it is a sparsely populated area.

that it was a detached wind cloud. This thing was in the center and was moving up and down. . . ."

From this and other reports throughout history it appears that lightning often accompanies tornadoes. However, the relationship between lightning and tornadoes is not yet fully understood – there is some doubt as to whether the lightning is a result of the tornado or whether it plays an active part in the production of the tornado. At one time it was generally believed that tornadoes were themselves a form of electrical activity, but this theory has now been discredited. They do appear as luminous columns on photographs that have been taken at night, which may well be due to lightning flashing inside the column and being hidden from direct view by clouds that compose the funnel. Ancient references to whirlwinds often use terms such as "fiery", probably as a result of this phenomenon.

Tornadoes that occur elsewhere than central North America may perhaps not inspire the overwhelming terror of a Midwest "special", but they are nevertheless quite capable of doing considerable damage such as ripping off roofs, demolishing small buildings, uprooting trees and causing expensive damage to crops and livestock in farming areas. Injuries and deaths may be fortunately rare in Europe, but there have been a number of very serious tornadoes in the Far East. In April 1981 a tornado in southern China killed four people, injured nearly 150 and wrecked more than 2000 homes. And in both India and Bangladesh – densely populated areas, with millions of people housed in flimsy buildings, with no cellars and poor emergency services – devastating tornadoes have occasionally ripped through towns causing huge losses of life.

Throughout Man's written records there are reports of strange "rains", including frogs and fishes, jellyfish and clods of earth, tadpoles, rats, lizards and stones. Some may be pure imagination or superstition: most are likely to be the results of the powerful suction effect of a tornado. For example, in a storm in 1978 a large number of geese were caught up in the updraught of a tornado, later to be dropped out of the clouds in a line stretching for 45 kilometres (28 miles) across Norfolk, England, and this phenomenon is by no means uncommon. The sucking up of red-brown mud may likewise explain some of the many ancient references to the skies "raining blood" and other strange deposits falling from the sky.

The spectacular collapse of the Tay Bridge on 28 December 1879, causing the loss of an entire train and everyone on board, may have been caused by gale force winds reaching tornado speeds.

Fire-devils (*above*) are caused by locally heated hot air escaping upwards into the atmosphere from a forest fire.

Inverted cone-shaped and slightly tilted dust-devils which rise to heights of around 61 metres (200 feet) are commonly formed during the hot summer months experienced in Kenya (*right*).

Dust-devils

Tornadoes have been known in Britain for many centuries, and almost without exception, and with good reason, are often referred to in ancient writings as manifestations of the Devil. In an age in which religion and superstition jointly ruled men's lives, and when it was still believed that the funnel cloud emanated from the ground, a blast from hell was the almost inevitable interpretation of the terrifying windstorm that could devastate farms and villages, causing death or injury to all in its path.

In 1165 an English monk wrote of the Devil, in the form of a black horse, striding across a hillside at Scarborough, Yorkshire, leaving footprints that were clearly visible a year later. The "footprints" were probably real enough – the suction marks sometimes made by a tornado as it passes across soft ground. But the most famous tornado that hit Britain was that of 31 October 1638. It struck the parish church at Widecombe, in Devon, in the middle of Sunday service, killing several of the congregation. The tornado is depicted in a contemporary drawing as a Devil's head on a long neck.

The name "devil" has persisted through the ages and is still used for the smaller whirlwinds, of which the most familiar is probably the dust-devil. These are common enough on hot days in many arid and semi-arid regions of the world. Dust-devils are generally less violent than tornadoes, but they can be quite powerful. There have been several reports of devils overturning cars and caravans, and in the arid American southwest, where devils have been observed extending up to a kilometre (3280 feet) into the air, buildings have sometimes suffered major damage.

The dynamics of a dust-devil are similar to those of a tornado, except that the system is not connected in any way with clouds. The devil's energy comes from intense heating of the dry ground and the layer of air in contact with it. Convection currents develop as hot air bubbles rise and air is sucked in at the ground, concentrating the rotation and accelerating to produce a whirlwind. Despite the powerful uplift, cloud is very rarely present due to the extreme dryness of the air.

Dust-devils are just one type of land-devil – a type made immediately visible by the load of dust carried in its swirling winds. In the absence of dust or loose leaves, a land-devil may hit without warning.

Fire is naturally an efficient generator of strongly rising air currents: the hotter the fire, the more powerful the updraughts. Predictably, fires tend to produce their own whirlwinds, called fire-devils. Once formed, a fire-devil can spin away from the main fire spreading heat, sparks and hot ash wherever its random wanderings may take it. Violent whirlwinds were observed around the billowing clouds of ash and steam belching from the recently formed volcanic island of Surtsey when it erupted off Iceland in 1965.

Nor can Man pretend his innocence in all this. Some of the most horrendous wartime bombing offensives of the Second World War, notably against Hamburg and Dresden, were deliberately conceived and planned to generate devastating firestorms in those cities. Similar firestorms contributed to the destruction that followed the earthquake in Tokyo in 1923.

Water-devils may form if land-devils wander out over water, but this type of water-devil soon dies out because of the lack of a heat supply. Some water-devils are generated when cool air moves out over a warm water surface. This is unusual though, because land surfaces are usually warmer than water.

A whirlwind can only be seen when dust and other material is sucked into it. The example shown here, caused by a local hot spot in Devon, in southern England, is made visible by wind-tossed hay.

Waterspouts

A waterspout is simply a marine tornado, formed in very similar conditions to a land tornado but, provided the sea is warm, more readily. A warm sea surface aids the formation of a tornado in two ways; firstly in warming the air close to the surface, and secondly in providing a ready supply of moisture. Both factors contribute to any instability in the atmosphere and so encourage the development of a vortex. Waterspouts never reach the intensity of the giant land tornadoes of the American Midwest, but they are still impressive and can present a serious hazard to small boats. Most at risk are sailing boats, because in conditions suitable for waterspout formation it is very likely that the general surface wind will be very light, leaving the craft with no means of taking evasive action.

In ancient times, waterspouts were believed to be sea monsters. The term itself rather implies that a fountain or column of water is somehow thrust upwards from the sea, but this is not so. Like a tornado, the waterspout forms as a funnel of whirling air descending from a storm cloud. When the funnel finally makes contact with the water surface, great quantities of water are sucked up and swirled around in the violently spinning tube, making it visible as a dark, grey, sinuous column. Sometimes a vortex of spray may appear on the surface of the sea before the cloud funnel becomes fully visible: such sightings are rare, but if such a tell-tale sign is seen it should be seriously regarded as a warning because the waterspout is certainly imminent.

One of the earliest references to a waterspout at sea was made by William Dampier in 1687, when he wrote: "A spout is a small ragged piece of a cloud hanging down about a yard, seemingly from the blackest part thereof. Commonly it hangs down sloping from thence. When the surface of the sea begins to work you shall see the water for about a hundred paces in circumference, foam and move gently round till the whirling motion increases; and then it flies upward in a pillar. Thus it continues for the space of half an hour, more or less, until the sucking is spent. Then all the water which was below the spout falls down again into the sea, making a great noise with its fall and clashing motion in the sea."

Like clouds, waterspouts move with varying speeds, but 5 to 10 metres per second (11 to 22 mph) is typical. The diameter of the waterspout column may be as little as 1 metre (3.3 feet) or it may reach 200 metres (650 feet) across. Typically, waterspouts tend to last for between 15 and 30 minutes. Very often the waterspout will writhe about and some have even been observed to start coiling up rather like a serpent. This, however, indicates that its energy is diminishing: as soon as the column coils up on itself it begins to disintegrate because it is impossible for the rotation of the air to be maintained. To be near a waterspout at the moment of disintegration is particularly dangerous, sometimes even more so than being near the spout itself, for as the spout fails, all the water held in suspension is suddenly released and drops in a torrential deluge that is quite capable of overwhelming a small boat.

Sea-water rises to form a narrow funnel-cloud of water droplets, spiralling in an anti-clockwise direction, here seen off Spain's Costa Brava coast on 2 September 1965. The funnel is composed mainly of droplets extending downwards from cumulonimbus cloud rather than water sucked up from the sea. The spiral nature of a waterspout has meant that it has often been mistaken for a long-necked sea snake.

Several methods of dispersing waterspouts have been tried and they vary from the firing of guns to shouting and stamping on deck; but of this method even Dampier commented, "I never did hear that it proved to be of any benefit." So far all attempts have been futile and the only sure way of avoiding trouble is to avoid the vicinity of imminent waterspouts completely.

Though particularly common in warm waters, and very much associated with oceanic areas such as the Gulf of Mexico and the Bahamas, waterspouts can form almost anywhere. They are most often seen under conditions which suggest that a main contributing factor might be a relatively cool wind blowing off the land. They are, however, generally rare in the cool conditions of northwest European waters and, being usually quite small, when they do appear they excite wonder and amazement rather than fear.

Waterspouts frequently appear in "families", three or four in the same area within a few minutes of each other being fairly common, while one writer described an occasion when nearly 50 were in sight at the same time.

MONSTERS OR DEVILS?

Water devils often emit a gentle hiss or even a muffled roaring as they pick up spray and waterweed, throwing it high into the air and because of this it has been suggested that these localized rotating storms may be at the heart of many monster legends. The great sea serpent of Lake Victoria in East Africa "announces its coming with a terrible roar and emerges from the lake at certain times to swallow up human beings, canoes and everything in its path"; a description that is compatible with a strong local water-devil that occurs on the lake. Lake Ogananagain in British Columbia and Loch Ness in the Scottish Highlands are also among the many great lakes reported to contain monsters and where water devils could occur: however, photographs of the Loch Ness monster (*right*) do not resemble waterspouts.

A swarm of waterspouts generates waves and sea spray, surging upwards and outwards from the base.

WORLD WEATHER

"Her [England's] fields a rich expanse of wavy corn
Pour'd out from plenty's overflowing horn;
Ambrosial gardens in which art supplies
the fervor and the force of Indian skies:
Her peaceful shores, where busy commerce waits
To pour his golden tide through all her gates:
Whom fiery suns that scorch the russet spice
Of eastern groves, and oceans floor'd with ice,
Forbid in vain to push his daring way
To darker climes, or climes of brighter day;
Whom the winds waft where'er the billows roll,
From the world's girdle to the frozen pole. . . ."
William Cowper – Expostulation

The Earth's climatic zones are among the most important characteristics of the planet, determining landscape, vegetation and animal life and setting a limit to Man's exploitation of the environment. They have a profound effect on human culture and on the way that people think and behave. Climatic conditions have a fundamental influence upon levels of economic activity, and it is no accident that the industrially developed countries are almost without exception located within the temperate climatic belt – and that the Third World lies largely within the tropics.

Clouds shroud Niederen, in Germany, in a veil of moist water droplets.

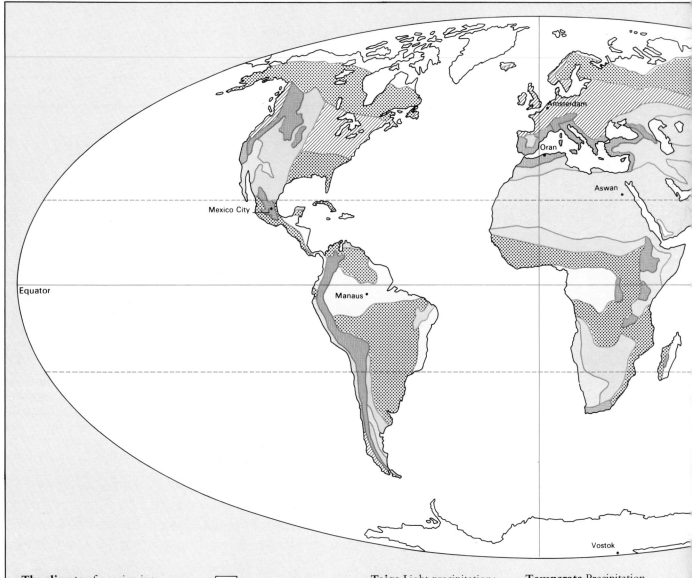

The climate of a region is a
summary of the day-to-day weather
that is characteristically
experienced through the seasons of
the year. As small fluctuations in
local weather conditions are
difficult to describe, all climates
with similar features are grouped
together and shown on the world
map; the climate graphs (right) are
used in conjunction with the map
to illustrate the typical average
temperature and rainfall of each
climatic region. The map shows
the tropical rainy climates of South
America, Africa and the Far East,
the world's great deserts that
straddle the subtropical latitudes
and the mosaic pattern of mid-
latitude climates – the temperate,
steppe, monsoon, mediterranean
and mountain belts that eventually
become simplified by the
continental taiga and then fringed
by the polar regions.

- ☐ Polar
- ▨ Taiga
- ▨ Mountain
- ▨ Temperate
- ▨ Monsoon/ Subtropical
- ▨ Steppe/ Savanna
- ☐ Tropical
- ▨ Mediterranean
- ☐ Hot Deserts

Taiga Light precipitation;
short, cool summers, long,
very cold winters.

Temperate Precipitation
in all seasons; temperatures
vary with location.

Polar Extremely long,
cold winters. No precipitation records for Vostok.

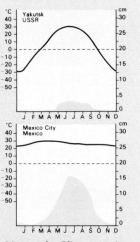

Mountain Climate varies
widely with elevation,
latitude and exposure.

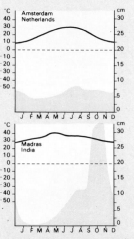

Monsoon and subtropical.
Often dry and wet seasons,
all months being hot.

124

Climate

The climate or long-term weather pattern of a region depends on several factors: latitude, which determines how hot or cold an area is, and the extent and influence of its seasons; the properties of the prevailing air masses that may be hot, cold, moist or dry; and physical factors such as the relative distribution of land, sea, mountains, valleys, forests and glaciers.

Equatorial regions are warm all year round because the air masses that affect them are warm and moist, and bring steady rain throughout the year. The monsoon climates of India and Southeast Asia and China occur when seasonal winds blow from almost opposite directions; warm, moist winds alternating with warm, dry ones to give cloudy, wet summers and drier winters.

Desert climates, found in broad zones on either side of the equator, are located in anticyclonic, stable regions of high pressure, where warm, dry air brings cloudless skies and little rain. In the middle latitudes of both hemispheres warm subtropical air is often juxtapositioned with cool subpolar air and they may often be in conflict. Areas in these zones have a temperate climate – they may bask in subtropical air in summer but suffer from occasional draughts of cold subpolar air in winter.

The Mediterranean climates of California, southwestern Australia and the Mediterranean region itself are generally found on the western flanks of continents that tend to be dry in summer and have mild, damp winters. Nearer the poles, the climatic regions are controlled by polar air masses that bring cold and dry weather throughout the year with brief sunny summers.

The pattern of the world's climatic zones has had a profound influence upon life on Earth. Before Man became a settled creature, his nomadic lifestyle followed the animals and vegetation as it came and went with the rains. When he first settled he built his towns in those latitudes where neither extremes of cold nor heat were to be found, but where there existed a happy mean. Thus the most favourable places for the first settlements were within Mediterranean climatic regions, in the "fertile crescent" where summer drought and dryness – the greatest threat to life – was alleviated by the presence of major rivers, such as the Nile, Tigris and Euphrates, which flooded each spring. In the same way the Indus and Yellow rivers cradled early civilizations of the East.

As populations increased and food supplies became more critical, people migrated towards the temperate zones, where rainfall, the crucial factor, was found to be more plentiful but where the climate was less predictable. The landscape and conditions encouraged a degree of preparedness for the future. Here people could not rely on the summer harvests with the same certainty but had to anticipate harsh winters and crop failures.

The climate dictates every facet of human life – architecture, clothing, food and even culture and temperament. The colours, ideas, pace of life and even certain lines of behaviour that are found to be typical of phlegmatic people in northern latitudes and the more volatile people of the lower latitudes are reflected by the weather that they are accustomed to.

Steppe Light precipitation, summers warm, some locations have cool winters.

Mediterranean Light precipitation, mild winters, dry summers; warm.

Tropical Heavy rainfall, often only one or two dry months; all months hot.

Hot Deserts Negligible precipitation, all months hot.

125

The Poles

The Arctic is an ocean of permanent pack-ice surrounded by Greenland, North America and Eurasia, its boundary being the 10°C (50°F) July isotherm. At the other extreme the Antarctic is a continent covered with ice; both have a world-wide influence.

Both the Arctic at the North Pole and the Antarctic at the South Pole present severe environmental conditions for any form of life. As the Antarctic is the coldest and windiest of the world's continents, it is not surprising that no indigenous land mammals have ever lived there, nor has there been any permanent human settlement. In contrast, the circumpolar Arctic has been inhabited for hundreds of years by the Eskimos of North America and Greenland and peoples of other cultures such as the Lapps of Eurasia. Besides the indigenous human population the Arctic also supports a large number of other mammals, birds and fish.

The first exploring ship to winter in the Antarctic was the *Belgica*, under the command of the Belgian Lieutenant Adrien de Gerlache de Gomeroy. The ship remained trapped in the ice for 347 days from February 1898. As winter set in, the crew began to suffer from anaemia due to unsuitable rations and from depression brought on by the appalling monotony of the environment. Besides the extreme cold and horrific winds their physical and mental deterioration was accelerated by their isolation and the darkness of the interminable night.

A few years later the 1901 to 1904 expedition in the *Antarctica* met with disaster and was forced to winter on the Antarctic Peninsula. One group miraculously sur-

People managed to cross the ice and reach the North Pole only when clothed in traditional Eskimo garments and drawn by huskies, hitched to sleds by harnesses made of walrus skins. Thick fur insulates the dogs so that they can sleep in the snow even when the temperature drops to −57°C (−71°F). They are able to pull sleds at speeds of up to 32 kilometres per hour (20 mph).

vived in an average temperature of −20°C (−4°F) by building a hut and killing penguins for meat and burning seal blubber for fuel. However, for other early explorers it was quite a different story and many, like Captain Scott in 1912, paid the penalty of death for venturing to the South Pole without previous experience of polar regions.

Today a Russian research station is situated at Vostok, deep in the interior of the Antarctic, 3488 metres (11,439 feet) above sea-level and holding the world record for the coldest temperature −88°C (−126°F). Some research bases are actually constructed almost entirely underground within the ice and the inhabitants pass the long winter in a troglodytic manner, living in their insulated quarters and working in their quite sophisticated laboratories in relative comfort.

The various forms of life, apart from Man, that are found in the Antarctic have evolved sundry adaptations that enable them to cope with the severe conditions. The remarkable Emperor Penguin breeds almost exclusively on sea-ice off the coasts of the Antarctic continent, and is the only living species of animal to breed in the Antarctic winter. The single egg is held on the feet and incubated only by the males, which huddle together tightly throughout the coldest months of winter, when temperatures frequently fall as low as −60°C (−76°F). The eggs take some two months to hatch – during which time the males live off their fat reserves – and the chicks emerge into an uninviting world of perpetual darkness and no food. At first they are fed by the returning females and later by the males as well. They grow rapidly and reach independence in December or January, when the sea-ice is dispersing and food is easily obtainable.

In the Arctic, the original Eskimo way of life was based entirely on a subsistence economy, relying on the indigenous wildlife for food and clothing, the Eskimos migrating with the animals. Sealing, whaling, caribou hunting and fishing are some examples of native activities. Within recent years the opening up of the Arctic regions has brought changes to such an extent that most native communities now have some degree of cash economy, and the old traditional life-style is disappearing. Even so, until recently inland Eskimos of Alaska survived through the winter living in dome-shaped tents made of caribou hides. Inside these small and well-insulated enclosures, a small fire of twigs or animal fat kept them warm and overnight the heat from the sleeping inhabitants was enough to keep temperatures above freezing point. There was, of course, a variety of other structures of local design, some built partly below ground and covered with carefully selected dry sods to conserve heat.

Eskimos and Arctic American Indians have certain physiological advantages, such as an extra insulating layer of fat, which provides some protection against the extreme cold – their thinner brethren, who live in more temperate latitudes, tend to feel the cold more acutely. However, the Eskimos' secret of success in coping with their severe environment lay very largely in their clothing, transport and behavioural adaptations. A large array of clothing and footwear was required for each

season. Fur was selected from various animals, and in general clothing, footwear and mittens were very basic. However, protected by imported clothing and shelter, the new generation of Eskimos, along with the white newcomers to the Arctic, do not need to exercise the skills with which their ancestors so accurately appraised the surroundings and which enabled them to survive its harsh influences.

Arctic species of wildlife have evolved various strategies to cope with the climatic conditions. Water-fowl, for example, are present only during the short summer, leaving before the freeze-up returns – a simple solution to the problem of cold. Some small mammals, such as the Arctic ground squirrel, hibernate throughout the winter period, during which time their body temperature drops considerably. Other animals are active throughout the winter, and some, such as the Arctic Fox, grow a thick white coat for the winter period. Other species, such as Caribou and Dall Sheep, acquire a thicker coat but do not change colour. There are, of course, various other adaptations for survival. In the case of the Caribou, for example, growth in bulk occurs mainly in summer, while the longer winter finds them just maintaining weight and apparently economizing by diminished levels of activity.

Adélie Penguins breed in the Antarctic and can survive for weeks beneath the snows of spring and summer blizzards. They huddle together to conserve body heat.

Modern technology allows people to live and work on research stations in the Antarctic in spite of the cold conditions that are beyond the extremes of normal experience.

The Taiga

The taiga stretches without interruption across Eurasia and North America. Its northern boundary is the 10°C (50°F) July isotherm and its southern boundary is marked by areas that have more than four months in a year above this temperature.

Climatic conditions of the northern forests, known by the Siberian term of taiga, are severe; the long, cold winters are interrupted only by short, warm summers. Precipitation is low, totalling less than 50 centimetres (20 inches) and is usually concentrated in the warmer months. No other climate has such a wide annual range of temperature – the most extreme values occurring in the interior of the largest landmass, Eurasia.

The world record for the greatest temperature range is held at Verkhoyansk, where the coldest month, January, has an average temperature of −47°C (−53°F), and the warmest month, July, has an average temperature of 16°C (61°F) – a difference of 63°C (114°F) between the two extremes. Verkhoyansk and Oymyakon, situated about 640 kilometres (400 miles) to the southeast, hold the record for the lowest temperature observed on the Earth's surface outside Antarctica, −68°C (−90°F).

These places are located in valleys in northeast Siberia at the "pole of cold", and the exceptionally low temperatures are produced by a combination of katabatic winds and radiative cooling, particularly during the long nights experienced near the Arctic Circle in winter.

Since trees and plants do not come into growth until the average air temperature has risen above 6°C (43°F), the growing season in the taiga is short and only lasts between one and three months. Coniferous trees are best adapted to this restriction and so taiga forests are dominated by pine, spruce, fir and larch, together with a scattered population of hardy deciduous species such as birch and aspen.

The life cycle of leafing, flowering, fruiting and seeding is relatively lengthy in trees, and most coniferous species retain their leaves all though the winter to save time in the spring. However, summers in the taiga are still too short for trees to produce fruit and seeds in one growing season, and the life cycle has gradually been adapted so that coniferous trees can survive without bearing fruit. Instead, the seeds are carried on the outside of cones, which take about one and a half seasons to ripen. Thus, by the early summer of alternate seasons the cones are ready to cast seeds from which the next generation of trees is formed.

Other special features of coniferous trees include hard, needle-shaped leaves that decrease resistance to the wind and also have waxy surfaces with very few pores so as to reduce transpiration to a minimum. A thick resinous bark covering the trunks and branches provides protection against cold, drying winds and decay. The overall compact, conical structure of coniferous trees helps to increase their stability in strong winds and allows their branches to be laden with snow without breaking.

The taiga provides a habitat for a wide variety of wildlife, including the bear, wolf, fox, lynx, deer and elk or moose. However, fur-bearing animals such as the sable and marten, having been hunted for centuries, now occur in appreciable numbers only in the more remote parts. With its fur coat turning pure white in the winter, the ermine displays a striking adaptation to the seasonal transformation of the landscape.

The taiga rivals the deserts and polar regions in its lack of human habitation; it constitutes 10 per cent of the world's land area, but is occupied by only about 1 per cent of the world's population. Some of its earliest arrivals were Asian steppe nomads, who originally migrated northwards, seeking refuge in the taiga from the periodic droughts of the grassland regions and belligerent neighbours. Perhaps the most adaptable of these nomadic tribes were the Yakuts, who occupied the Lena River basin in the heart of the "pole of cold". They learned to supplement their meat diet with fish and game, and to sell their farm products to later Russian settlers and even to act as traders between the Russians and the Asiatic peoples living in the more remote parts of the taiga. The Indian tribes of the Canadian boreal forest, who lived only by hunting and fishing, are also believed to have migrated from Asia through Siberia and Alaska.

Peoples of European origin are increasingly extending their frontiers of settlement into the taiga, but unfortunately contact with the modern European way of life has disorientated many of the long-established "native" patterns and only the Yakuts in Siberia are still increasing in numbers. The first contacts between Europeans and the earlier Asiatic settlers in the taiga were made through the fur trade in the eleventh century. During the sixteenth and seventeenth centuries trading posts were established by Europeans, both in the Old and New World taigas, mostly at river mouths, to which the "natives" brought their loads of skins after the snow had melted in spring. In Canada the Hudson's Bay Company gradually established posts farther inland from the western shores of the Bay, whilst in Asia the Russians pushed their trading activities eastwards into Alaska, which the United States purchased from them in 1867.

Although agricultural scientists have recently made great progress in breeding special strains of quick-ripening crops, the amount of food grown in the taiga remains negligible compared with large-scale farming areas to the south. The sparse sprinkling of pioneer farms are literally islands in a sea of forest, and occur only where some local singularity of soil or climate has provided at least some small advantage to combat the brief and variable growing seasons.

Most of the people who make up the sparse population of the taiga today are not hunters, trappers or farmers, but workers in the lumbering and mining industries. The region has become noted for its vast quantities of softwood conifers, which are felled for the pulp and paper industries. The taiga also has important reserves of primary energy such as oil, natural gas and uranium, and minerals which are in great demand by the outside world.

The mink (*above*), native to the North American taiga, is prized for its lustrous brown fur coat.

Conditions for commercial logging are ideal because large stands of a single species of fast-growing coniferous tree grow in one area.

Only hardy and adaptable trees can survive in the bleak climate, where most of the water is locked in the ground.

Mountains

Mountain areas, mainly the Cordilleras of North and South America, the Alps of Europe and the Himalayas of Asia have a complex climate because they extend over a wide range of latitude and their temperature, rainfall and pressure vary with altitude.

One of the most important factors affecting mountain climates is the decrease of temperature with height. Averaging about 6·5°C per kilometre (3·6°F per 1000 feet), this factor is responsible for a vertical zoning of temperature, pressure and rainfall as well as several other climatic elements. In parts of tropical Latin America, for example, three zones can be distinguished: the *Tierra Caliente*, which includes the hot tropical coastlands and extensive pasturelands stretching from sea level to about 900 metres (3000 feet); the *Tierra Templada*, the subtropical zone in which temperatures range between 18°C (65°F) and 24°C (75°F), rising to 1800 metres (6000 feet); and the *Tierra Fria*, the temperate zone in which the mean annual temperature is about 13°C (55°F) and is 3000 metres (9800 feet) high – a zone which has proved popular for urban centres, including the capital cities of Mexico City, Bogota and Quito.

Although the changes of climate that occur with elevation on high mountains in the tropics may superficially resemble those experienced when travelling from the equator to the poles, there are some important differences; none of the climates of extra-tropical latitudes are exactly duplicated in tropical highlands as they are not affected by weather changes due to travelling storms or anticyclones; also the smaller annual of temperature in the tropics makes seasonal changes less marked.

The human body cannot perceive the comparatively minor changes in air pressure at sea level, but as one ascends a mountain the rapid decrease of pressure with height can easily be felt. The rate at sea level is approximately 1 millibar per 10 metres (1 millibar per 30 feet), but becomes less with increasing altitude. At altitudes above about 3000 metres (9800 feet) many people experience "mountain sickness" symptoms, which generally disappear after a week spent at this altitude. But at 6000 metres (19,600 feet) the pressure is so reduced, less than half of its value at sea level, that difficulty with breathing is permanent and acute, presenting a distinct physiological limit. Nevertheless, a group of Andean Indians living in mountain villages at about 5200 metres (17,000 feet) has developed lungs and hearts larger than those of people living at sea level, and over many generations they have probably achieved the ultimate condition in Man's ability to become acclimatized to high altitudes.

In tropical mountains, rainfall initially increases with height up to about 1500 metres (5000 feet), above which there is a distinct decrease. The effect is less evident outside the tropics, where precipitation continues to increase with height. Winds also generally become stronger with height because the movement of air becomes less affected by frictional drag with the Earth's surface.

The sherpas of Nepal are born to a life of porterage and are capable of carrying loads, equalling their own weight, up almost sheer rock faces at altitudes of more than 3030 metres (10,000 feet).

The invigorating climate and unrivalled beauty of the Alpine mountains that span across Europe attract tourists all year round.

La Paz, in Bolivia (*left*), the world's highest capital. It lies at an elevation of 3577 metres (11,910 feet) above the *Tierra Fria* in the *Altiplano*, a high intermontane plateau on which the Inca Empire flourished in the fifteenth century. The snow-capped peak of Illimani, 6462 metres (21,200 feet), in the background and the surrounding peaks give the city a rugged beauty.

Tea-pickers in the Darjeeling area of the Himalayan foothills form a basic economic framework, but the equable climate also enables the area to be used as a "hill station" by more fortunate inhabitants of the West Bengal plains. Many people move up here to escape the long, hot summers and to enjoy the magnificent view of Kangchenjunga, 8598 metres (28,208 feet) high.

The intensity of sunlight increases with height in the progressively cleaner, drier and less dense air of mountains. On a clear day about 75 per cent of the solar energy penetrates to 2000 metres (6500 feet), whereas only 50 per cent reaches sea level. Also with decreasing amounts of atmospheric filtering, the proportion of ultraviolet radiation increases with altitude, causing people to tan more quickly in mountain sunlight. In the Northern Hemisphere the north sides of valleys which run from west to east are much warmer, due to increased exposure to sunlight, than the south sides at the same altitude. These differences of temperature have resulted in contrasts of vegetation and settlement such as that found in the upper Rhône Valley in Switzerland, where the sunny and shady sides have been distinguished by the terms "adret" and "ubac", respectively.

Rainfall can be dramatically affected by local mountains. The heaviest rainfall occurs when warm, moist air is uplifted on windward slopes, for example the world's wettest known place is Mt Waialeale, 1548 metres (5079 feet), on Kauai Island, Hawaii, with an average annual rainfall of 1168 centimetres (460 inches). A striking rainshadow effect is also shown on the same island, where only a few kilometres away the rainfall decreases to 25 centimetres (10 inches) per year.

Snowfalls are heavier and more frequent in highlands because of lower temperatures; even at the equator some of the highest mountains in Africa and South America have snow-covered peaks. The snow-line – the lower boundary of permanent snow cover on mountains – becomes lower with increasing latitude and on windward and shadier slopes.

There is a tendency for a daily reversal of local wind direction in mountainous areas. Daytime heating of mountain slopes by the Sun causes an up-valley or anabatic wind, which sometimes triggers off thunderstorms. Night-time cooling of the slopes by radiation causes down-valley or katabatic winds. The draining of the cold air into valleys leads to frost-hollows and temperature inversions.

The amount of land available for cultivation in mountainous areas is limited because the highest slopes are often covered by snow for much of the year. Efforts to make the best use of land have led to a typical life-style of annual migrations called transhumance. For instance, in some Alpine and Norwegian valleys a series of journeys up and down the slopes has been developed with the animals being driven up to high pastures, "alps" or "saeters", during summer and down again in winter.

Because of the difficult terrain and rigorous climate, mountains have acted as barriers to people's movements and communications. Mountains have tended to isolate and separate communities both within the highland areas themselves and in lowlands lying on either side of mountain ranges. This insulating effect has hindered change and allowed traditional ways of life to be preserved in mountainous areas and has sometimes led to the development of distinct cultures that are separated by only a few kilometres.

Temperate zones

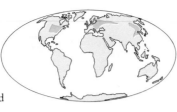

Temperate climates are found in most of Europe, on the northwest coast of North America and in parts of eastern North America, eastern Asia, Chile, Tasmania and New Zealand; they have a small annual range of temperature and an even distribution of rainfall.

Temperate climates may be divided into western marginal, continental and eastern marginal types. There is a distinct difference between the maritime climate of temperate western marginal regions, which are most strongly affected by the travelling storms of the westerlies, and the more extreme climates of areas situated farther inland and on the eastern margins of Eurasia and North America. Lying in the direct path of mid-latitude westerlies, the classic type of temperate climate, the western continental marginal type, is extremely equable due to the moderating influence of maritime air-streams advected from adjacent oceans by the prevailing winds. But besides this, the westerly winds cause day-to-day weather to be extremely changeable, for they carry along with them a succession of low- and high-pressure systems responsible for wet and fine weather respectively.

At times, a greater variation in temperature and rainfall is brought about when the normal westerly winds are interrupted by a "blocking high", which diverts the usual lows into other areas; blocking highs tend to develop either in the eastern North Atlantic or the eastern North Pacific. Both the prolonged drought which affected northwestern Europe during 1975–76 and the very cold winter over eastern North America in 1976–77

were due to persistent blocking activity in these areas.

In winter high-pressure systems tend to develop over the continental interiors, thus displacing the travelling storms and their moderating effects. However, in summer the formation of large-scale thermal lows over the same continental interiors allows the inflow of moist maritime air from the western and eastern seaboards.

The moderating influence of the oceans on temperate climates creates the typical cool summers and mild winters that characterize the climate. Temperate climate is most fully developed on the western margins of landmasses, especially in Europe, where the west-to-east alignment of mountain chains does not seriously impede the eastward penetration of Atlantic air. On the other hand, the annual range of temperature is particularly large in the eastern margins of Asia. This is due mainly to the low temperatures that occur in winter, when cold air masses flow out of the Asiatic high-pressure region. These persistent outblowing winds carry fine desert dust, which, over the ages, has produced a thick and extensive deposit of loess soil over northern China. This soil is particularly fertile and so encouraged settlement by early civilizations that were flourishing in China.

In winter the shores of western Europe are washed by the unusually warm waters of the North Atlantic Drift; the course of the 0°C (32°F) January isotherm illustrates the effect of the "gulf of winter warmth" that extends northeastwards over the British Isles to well within the Arctic Circle, keeping the coasts of Norway ice-free as far north as North Cape at latitude 71°N. In contrast, the other side of the North Atlantic does not benefit from a warm ocean current and so the St. Lawrence River, at

Deep, fertile, organic soils combined with a climate that is favourable for growing grain has meant that much of the original natural vegetation in temperate regions, particularly in eastern North America and Europe, has been cleared to make way for highly mechanized farming.

New Zealand (*above*) intercepts moist winds that encourage the growth of rich and varied temperate forests. Some of the warm temperate rain forest is protected from clearance because it occupies relatively inaccessible land with soil that is unsuitable for agriculture.

Caves (*below*) are dug into the cliff-like formations of wind-blown loess soil in the Shansi region of northwest China; caves are warm in winter and cool in summer, and since timber in this area is sparse, they have been used as dwellings since time immemorial.

higher latitudes than 50°N, is blocked with ice for several months in winter. The pattern of winter warmth is less pronounced off the coasts of British Columbia due to the relative weakness of the North Pacific gyre.

Along the western margins of landmasses, rainfall is mainly cyclonic, although there is a strong orographic effect in mountainous areas. Particularly heavy falls, over 250 centimetres (100 inches), occur on the exposed west-facing coasts and slopes of Scotland, Norway and South Island, New Zealand. Rainfall amounts tend to decrease steadily inland, although the effect of increasing precipitation on mountains is locally important.

Low-pressure systems are frequent and are usually more vigorous in winter, with the result that maximum rainfall occurs in many temperate western margins in this season. Orographic rainfall, on the other hand, tends to increase to a maximum in late summer or autumn due to warmer seas increasing the moisture content of the prevailing maritime air masses at that time of year. Farther inland convectional rainfall, which is mainly a summer type, becomes more important; also lows and their associated precipitation belts tend to penetrate more readily into continental interiors during summer. Snow is common in temperate latitudes, although it usually persists only in the interiors and eastern parts of continents, where it accumulates and accounts for most of the winter precipitation.

Temperate climates are clearly distinguished by a dormant season of one to five months, when the mean temperature falls below the threshold level of 6°C (43°F) necessary for plant growth. Over most of the region the rainfall is sufficient to support tree growth and the natural vegetation is broad-leaved deciduous forest, which includes oak, beech, ash and maple. As a protection against winter cold these trees annually shed their leaves, but where mean temperatures are lower or soils poorer the forest tends to become coniferous.

Although temperate regions comprise only about 7 per cent of the Earth's land surface they are occupied by over 40 per cent of the world's population. Parts of northern China have been continuously inhabited longer than anywhere else on Earth. Much of the original forested habitat has been cleared in eastern Asia and western Europe to make way for agriculture, which in turn has been replaced by industrialized urban complexes.

The reasons for the remarkable rise of industry and urbanization in temperate climate regions during the eighteenth century are complex, but it does appear that these developments were particularly encouraged by a combination of geographical and historical factors which strongly interacted within a particularly favourable set of climatic conditions. Access to deposits of coal and iron, fertile soils, geographical position and not least a climate suitable for agriculture on a large scale and human activity were major factors in the developing prosperity of these regions in the twentieth century, and so some of the world's greatest cities, such as London, New York, Berlin and Paris, have developed in the temperate zone.

Monsoon zones

Monsoon climates include the classical Indian monsoon lands, temperate monsoon lands and subtropical areas of Africa, Australia and South America. Warm weather prevails, mean temperatures being at least 18°C (64°F) with well-developed seasons.

The monsoon of southern Asia, the so-called "Indian monsoon", is the most impressive seasonal phenomenon of the tropics. The term is derived from the Arabic word "mausim", meaning season, and was first used by Arab navigators to describe the seasonal winds of the Arabian Sea that blow from the northeast for one half of the year and from the southwest for the other half. For centuries, ocean-going dhows have taken advantage of these wind systems, arriving in East African ports during January after voyages lasting five or six weeks from the Persian Gulf and returning northwards in April or May following the reversal of the monsoon winds.

The natural vegetation of southern Asia varies widely according to the rainfall. In areas of heavy precipitation, such as the Western Ghats and Khasi Hills of Assam, with over 200 centimetres (80 inches) per year, there are ever-green forests that resemble tropical rain forest. In the true monsoon forests, which occur where the rainfall is only moderately heavy, between 100 and 200 centimetres (40 and 80 inches), teak is the most characteristic tree. In the western Deccan and northwestern India, where rainfall totals are only 64 centimetres (25 inches) per year, the monsoon forests merge into scrub and thorn forests. Wildlife abounds in the jungle of the eastern Deccan.

The savannahs of Africa and Australia and the *Llanos* and *Campos* of South America are tropical lands with a climate dominated by a monsoonal effect. During the dry season, stable subsiding air masses of the subtropical anti-cyclones give cloudless skies with maximum temperatures of 27°C to 32°C (81°F to 90°F), sometimes rising to over 38°C (100°F) just before the summer monsoon rains. The weather can be very hazy at times in the Sudan when strong northeasterly winds – the Harmattan – laden with dust blow from adjacent deserts.

In the wet season the region is affected by unstable air masses of the Intertropical Convergence Zone (ITCZ). Although thick clouds and heavy, thundery rain slightly lower the temperature, conditions are still uncomfortable due to the high humidities. Annual rainfall varies between 75 and 150 centimetres (30 and 60 inches), decreasing with distance from the equator. Bordering the desert the annual rainfall becomes extremely variable.

The natural vegetation consists mostly of coarse grasses, which quickly grow to a height of several metres in the wet season. The grasslands are sometimes inter-spersed by scattered trees, which give the impression of an open "parkland" landscape. By developing large root systems, storing water in their trunks and shedding their leaves, trees such as acacias, baobabs and euphorbias have become adapted to withstand long seasons of heat and drought. For most of the year the vegetation appears to be almost dead, but soon after the first rains of the summer monsoon it becomes a blaze of colour.

The savannahs of East Africa comprise the natural habitat for some of the largest animals in the world. Carnivorous species such as lions and leopards prey upon the herbivorous species such as giraffes, zebras and antelopes, which rely upon their speed for protection. Both hunted and hunter have developed visually pro-tective coats, the markings of zebras and giraffes forming camouflage for the contrasts of light and shade on the open savannah, whilst the tawny coat of the lion is almost an exact match for the dry grass. In contrast the savannahs of South America and Australia are relatively deficient in wildlife.

The earliest inhabitants of the African savannah were probably Bushmen, primitive hunters, fishermen and collectors, who were attracted to the area by its varied

The power of elephants is harnessed to move precious hardwoods in Indo-Malaysia – where logging technology has remained unchanged for hundreds of years. The heavy summer rain encour-rages the growth of thick, luxurious and commercially valuable forests of teak and sal in this region.

and abundant fauna. Their use of fire in hunting probably pushed back the edge of the forest and resulted in the present parkland landscape of grass and scattered trees. Later, the Bushmen were forced to move southwards by Negroid tribes and a traditional relationship developed in the savannah lands of West Africa between the sub-sistence farming of the Hausa and the pastoral nomadism of the Fulani Bushmen. In the Middle Ages the mud-walled city of Kano became the southernmost terminus of caravan trading routes across the Sahara. New farming techniques and improved medical services, first introduced during the colonial period, have led to a great upturn in the population growth rate. Unfortunately the consequent demand for more food is putting pressure on the old ways of life; pasture lands used for centuries are being overgrazed by larger herds, leading to desertification and increasing vulnerability to the adverse effects of prolonged droughts. In equivalent areas in the New World, stock-raising on a commercial basis has been made possible

Hill rice is grown on flattened terraces in drier areas. Throughout southern Asia, the summer monsoon rains are vital for growing rice – sustenance for the ever-increasing population. Unfortunately, each year's summer monsoon is difficult to predict, drought and famine occurring in some years and floods and disease in others.

Swamp rice grows in well-watered, flat paddy fields, and to increase the yield it is intensively transplanted by Malaysian women.

where improved pastures have long been established.

Temperate monsoons are extensions of classic monsoon climates and occur on the eastern margins of landmasses in central China, Japan, the southeastern United States and eastern Australia. Unlike the classic version, rain falls all year round, and totals between 100 and 200 centimetres (40 and 80 inches), but a distinct summer maximum still occurs. The weather in the regions is dominated by tropical maritime air masses, hot and humid summers with occasional tropical cyclones and mild winters. In North America and Asia occasional incursions of polar continental air can bring unseasonably cold conditions. The natural vegetation is comprised of a rich, luxuriant growth of deciduous and coniferous trees, which at its densest resembles tropical rain forest. Giant eucalypts, "gum trees", that grow to a height of 120 metres (400 feet) occur in eastern Australia. A similar vegetation used to grow in the southeastern United States, but has now been cleared for cultivation.

Steppelands

Steppe climates of the Northern Hemisphere have warm, short summers and long, severe winters. Southern Hemisphere steppes are generally warmer and more equable, with light rainfall. Tropical steppes, found on the fringes of hot deserts, are semi-arid.

The steppes of Eurasia and the prairies of North America occur in the heartlands of the two great landmasses of the Northern Hemisphere. As they are far away from the moderating influences of the oceans they experience large diurnal and extremely large annual ranges of temperature and precipitation. During the warm, short summers, monthly mean temperatures vary between 17°C (63°F) and 20°C (68°F). The winter, on the other hand, is long and severe, with monthly mean temperatures well below freezing; blizzards occasionally occur, especially on the prairies of North America.

In contrast, the grasslands of the Southern Hemisphere – the pampas of Argentina, the veld of South Africa and downs of southeastern Australia – have a generally warmer and more equable climate than their equivalents in the Northern Hemisphere because they are nearer the equator and are affected by the moderating influence of the sea. The annual rainfall of all the temperate grasslands is light; the prairies are shielded from the rain-bearing westerly winds by the Rocky Mountains and the pampas by the Andes, while the steppes are sheltered by their great distance from the sea.

The light rainfall, together with its annual distribution, produces the characteristic cover of tufted grass. Tree growth is inhibited by the lack of moisture; winter snow cover in the Northern Hemisphere is a drawback for trees, but it does provide the grass with a protective cover against severe frosts.

The world's temperate grasslands are remarkably alike in their appearance – vast gently rolling plains stretching without break from one horizon to another. There is, however, a good deal of seasonal variation, from the fresh bluish-greens of spring to the yellowish-browns of late summer and autumn and, in the northern grasslands, the white blanketing of snow in winter.

Only small areas of natural grasslands of the temperate latitudes with herds of herbivorous animals, wild horse, bison and buffalo, exist today. The occupance by Man has also changed. During successive stages of settlement Man has followed three main ways of life: initially as a hunter, for example the Indians of the North American prairies. Later, Man domesticated animals and became a pastoral farmer, rearing sheep and cattle in the same way as the nomadic tribesmen of the Eurasian steppes. Next he began to till the soil and cultivate crops, first on comparatively small plots of land, using handtools, oxen and horse-drawn ploughs, and then on large-scale wheat-growing farms, using the most advanced agricultural machinery and technology.

This transformation of steppelands into the granaries of the world has been made possible by favourable climatic and physical characteristics; light rainfall in the form of showers in the growing season during spring and early summer; dry, sunny conditions in late summer, during the ripening and harvesting season; fertile soils – the famous "black-earths", or chernozems, that are rich in humus and plant foods – and a wide expanse of flat, rolling, open plains.

Tropical steppes occur in low latitudes on the fringes of hot deserts. They are usually affected by rain-bearing winds and associated disturbances for a short part of the year, resulting in semi-arid rather than completely desert climates. Here the annual rainfall varies from about 30 to 75 centimetres (12 to 30 inches) but is extremely unreliable from year to year, especially in the tropical steppes on the equatorward side of hot deserts. The natural vegetation is comprised of thorn bushes, scrub and succulent plants.

Steppelands have been drastically affected by recent changes in climate. The increase in mid-latitude westerly winds during the first half of the twentieth century led to contrasting rainfall patterns in the temperate grasslands of the Northern Hemisphere; while greater amounts of moisture were being carried into the interior of Eurasia, the "rain shadow" of the Rocky Mountains was increasing the dryness over the prairies of North America, culminating in the disastrous "Dust Bowl" drought of the 1930s,

Wildebeest roam the open grassy plains of east Africa. Unfortunately their numbers are decreasing due to the pressures of hunting and agriculture.

which was aggravated by the ploughing up of the topsoil cover of native grasses by European settlers.

The increased rainfall over central Asia in the first half of the twentieth century probably encouraged the USSR to extend their grainlands farther east. But since about 1950 the moisture-bearing westerlies have become less frequent, resulting in decreased and more variable rainfall over central Asia. Thus despite improved agricultural technology there have been some serious shortfalls of cereal production due to droughts during the 1960s and 1970s. These have forced the Russians to make large purchases of grain from North America.

There were changes in the rainfall patterns of the tropical steppes between the early 1950s and the late 1960s. The decline in the westerlies appears to be symptomatic of global changes in atmospheric circulation which have affected the seasonal migration of the Intertropical Convergence Zone (ITCZ) and resulted in more frequent failures of the summer monsoon rains over West Africa. These have been particularly severe in the Sahel region, the tropical steppelands bordering the Sahara on the south, where a long series of droughts beginning in the late 1960s caused the deaths of hundreds of thousands of poverty-stricken people and even greater numbers of cattle and wild animals.

The Australian mallee scrublands (*above*) are composed of dwarfish eucalyptus and acacia trees. A host of birds and marsupial mammals, whose future depends on the survival of this habitat, are partial to browsing among the trees.

The Khalka pastoral nomads (*below*) of the Eurasian steppes developed the art of horse-riding in response to the distances they had to travel across the grasslands to keep up with the annual migration of bison.

The tropics

Tropical climates lie in a band between 10°N and 10°S of the equator. Average temperatures are 26°C (79°F) with an annual range of less than 3°C (5°F). Heavy rainfall occurs evenly throughout the year with annual totals of at least 150 centimetres (60 inches).

Amazonian Indians (*above*) pile up their crops of yams, manioc and bananas – the staple food. Tapioca is prepared by extracting prussic acid from manioc roots and drying them in the sun.

Positioned in the zone of maximum insolation the tropical daily pattern of weather is reliable and regular; as the Sun ascends during the morning there is a rapid rise in temperature and early morning mists clear quickly. Cumulus clouds form later and develop into cumulo-nimbus during the mid-afternoon, leading to torrential showers, often with thunderstorms, in the late afternoon. The downpours are commonly followed by fine evenings. It has often been said that night-time is the winter of the tropics. The humidity, which is continually high, is alleviated in coastal areas by sea breezes, which occur with almost clock-like regularity, sometimes extending 160 kilometres (100 miles) inland.

One of the world's most notable climatic anomalies occurs westwards from the coasts of Ecuador and Peru to between longitudes 160°E and 170°E. In this area rainfall totals are lower than elsewhere in the tropics – less than 25 centimetres (10 inches) in the east to 76 centimetres (30 inches) in the west. These unusual conditions are believed to be brought about by the Intertropical Convergence Zone (ITCZ) splitting into two branches, which consistently remain north and south of the equator.

Heat and heavy rainfall create the typical vegetation of the region, tropical rain forest, which in its most extreme form is represented by the *selvas* of the Amazon Basin in South America. Other main forest areas occur in the

Congo Basin of Africa and in parts of Indonesia. There is a wide variety of forest types, but the popular image of a dense, impenetrable jungle is a myth; away from the tracks and riverbanks tropical forests are dark and shady with little undergrowth.

The vegetation is well adapted to the wet conditions. To increase transpiration rates, plants typically have numerous stomata and long, drooping points for excess water to drip from. Competition for light causes trees to grow to great heights, some giant species growing to 60 metres (almost 200 feet) high and carrying a dense canopy of leaves. The forests have a great variety of trees; mahogany, rosewood, rubber and palm are common, with often as many as 100 different species of trees growing within one hectare (2·5 acres). Epiphytic and parasitic plants grow prolifically on trunks and branches. There is continuous growth and the plants have their own seasons of flowering, fruiting and leaf shedding. Where tropical forests meet the coasts, especially along the mouths of the Congo and Amazon rivers, there exists a strange world halfway between land and water where salt-tolerant trees, known as mangrove, advance out to sea.

Food for wildlife is plentiful, but only those animals which have become adapted to the specialized conditions survive. Insect life is especially varied and human settlement in some areas may have been more restricted by the presence of certain insects, such as malaria-carrying mosquitoes, than by the difficult climate.

Tropical rain forests are sparsely populated, the original inhabitants that managed to live in harmony with the forest, such as the Indians of the Amazon Basin, the Pygmies of the Congo Basin and Papuans of New Guinea having always been scattered in small isolated groups. Some tribes survive solely by hunting and gathering and others practise shifting cultivation, making small clearings to grow manioc; after a few seasons the soils become so exhausted that they have to move on.

Increasing contacts with the encroaching modern world have resulted in the numbers of forest dwellers being reduced by epidemics of imported diseases against which they have no immunity and a decline in their primitive but self-sufficient ways of life, which have survived for countless generations in the past. The inevitable acculturation and integration now taking place probably means that little will remain of these early human patterns of existence in a decade or so.

People who are not acclimatized to the environment find the continual damp heat enervating and unhealthy, and tropical diseases debilitating. Domestic animals are difficult to keep because the rank and coarse grass that can be grown is not nutritious and insects, such as the tsetse fly, plague animals almost as much as Man.

The effects of deforestation on climate are particularly striking in the Amazon Basin, where vast areas are being cleared for commercial forest products, agricultural land and human settlements, especially along the rivers and new highways. The discovery of oil and an expanding tourist industry are also boosting developments. It has recently been estimated that perhaps as much as a fifth to a quarter of the Amazon rain forest has already been cut down and the rate of deforestation is accelerating.

Programmes to deforest and develop tropical rain forests should be carefully weighed against destroying, perhaps irreversibly, an ecosystem in which, due to a relative absence of major changes of climate in the past, a great diversity of species has evolved uninterruptedly over millions of years.

Tropical rain forests play an important role in the carbon cycle and any large-scale deforestation schemes can turn an important carbon dioxide sink – in the form of carbon stored in the tree-trunks – into an equally large source, derived from burning the wood to produce carbon dioxide in the atmosphere. This could result in a stronger "greenhouse effect" and significant changes in temperature and rainfall patterns in other parts of the world. Tropical rain forests also play a vital role in another natural cycle – that of water. Cutting down the trees reduces the capacity of the soil to absorb rainfall and the local recycling of water vapour into the atmosphere by transpiration is reduced. Another climatic effect is that when forest cover is cleared and replaced by lighter-coloured crop land or pastures, the albedo, or reflectivity, of the surface is increased, leading to less insolation being absorbed and thus to changes in the global terrestrial heat budget.

Isolated by the forest and perfectly self-contained are the malocos or dome-shaped dwellings of an Indian village in the Xingu region of the Amazon Basin (*left*). Space for the village is created by cutting and burning a patch of rain forest.

A tribesman in the rain forest of Borneo carrying bamboo for mending his boat. The nomadic tribes that live in this region rely on wild sago palms for their staple starch food and thatching material for their temporary shelters.

Mediterranean

Mediterranean climates are found on the fringes of the Mediterranean Sea, and also in parts of California, Chile, South Africa and south-western Australia. They have hot dry summers, mild wet winters and ample sunshine all year round.

Lying between the subtropical anticyclonic belt and the travelling storms of the middle latitude westerlies, the climates of Mediterranean regions are determined by the seasonal shift of these atmospheric zones giving subtropical aridity in summer and temperate storminess in winter. The extended inland penetration of Mediterranean climates is found only in Europe; both in North and South America, chains of mountains running north to south terminate this type of climate a short distance from the coast. In South Africa and Australia the poleward tapering extensions of these continents are barely far enough south to reach latitudes that would produce Mediterranean climates.

Typical monthly mean temperatures are usually between 21°C (70°F) and 27°C (80°F) in summer and between 4°C (39°F) and 13°C (55°F) in winter. The light to moderate annual rainfall varies between 38 and 76 centimetres (15 and 30 inches) and occurs mostly in the winter. There is a high incidence of clear, sunny weather; even in winter, days without any sunshine are quite rare, since the rain usually falls in short-lived spells.

The occasional frosts that do occur in winter are usually the result of nocturnal radiational cooling following the advection of cold polar air. Sensitive crops, such as citrus, are commonly planted on slopes to avoid being affected by the cold air which collects on the valley floors. Burning oil cans or "smudge pots" were formerly used in citrus groves to provide extra protection against frosts, the smoke serving as a blanket to reduce radiational heat losses. However, because of air pollution these oil burners have generally been replaced by smokeless heaters that are fuelled by natural gas.

A number of distinctive winds – the Scirocco, Mistral, Bora, Etesian and Santa Ana – are associated with Mediterranean climates. The Scirocco is a hot, dry and sometimes dust-laden wind which originates in the Sahara Desert and blows northwards over the Mediterranean. As it does so, it picks up a great deal of moisture and brings very warm, humid and enervating conditions to Spain, Sicily and Italy, withering vegetation and damaging crops in its path, especially if it blows while the olive trees and vines are in blossom.

The Pyrenees, Alps and Balkan ranges form a mountain barrier to the general penetration of polar air into the Mediterranean Basin. However, there are gaps through which the cold air is channelled, sometimes with great force, resulting in local winds such as the Mistral of the Rhône Valley and the Bora of the Adriatic. The Mistral can blow continuously for several days, drying out the soil and causing serious damage to crops. It has been the scourge of farmers for centuries and in 1769–70 it was

The ancient craft of wine-making was first practised in the Mediterranean region, where gently sloping vineyards are traditionally terraced into impressive steps held in place by walls of stones to prevent soil erosion (*above*).

The techniques and implements that have been used here since the first civilizations farmed the area have remained unchanged in many parts. A piece of timber here serves as a simple but effective harrow (*below*).

The bark of the cork oak tree is unique – it can be peeled off without damaging the tree. Cork has been harvested from the forests that surround the Mediterranean for more than 2000 years; today world demand for its special properties and versatility is continually increasing.

reported to have been the dominant wind for 14 months. Hedges of cypress trees have been planted to act as windbreaks for protecting the fields and orchards.

The constant northeasterly or northerly Etesian winds that blow over the eastern Mediterranean in summer are relatively dry. However, they sometimes bring overcast skies, and in places such as Athens they may raise suffocating clouds of dust. In the coastal plains of Southern California the hot, dry Santa Ana wind, which blows from the high inland desert plateaux via the narrow mountain passes around Los Angeles, is named after a particular canyon where it is commonly experienced. Its dry, dusty heat damages vegetation and crops, increases the risk of brush fires and causes much discomfort.

Due to clearance by fire, cultivation and browsing goats, almost all of the original open evergreen woodlands and intervening herbage have disappeared from Mediterranean regions. In areas of lower rainfall or poorer soils a scrubland type of vegetation now predominates; this is mostly comprised of small evergreen trees and shrubs, collectively known as maquis in Europe, chaparral in the western United States and mallee in southern Australia. In the wetter parts typically Mediterranean fruits are cultivated, such as the native olive, fig and vine, and the more recently introduced orange, lemon and grapefruit; deciduous fruits such as peach, apricot and plum often require some irrigation and strains of winter wheat and barley have also beome well adapted to the climate. Cultivated in the Mediterranean Basin for some 3000 years, the olive tree is often regarded as the natural

vegetative index for the distribution of Mediterranean climates and has become a familiar part of the landscape. Olive trees are typical of evergreen Mediterranean plants that have developed special characteristics to withstand the summer drought. They have lance-shaped leathery leaves covered with fine hairs and a thick bark which protects them from excessive heat. The vine and some other Mediterranean plants have unusually long roots, and some trees such as the orange have leaves coated with wax to prevent desiccation.

Air pollution is causing increasing concern in many urban and industrial areas of the Mediterranean climatic regions. The effect is particularly severe during the summer, when the dispersal of pollutants emitted from industrial and domestic sources is inhibited by the presence of a strong and persistent temperature inversion associated with the subsiding air masses of the subtropical anticyclonic belt. In California, the brownish-coloured photochemical smog of Los Angeles is seriously affecting nearby citrus groves and woodlands, as well as causing ocular irritation and respiratory distress to the inhabitants. In Europe, air pollution is damaging many famous monuments and buildings in historic cities.

As with the temperate zone, some of the world's greatest cities, such as Los Angeles and Santiago, have developed in these regions. The warm and sunny climate has also led to the establishment of holiday resorts, originally centred on the Riviera coast; this development has now expanded, and the tourist industry is important in the economy of many Mediterranean countries.

Deserts

Deserts lie where annual rainfall is less than 25 centimetres (10 inches). "Hot" deserts such as the Kalahari and Sahara have no cold season, but "cold" deserts such as the Gobi and Great Basin have at least one month where the mean temperature is below 6°C (43°F).

Besides being the hottest regions on Earth, hot deserts also experience the most extreme ranges of temperature. A common feature expressed in the journals of early desert explorers is the experience of freezing cold nights followed by scorching hot afternoons. The high temperatures and the high daily range result from the lack of humidity and lack of cloud; by day, temperatures build up because of uninterrupted insolation and by night, without a protective blanket of cloud, surface heat can freely radiate away.

In environmental terms there is one factor above all others that governs life in the desert – water. Water is deficient in the desert simply because the amount of evaporation greatly exceeds the annual precipitation. In the case of birds, for instance, water loss by evaporation in deserts is the most serious factor limiting their distribution in arid regions. Also, moisture is the most important factor restricting plant growth in desert soils. In addition to water shortage, the prevalence of hot, drying winds increases the problems of animals and plants in combating desiccation and obtaining enough moisture.

Nowadays Man can live in the desert in relative comfort. Little more than commonsense precautions are required to prevent heat stroke, desiccation or salt imbalance, and modern technological aids take care of everything else. Not long ago almost all native desert people lived in a rather specialized and primitive way, and a good many still do so. A large proportion of them survived only with difficulty; the scarcity of water and the sparseness of desert vegetation obliged them to adopt a nomadic way of life, moving from place to place in search of food and water for themselves and their animals. This nomadic life-style was discovered, for example, among the Aborigines of the Great Australian Desert, in the Bushmen of the Kalahari and among the Bedouin and Tuareg and other tribes of the Middle East and North Africa, who, until recent attempts to settle them, roamed back and forth without reference to political boundaries. There are still many areas where the nomadic way of life continues, but the advent of mechanized travel has for the most part irrevocably changed this traditional pattern.

In contrast some desert people of the Sahara and the Sahel have a sedentary way of life, having learned to exploit meagre water and soil resources by either developing a linear pattern of agriculture along the wadis or one centred around oases. Although these settled populations have been able to solve the problem of existing in the hostile conditions of the desert, their solutions have limited application. Just how precarious life can still be in the desert was demonstrated by the great Sahel drought

The traditional lifestyle of the Tuareg, a tribe of 300,000 nomadic herdsmen that live in the Sahara and whose economy is based on camels, is threatened by recent political development and droughts. From puberty, Tuareg men are veiled, using a cloth some 5 metres (16 feet) long for protection from the sun and wind-blown sand (*above*). The style of dress, although appearing restrictive, has become ritualized, so that even in camp the veil is rarely removed.

of the early 1970s, in the regions bordering the southern fringes of the Sahara Desert, which caused the deaths of hundreds of thousands of humans and livestock.

From evidence accumulated in recent years we know that most of the world's desert regions, including the Sahara, are not simply the result of climatic change, but are largely man-made and are expanding rapidly. To a great extent the nomadic way of life that many peoples are obliged to adopt is precisely what leads to the spread of desert conditions. The major factors contributing to desertification are the felling of trees and shrubs for fuel, and overgrazing by domestic stock, especially by goats, which will eat virtually anything that grows.

Many animals have adopted their own strategies to survive desert conditions. Some increase their water intake by eating plant tissue with a high water content; others produce metabolic water from the respiration of food and many reduce their water loss by excreting concentrated urine and nearly dry faeces. Water loss is also reduced by adopting an inactive life-style, using shade effectively and, in the case of arthropods, by taking up water directly from the air. Small desert mammals are not able to regulate their body temperature by sweating, and avoid extremes of desert conditions by remaining in their burrows during the heat of day and foraging for food at night. Within a burrow the moisture content of the air may be several times higher than that of the atmosphere outside. Also, because microclimatic conditions in caves and rock fissures are relatively uniform, they have become the natural habitat for a large number of desert animals.

Some animals are able to live in areas of desert in which no plants grow, and form part of a food chain based on dried vegetation and seeds: the jerboas of North Africa, for example, survive by sleeping with their tails held over their nose to trap exhaled moisture, which is breathed in again. The camel and the kangaroo rat reduce their body temperature as it approaches a lethal level by foaming at the mouth. The foam wets the skin and, as the moisture evaporates, the temperature is reduced. The camel also stores water in special stomach compartments and derives some water from oxidation of fats accumulated in its hump. Yet another animal adaptation is dormancy – some desert snails have been known to remain in this state for five years or more.

Desert plants are sparse not only because of the lack of water but also because of the saline nature of desert soils; due to the high rate of evaporation salts are precipitated in the upper layers of the soil and they accumulate because there is insufficient rainfall to wash them away. As annuals have a remarkably short life cycle they comprise some 60 per cent of desert floras. Their seeds survive during the long dry spells and are ready to germinate when the rains come. The plant then quickly flourishes, scatters its seeds and withers away. Other desert plants have long root systems, spiky leaves that may be coated with wax or efficient water storage organs that help them to survive the aridity of the desert.

Sagaro cacti (*above*) are succulent plants that manage to survive successfully in rigorous desert conditions because they store water in their stems.

The oasis at the Gorges du Todra in Morocco is formed by a high water table providing a fresh water supply all year round. Date palms flourish in the locality, and create a fertile island amidst the surrounding barren desert.

Microclimates

Microclimatology is the detailed, small-scale study of atmospheric conditions in the shallow layer of air that lies immediately adjacent to the Earth's surface. Without actually naming the subject, the German botanist Gregor Kraus, who lived between 1841 and 1915, can be regarded as the founder of microclimatology. The subject was developed and quantified into a branch of climatology through the research of the German meteorologist Rudolf Geiger, whose treatise *Das Klima der bodennahen Luftschicht (The climate near the ground)*, first published in 1927, remains the classic text for providing an initial survey of microclimatology and the effects of microclimate on plants, animals and Man.

The layer of air adjacent to the ground was long neglected, but since it was realized that the interface between the Earth's surface and the atmosphere is the seat of some very important exchanges of energy and moisture, investigations of the atmospheric processes in this layer are now being actively pursued by both meteorologists and microclimatologists. Special instrumentation developed to obtain micrometeorological data reveals that atmospheric conditions often vary more between a person's head and feet than they do horizontally over hundreds of kilometres.

The diurnal range of temperature near the ground is very large. For example, if a meteorological station observes a daily range of 10°C (18°F) at a height of 2 metres (6 feet) the value at ground level could be three or four times as great. Differential weathering according to height in rocks and buildings gives visible evidence of this effect. Rapid fluctuations in humidity are also a characteristic feature of the surface layer of air below 2 metres (6 feet) because moisture is derived from near the Earth's surface through evaporation of precipitation, sublimation of ice and snow and transpiration by plants, and so water vapour generally decreases with height.

Forests have a notable moderating influence on climate. The leafy crowns of a high, dense forest form an almost unbroken surface, which to a large extent takes over the function of the ground. During the daytime most of the solar radiation is absorbed at crown-level, resulting in the highest temperatures of the forest occurring at the top of the canopy. Owing to the shading effect of the trees, temperatures decrease downwards and forest floors are generally cooler than the surrounding open country; on a warm summer's day the temperature difference at midday can be 5°C (9°F) or more. At night forests are warmer than the surrounding country.

Humidities are generally higher inside forests, where the air flow is greatly reduced. Wind speeds are reduced by the canopy and become very light near the ground. The effect on rainfall is less definite, since it is very difficult to measure precipitation in forests. However, when forests are cleared, the rainfall can no longer be contained so effectively within the region and the increased run-off results in flash-floods, which cause soil erosion and damage the landscape.

An increasing percentage of the world's population lives in large cities and the widespread replacement of natural and agricultural landscapes by urban environments has produced some notable changes of weather and climate over the past century.

The physical and chemical properties of the surface layer of air over cities have been altered to produce a distinctive type of microclimate. Meteorological elements such as temperature, visibility and wind differ markedly in cities compared with rural districts.

Heat imprints from the two aircraft that have already flown off (in the top row), detected by infra-red cameras, illustrate heat energy produced at ground level.

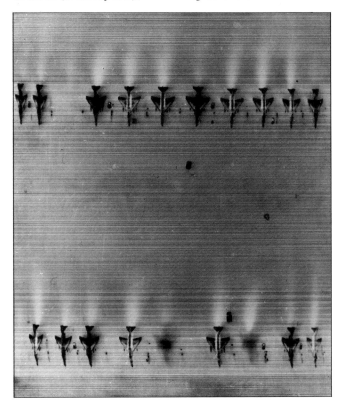

The most striking departure from natural conditions within urban areas is the high concentration of pollutants. These not only influence atmospheric conditions but also adversely affect human health, plants and animals. Besides these detrimental effects, the increasing concentration of carbon dioxide over cities influences global climate by producing a stronger "greenhouse effect": the pall of pollution affects the radiation balance by screening insolation during the day and reradiating terrestrial radiation at night. Also, in winter the artificial heat produced by burning fuels sometimes exceeds that received from the Sun, creating an imbalance in radiation.

Apart from pollution, more attention has been given to the study of urban temperature than any other meteorological element. Most cities are enclosed by a mass of warm air which extends up to a height of about 120 metres (400 feet), and is known as a "heat island". Urban-rural temperature differences of up to 6°C (11°F) are common, with maximum differences (11°C/20°F)

occurring at night and it is only when wind speeds increase to above 24 kilometres per hour (15 mph) that the ventilation becomes strong enough to dissipate this warming effect. Heat islands are produced by a combination of factors such as combustion processes, higher heat capacity of buildings and of airborne pollutants.

Urban visibilities are often less than those of rural areas because of the increased concentrations of suspended pollution particles, which increase atmospheric turbidity by their own screening effect and by acting as condensation nuclei for fogs. Because of increased surface friction, wind speeds in large cities are about 25 per cent less than in rural areas, the reduction being most noticeable when the winds are strong. However, the uneven surface of built-up areas increases turbulence and the eddies and funnelling effects produced by tall buildings can be troublesome. Urban-rural differences of precipitation are more difficult to determine, but it appears that urbanization has increased rainfall over many large cities.

A self-sustaining garden in a bottle contains a microcosm of the atmospheric processes that occur near the Earth's surface.

The Stevenson Screen, the standard housing for thermometers, must, for accurate temperature readings, stand at a height of 1·2 metres (4 feet) above the ground, and be well away from buildings or similar obstructions. The sides of the screen are louvred to provide an even flow of air past the thermometers.

145

THE CHANGING CLIMATE

"There is a toy, which I have heard, and I would not have it given over, but waited upon a little. They say it is observed in the Low Countries (I know not in what part), that every five and thirty years the same kind and suit of years and weathers comes about again; as great frosts, great wet, great droughts, warm winters, summers with little heat, and the like, and they call it the prime; it is a thing I do the rather mention, because, computing backwards, I have found some concurrence."

Francis Bacon – *Essay LVIII*, 1625

The Earth's climate has not always been the same; significant changes have taken place even during recorded history, although they are slight in comparison with those that have occurred over the millions of years of the Earth's history. The problem for scientists has been to establish how these changes take place. Some can be accounted for by alteration in geography due to continental drift, but these great movements do not account for variations over the comparatively short time of a few hundreds or thousands of years. Is it change on Earth or within the Sun? The problem is that there are so many aspects to look at – sunspot cycles, volcanic eruptions, alterations in the Earth's magnetic field or angle of orbit – all of which are possible candidates. The combination of factors that may influence our delicately balanced climate and how scientists foresee our future is a fascinating story.

Smoke and dust particles, seen here at sunrise, may well have an effect on natural climatic changes.

Ice ages occur not because the Earth as a whole is plunged into a deep freeze with ice extending down to the equator, but because during the Earth's evolution, the slow process of continental drift carries continents to high latitudes, where snow can fall and build up into great ice-sheets.

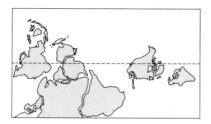

The supercontinent, "Pangaea I", lay across the Southern Hemisphere in the Cambrian, 510 million years ago.

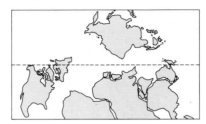

Life moved from the ocean and began to flourish on land during the Devonian, 380 million years ago.

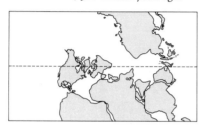

A single land mass, Gondwanaland, existed in the Southern Hemisphere in the Carboniferous, 340 million years ago.

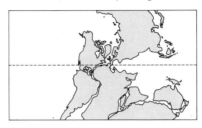

An ice age occurred in the southern continents, grouped around the pole, in the Permian, 250 million years ago.

A rift appeared in "Pangaea II" as it began to crack during the Triassic, 220 million years ago.

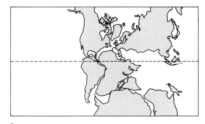

The continents began to drift towards the poles again during the Jurassic, 170 million years ago.

A warm and equable climate prevailed during the Cretaceous, 100 million years ago.

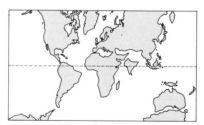

By Tertiary times, 50 million years ago, conditions were similar to those of today and suitable for ice-caps to form.

The extent of ice 18,000 years ago, during the fiercest stage of the last Ice Age. The ice encompassed northern Europe, Canada and the USSR – regions that are among the most heavily populated today. The natural state of the world is still under the influence of ice, although at present we are experiencing a brief and temporary respite from its grip – an interglacial.

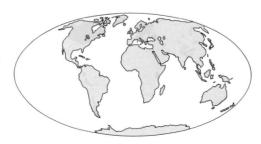

What we think of as the normal situation on Planet Earth – the conditions that have persisted for the past five million years or more, during which mankind has emerged as an intelligent species – is in fact highly unusual. The face of our planet is constantly changing as the continents drift about the surface of the globe, and this geography has been crucial in producing the pattern of climate experienced on Earth – ice ages separated by slightly warmer "interglacials". We live in an interglacial now; these periods have contributed directly to human evolution over the past few million years.

We think it is "normal" to have ice-caps at the poles. Yet during the history of our planet (4500 million years) the presence of just one ice-cap has been a rare and brief occurrence. The reason is simple. Most of our planet is covered by water, and warm water is very efficient at carrying heat from the tropics to the poles. Normally, warm tropical water circulates to the poles and keeps them ice free. But occasionally a continent, such as Antarctica today, blocks this warm water route. In the course of its slow drift a continent may spend a few million years sitting over one of the poles, blocking out the warm tropical water and allowing an ice-cap to grow.

Even more rarely, a group of continents may drift into a peculiar position where they surround one of the poles, blocking off the flow of warm water and leaving a land-locked polar sea to freeze. This has happened in the Arctic, where the warm waters of the Gulf Stream are sealed off from the Arctic Basin by Greenland and Iceland. So today – uniquely in the history of our planet – we have two polar ice-caps. This has never happened before, and may never happen again; geography suitable for even one polar ice-cap happens only for five or ten million years out of every 300 million years or so, that is less than 10 per cent of the time. Frozen polar caps at both ends of the Earth is indeed a rare and bizarre combination. Yet this combination is the dominant factor in determining our present patterns of weather and climate – warm tropical regions, cold poles, a flow of air from one to the other and back again, plus, in the Northern Hemisphere at least, a lot of land around the frozen polar region, land where snow can fall and lay when conditions are just right.

As a result, for the past few million years, the Earth has been uniquely susceptible to very small changes in the balance of radiation arriving at the surface from the Sun. We would be living a full ice age, with ice-sheets and glaciers stretching down to Chicago, London or Paris but for the fact that all the variable factors which affect the climate have conspired to pull the Earth towards warmth, and this interglacial, the comparatively mild spell between ice ages that has persisted for the past 10,000 years or so, has seen the rise of human civilization. For millions of years, the pattern of climatic change has been one of long ice ages, lasting in round terms for 100,000 years, divided by short interglacials, some 10,000 years long. Until the geography changes, the pattern will persist. 50 million years from now, the North Atlantic will have widened so much (at present North America and Europe are separating at a rate of 2 centimetres a year) that warm water will flow into the Arctic and keep it warm, destroying the pattern. But for us, the pattern can be regarded as permanent – carrying with it the implication that the present inter-glacial, already 10,000 years old, must be due to end. The "next" ice age is perhaps only 1000 years away.

Causes of climatic change

Climatic patterns can be explained in terms of changes in the way the Earth tilts and wobbles as it moves around the Sun, changing the distribution of heat reaching different latitudes in different seasons. But other factors also affect the climate, and with special force at a time when the geography has made our world so prone to climatic fluctuations.

Firstly, the forces which change the geo-graphy of the globe also produce earthquakes and volcanic eruptions. Volcanoes can belch dust high into the atmosphere, where it acts as a sunshield, blocking out the Sun's heat and sending the Earth shivering into a little ice age. For most of the twentieth century, the Earth's volcanoes have been unusually quiet. But between 1960 and the early 1980s many rumbled into life, including Mt Agung in Bali and Mt St Helens in Washington State, in the USA. Could this be the harbinger of a cycle of volcanic activity cooling the whole globe in the decades ahead?

Secondly, to the undisguised astonishment of many astronomers, proof came during the first half of 1980 that the Sun itself varies. Between 1976 and 1979, the Sun's output increased by 0.4 per cent, during the phase of increased sunspot activity we are now living through. Climatologists had already noticed that during the seventeenth century a period of bitter cold, when the River Thames, in England, froze solid during many winters, coincided with a complete absence

Cliffs of Old Red Sandstone at Stockholm Island, off the coast of Sweden, show that this area was situated within the tropics during Carboniferous times, 340 million years ago, and was once a hot, sandy, windblown desert with little or no rainfall, supporting no form of life. Through the process of continental drift, this land has moved northwards to its present position of 60°N.

FOSSIL TREES
Evidence of lush tropical forests that once covered the present-day temperate lands of the Northern Hemisphere is found either in the form of fossil tree trunks, whose wood has been replaced by another mineral, or as coal. Preserved relics of palm and banana trees have been found way beyond their present limits of growth, as far afield as Greenland, within the Arctic Circle. Forests that were gradually buried by sediments and then compacted form most of the world's coal resources today.

The sole survivors of a once wetter climate in Australia's great deserts are the *Livistonia mariae* trees (below), in the arid sandstone gorges of Central Palm Valley.

149

of the dark spots which often mark the surface of the Sun. They suggested that the Sun might be 1 per cent cooler when it had no spots, only to be laughed at by astronomers. Now rockets and satellites have measured exactly the amount of solar variation needed to fit the climatologists' claims, and astronomers have been forced to take their theory seriously. How can these newly discovered fluctuations be used to forecast climatic changes in our lifetimes?

How will Man himself affect the climate? Will dust from pollution act like a "human volcano" and hasten the next little ice age? Or will the carbon dioxide released by burning fossil fuel and by destroying the tropical

Cave paintings found in the Sahara Desert vividly portray that towards the end of the last Ice Age wetter and more fertile conditions prevailed, which allowed the Neolithic – New Stone Age – people time to develop art and culture.

forests act like a blanket around the Earth, warming it like a greenhouse? We have to live on a planet balanced on a climatic knife edge; in the immediate future it may be as important for our global society to understand climatic changes as to know how to find new sources of energy and food. Fortunately, we seem to have discovered the mechanisms which drive climatic change.

On a timescale that is relevant to Man, climatic changes caused by the movements of the continents around the globe can be ignored. We have to live with the present-day geography of our planet, and the fact that this is an unusual geography on the long timescale of the Earth's history is merely an abstract, although interesting, fact. The whole history of the human race as a separate species is contained within the past few million years of ice age, or approaching ice age, conditions on Earth. This is no coincidence; palaeoanthropologists now agree that the selection pressures resulting from the harsher and colder conditions on the surface of the Earth were among the key factors that contributed to the unique human attributes

of adaptability and intelligence that were so valuable to our ancestors. In human terms, ice age conditions are normal.

The rigorous conditions that prevailed during the last Ice Age coincided with an important stage in human evolution and encouraged its development in several ways. *Homos erectus,* or upright man, our direct ancestor who lived half a million years ago, did not seem to have been deterred by the cold – in fact it probably instigated his most fundamental discovery, fire. As plant foods in the form of fruits, berries, nuts and leaves were becoming less abundant due to the cold, early hominids learned to use weapons for killing wild animals to supplement their diet. To do this they had to master the art of making axe heads, and it also inspired them to co-operate in a group and thus encouraged the rudiments of speech. As much ocean water was locked up as ice, many new areas of dry land were exposed, creating land bridges such as Beringia – linking Siberia with Alaska – over which the first people reached North America.

Whether we want to understand the changing climatic patterns of the recent past, or forecast how climate will vary in the immediate future, we have to work within the framework of a planet with ice at both poles. The longest timescale relevant to these discussions is the cyclic rhythm with which the ice first advances, bringing a full ice age that lasts for 100,000 years and then retreats, bringing a temporary lull, an interglacial, that lasts for about 10,000 years.

This may still seem a timescale of only abstract interest. Who really cares what happened 100,000 years ago, or what may happen in 10,000 years' time? But one fact brings these cycles into sharp focus. The present interglacial began just over 10,000 years ago. If the cyclic pattern continues to hold, the next ice age could begin at any time. And even though by "any time" climatologists mean any time within the next 1000 years, it is still a chilling thought, which makes the whole business of climatic study take on a much more significant appearance.

Rhythms in Earth-Sun geometry
What causes this underlying rhythm of climatic variation? During the 1970s a combination of several pieces of evidence fell into place, confirming that the driving force behind this pattern is the way the Earth's orbit around the Sun changes. This slight eccentricity changes the pattern of heat received at different latitudes in different seasons. This hypothesis for the cause of ice

Glaciers, tongues of plastic, flowing ice, still exist in the world's mountain ranges and remind us of the advancing ice-sheets that once covered Canada and northern Europe. The terminal morraine beyond the snout of the glacier represents its extent some 50 years ago.

Ice acting like a giant chisel is responsible for creating many features of our landscape such as the familiar U-shaped valley that appears to be too large for the meagre river that runs through; it was originally gouged out by glaciers.

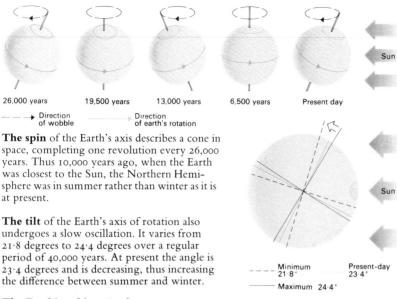

| 26,000 years | 19,500 years | 13,000 years | 6,500 years | Present day |

- - - → Direction of wobble   —— Direction of earth's rotation

The spin of the Earth's axis describes a cone in space, completing one revolution every 26,000 years. Thus 10,000 years ago, when the Earth was closest to the Sun, the Northern Hemisphere was in summer rather than winter as it is at present.

The tilt of the Earth's axis of rotation also undergoes a slow oscillation. It varies from 21·8 degrees to 24·4 degrees over a regular period of 40,000 years. At present the angle is 23·4 degrees and is decreasing, thus increasing the difference between summer and winter.

The Earth's orbit varies from an almost perfect circle to a marked ellipse. When in the ellipse phase the Earth is nearer to the Sun at one particular season. A complete orbital cycle from the near circular-shaped orbit to the elliptical shape and back again takes between 90,000 and 100,000 years.

--- Minimum 21·8°   Present-day 23·4°

—— Maximum 24·4°

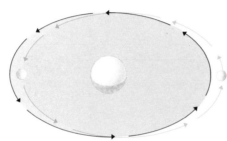

the orbit of the Earth around the Sun changes, "stretching" from a nearly circular shape to a more elliptical one, and back again. When the orbit is circular, the distribution of heat is even through the year; when the orbit is elliptical, the Earth is closer to the Sun, and therefore warmer, for parts of the year. Depending on other factors, this may either alleviate the cold of winter or enhance the warmth of summer.

The "other factors" involve the way the Earth is tilted on its axis relative to a line joining the Earth to the Sun. The pole that points towards the Sun gets more heat, while the pole that points away from the Sun gets less; this is why we have seasons. But the degree of this tilt varies, with the Earth nodding up and down with a rhythm some 40,000 years long. When the tilt is more pronounced, there are strong seasonal changes in the course of each year; when the Earth is more upright, there is much less difference between summer and winter.

Finally, the gravitational pull of the Sun and Moon on the bulging equatorial regions of our planet makes it wobble like a spinning top, with a period of 26,000 years.

The combined effect of all these rhythms produces the overall change in the way that heat is distributed in different regions of the globe at different times of year. The pattern is complicated, which is one reason why it has taken so long to confirm that the history of climate on Earth really does fit a pattern – one that shows two distinct features: very cold spells, or ice ages of about 100,000 years in duration, that are separated by less cold intervals, interglacials of about 10,000 years in length.

It is simple to see how the pattern works, although much harder to make the precise calculations necessary to test the theory properly. In the Northern Hemisphere, there is plenty of land surrounding the frozen polar sea, and snow that falls in the winter will settle on the cold land. If the summers are cool, the snow will persist until the next winter, and each year a new layer of snow will be added to what has become a growing ice-sheet. In fact, this is a rather parochial viewpoint based on our everyday experience of life during an interglacial. It is much more realistic to turn the argument on its head. Given the present-day geography of the Northern Hemisphere, the only way to stop an ice age developing is to have all the orbital factors working together to bring unusually warm summers that will melt the winter snow and so enable the present interglacial to persist.

ages was originated by a Yugoslav astronomer called Milankovitch in the 1930s; in fact, the basic idea is far older, and among others who supported it before Milankovitch's day was Alfred Wegener, better known today as one of the originators of the concept of continental drift. But there were good reasons why the "Milankovitch Model" remained unproven until very recently.

The theory itself is simple enough. Three separate cyclic changes in the Earth's movements through space combine to produce the overall changes in the pattern of solar radiation falling on Earth. There is no change in the total amount of heat received from the Sun over a whole year (unless the output of the Sun itself changes, and this is considered later). But the distribution of heat over the year is altered, bringing, for example, a pattern of hot summers with very cold winters, or a pattern of cool summers and relatively mild winters. It turns out that a key to the cause of ice ages is a pattern of cool summers and autumns in the Northern Hemisphere which do not allow the snow that has fallen the previous winter to melt before the following winter's snow comes along to fall on top of it.

Over a period of 90,000 to 100,000 years,

Because shiny white snowfields reflect away a lot of heat, this is very difficult to achieve and interglacials are rare. Once an interglacial is established, it can persist for a while because the darker snowfree ground absorbs more warmth from the Sun and helps to keep the snow at bay. But today we have reached a stage where, if the snow returned over a wide area of the Northern Hemisphere, the Sun's heat would be much too feeble to melt it again. Most climatologists are still reluctant to say that this means a new ice age could begin in the space of one winter. But ice ages seem to occur within a few years – starting from a "snowblitz" when winter snow fails to melt, rather than slowly developing over thousands of years with glaciers creeping down from the polar regions. So a persistent run of bad winters over a few decades could initiate the onset of the next ice age.

But what of the Southern Hemisphere? Surely the seasons are opposite there, so that cool northern summers correspond to severe southern winters, with correspondingly mild southern summers to melt the snow? The argument does not necessarily follow because the geography is different in the south. Around the south pole there is a great landmass, permanently covered in snow and ice, Antarctica. The polar continent is surrounded by the sea and any snow which falls on the sea is likely to melt. It simply does not matter if summers are warm or cold, because there are no snowfields to melt anyway. A vital factor in the south is ice. The more ice there is, the more its shiny surface will reflect away heat from the Sun and keep the region cold. If a series of very severe winters occurs, the large amounts of seawater may freeze into a growing ice-sheet.

Because of the highly unusual geography of the globe today, with one landlocked polar sea and one pole with a continent sitting over it, the same pattern of orbital variations that causes mild summers in the Northern Hemisphere also causes severe winters in the Southern Hemisphere.

The calculations confirming that there is enough variation in the amount of heat received by the high latitudes in different seasons to produce the pattern of ice ages and interglacials were only made in the mid-1970s. Whatever the theory might say, no one was ready to accept the Milankovitch Model until there was evidence that the calculated pattern of variations matched up with the Earth's actual climatic fluctuations. That

The white, highly reflective surface of snow, clearly seen in this photograph, acts as an effective cooling agent.

153

These shells are the remains, magnified 75 times, of marine animals, foraminifera, that once lived in the Mediterranean Sea. When the animals died their shells sank to the bed of the sea and today their sediments are being dredged up and used by climatologists to help reconstruct past climates. By counting the different species of foraminifera, each of which prefers different water temperatures, a reliable guide of past temperatures can be obtained.

The grains of pollen floating on the surface of this lake in the Rocky Mountains have been derived from the cones of the surrounding pine trees and will eventually sink to the lake floor. Sediments formed in the same way, that have accumulated over thousands of years, can be analysed, and the species of plants that they contain, when dated, reveal the history of the climate of the region.

154

means one needs a reliable record of how the temperature on Earth has fluctuated over at least the latest cycle, of the past 150,000 years or more. The breakthrough came in 1976, from an analysis of the remains of fossilized sea creatures excavated from the bed of the Antarctic Ocean by drilling operations undertaken from a special research vessel. The shells of these tiny sea animals fall to the sea bed as they die, and over millions of years build up into layers that form white, crumbly rock known as chalk. Chalk is basically calcium carbonate, rich in oxygen, and palaeoclimatologists are able to use the oxygen atoms in the chalk, which is made of the tiny seashells, as a thermometer indicating past temperatures of the Earth.

This is based on the fact that there are two kinds of oxygen in the air we breathe, oxygen-16 and oxygen-18. Oxygen-18 is slightly heavier than oxygen-16, and as a result water molecules which happen to contain oxygen-18 do not evaporate from the sea as easily as water molecules which contain oxygen-16. Some of the molecules of water in the air are incorporated into the water cycle and fall as snow over the polar regions and are eventually locked up in ice-caps. When the weather is colder during an ice age, the heavier oxygen-18 water molecules tend to be left in the sea without evaporating, and the oxygen-16 water molecules tend to be the ones that get locked up in the ice-caps. By measuring the ratio of the two types of oxygen (the isotopes) in the sediments drilled from the sea floor, climatologists can deduce the temperature of the distant past. To clarify exactly when in time temperature changes occurred, the fossil remains are then dated accurately.

In 1976, a team from the Lamont-Doherty Geological Observatory in New York produced an analysis of temperature fluctuations for the past 500,000 years, ample time over which to test even the longest cycle of interglacials interrupted by ice ages. They found exactly what the Milankovitch Model forecast – a cycle, 100,000 years long, modulated by shorter cycles around 42,000 and 24,000 years long. These results imply that, given the present geography of the globe, any changes in the orbital geometry of the Earth are the fundamental cause of ice ages.

From this perspective, our present interglacial can be understood. It began when the Earth had a more circular orbit, which coincided with a shift in the wobble, which made June the month of closest approach to the Sun, boosting the warmth of northern summers and melting ice-sheets that had

existed for 100,000 years. At the same time, the tilt of the Earth reached a maximum, putting the Sun high in the sky in summer and boosting the warming effect. But peak warmth in summer was reached about 6000 years ago. Since then, all these factors have turned around and are becoming less favourable. The tilt is decreasing, cooling our summers and warming our winters; the orbital changes are working against us; and slowly the month of closest approach to the Sun is changing. The end of the present interglacial is in sight.

Recent climatic patterns

It is against this overall background that our attention is turned to smaller-scale climatic fluctuations – the changes that occur on a timescale of thousands of years, centuries or decades, within the present interglacial and during recorded history.

The most recent phase of glaciation – the latest, but not the last Ice Age – ended about 10,000 years ago. Since then there have been four main climatic epochs, identified by geological changes, measurements of isotope ratios, like those which pinned down the Milankovitch cycles, and remains of living species. Pollen grains from trees, for example, are deposited and preserved in many sediments, including the mud in lake beds. Each year the mud records which species of tree, herb or flower was prominent around lake shores, and as the climate changes, different species inhabit the vicinity. Today, a climatologist can extract a core of mud from the lake bottom and analyse the changing layers of pollen to determine how climate has changed. These and other techniques provide a good guide to climate over the whole of the present interglacial. The record is more detailed and complete the closer we come to the present, and for the past few hundred years we have direct measurements of temperature and rainfall.

From about 18,000 years ago, a combination of orbital factors began to pull the Earth out of the Ice Age, although the interglacial proper did not begin until about 10,000 years ago. With the modern understanding of the Milankovitch Model, it is clear that only the warmest possible northern summers stop ice ages while the continents are arranged in their present geographical position, so it is no surprise to discover that the warmest period of the whole interglacial was just after the ice melted, and peaked between about 7000 and 5000 years ago.

During the Iron Age there was a colder climatic epoch which reached its harshest

Tree rings laid down annually represent the growth of a tree and are used to decipher the climate during the tree's lifetime; a narrow ring represents poor growth and harsh conditions. The age of the tree is derived by counting the number of rings, which is correlated with the varying thickness of rings.

155

conditions between about 2900 and 2300 years ago, and this was followed by a secondary climatic "optimum" peaking in the early Middle Ages, roughly between AD 1000 and AD 1200. Since then, we have experienced the Little Ice Age, a return to harsher conditions which peaked in western Europe during the seventeenth century, and which may or may not yet be over. The pattern is one of waves of relative warmth and relative cold, with each warm interval a little cooler than the one before, and each cold spell harsher than the one before, until in one or two cycles' time we can expect a cold spell so severe that it initiates the next ice age proper. The exact combination of causes producing each of these epochs is probably different; but at one time or another factors such as the amount of dust put into the atmosphere by volcanoes, changes in the Sun's activity, and changes in the Earth's magnetic field have probably all played a part.

During the post-glacial warmest times, sea-level was around 3 metres (10 feet) higher than today, and temperatures in Europe in summer averaged 2–3°C (3.6–5.4°F) higher than corresponding temperatures today. In the cold epoch during the Iron Age, conditions were colder than today, but techniques of palaeoclimatologists have revealed that there is a great increase in rainfall across Europe from Ireland to Germany and beyond. The forests of Russia spread farther south, and the Mediterranean region was drier than in the warm epoch, but wetter than it is today. There are reliable historical records by the time of the secondary optimum. As the Arctic pack ice melted, new sea routes were opened up to the Norse voyagers, who colonized Iceland and Greenland, and visited North America. In western and central Europe, vineyards extended 3–5° of latitude farther north than today, which means that temperatures must have been about 1°C (1.8°F) higher than those that are now considered normal.

But the Little Ice Age, generally taken as the period from about 1450 to 1850, changed the picture dramatically. The Arctic pack ice expanded considerably, soon bringing an end to Norse voyages to America, and eventually bringing the death of the Greenland colony. By about 1800, temperatures across the North Atlantic north of 50°N seem to have been 1–3°C (1.8–5.4°F) below those regarded as normal. By the early nineteenth century, we have direct records of temperature. But evidence suggests that these low temperatures had been reached by the early seventeenth century.

Gathering grapes in an English medieval vineyard was not unusual prior to the onset of the "Little Ice Age", which began in about 1430 – as this illustration from the Peterborough Psalter shows.

The pattern of temperature changes for the past 1500 years is shown very clearly by a remarkable study of an ice-core drilled from the Greenland ice-cap. Willi Dansgaard, a Danish climatologist, and his team have analysed the oxygen isotope ratios in this core to provide a continuous record of the average temperature each year. The broad sweep of the secondary optimum and the Little Ice Age shows up, together with ripples indicating fluctuations of temperature over shorter periods of time, decades rather than centuries. Dansgaard's analysis shows a hint of two main rhythms in this 1500-year record, one a cycle lasting about 180 years and the other cycle lasting roughly 80 years. The two cycles combine, like the various cycles of the Milankovitch effects, on a longer timescale, to produce a complex but predictable pattern of warm and cold decades. Even without knowing what causes these regular fluctuations, they can be used to provide a forecast for the decades ahead – and it is a grim one. We are entering a period when both the 80-year and 180-year cycles

The success of the Vikings during the "climatic optimum", between AD 1000 and 1200, is shown by this hoard of silver found in the Viking town of Birka.

Norse picture stones show how the period of warmth encouraged the spread of Norse colonies across the Atlantic, only to be destroyed by the "Little Ice Age".

are heading downwards, and may possibly plunge us back into the full rigour of the Little Ice Age. To envisage this, one need only go back in history to just over 300 years ago to the times of William Shakespeare, Isaac Newton and the Great Fire of London, an era of regular Frost Fairs on the River Thames, which often froze solid in winter, in the heart of London.

This was the time when the scientific recording of weather began. It was the coldest century of the Little Ice Age in England, where science was flourishing, and also the time of great diarists, who recorded the events of day-to-day life. John Evelyn speaks of "great drought" (June 1681), "intolerable severe frost" (1683–84), "excessive cold" (November 1684), and "backward spring" (1688), among many other references. Shakespeare refers to the time "when milk came frozen home in pail", and the great fictional winter described in the book *Lorna Doone* is based on the real winter of 1683–84, when the greatest of all Frost Fairs was held upon the frozen River Thames.

Celtic communities spread throughout northern Europe during the "Iron Age Cold Epoch" and the drawings depicted on their artefacts, such as this bowl, show how animals typical of the time were specially adapted to a colder climate and how the Celtic culture was tuned to cope with severe cold.

157

A tent city was once a regular winter feature of the frozen River Thames – complete with swings, sideshows and food stalls. This painting by Luke Clement shows the Frost Fair of 1813–14, the last of its kind.

Frost fairs

As there are no official temperature and rainfall measurements prior to 1840, the most useful information on conditions during the "Little Ice Age" comes from historical records, particularly reports written about the frequent freezing of the River Thames in England.

Between 1407–8 and 1564–65, the river froze no fewer than six times; during the winter of 1564–65 Queen Elizabeth I took regular strolls on the frozen river and people even began to play football on the ice, initiating the river as a regular winter sports attraction in the seventeenth century. The first "Frost Fair" ever was held in the winter of 1607–8, and according to legend the sport of ice skating was first introduced in Britain in 1662–63, when the king watched a demonstration of the new sport upon the frozen river. The greatest ever Frost Fair was held in the winter of 1683–84, when the ice was 26 centimetres (10 inches) thick in places and the river was completely frozen for two months.

The eighteenth century was less spectacularly cold overall, but still the river froze ten more times between 1708–9 and 1813–14 – the year that the last Frost Fair was held. It only lasted for a few days, but the ice was hard enough for the *Morning Post* to report on 3 February: "An elephant on the ice. . . . Yesterday a very fine elephant crossed the Thames a little below Blackfriars Bridge; the singularity of such an animal on the ice attracted a great concourse. . . ." The ice gave way on 6 February and the river has not frozen since.

Entertainments on the thick ice of the frozen River Thames during the typically severe winter of 1720.

159

RETRAITE DE MOSCOW.

Napoleon's army, the largest that Europe had ever seen, advanced on Russia in 1812, but was badly affected by the harsh winter of that year – typical of many that occurred as the Little Ice Age drew to a close. Napoleon attempted to retreat at the first signs of cold, which was followed by alternate thaws and frosts until early December, when bitter cold set in. The French forces only managed to retreat by crossing the unreliable ice on the River Dnieper.

The last real bite of the Little Ice Age came in the early nineteenth century, when among other things the severe weather played a part in destroying Napoleon's army at the gates of Moscow. In addition, the early 1800s saw a much more frequent occurrence of white Christmases in England than at any time since, and it happens that this coincided with the youth of Charles Dickens. His memory of these Christmases went into many of his books, including *A Christmas Carol,* and established the Victorian image of Christmas, which has since been inherited. Even though snow at Christmas in England has been rare recently, the image persists on our Christmas cards, and has spread to the rest of the world.

An improvement of climate after about 1850 saw first what may have been the end of the Little Ice Age, and then a much more remarkable warming. The most striking conclusion from the historical and "proxy" evidence (such as ice cores, pollen remains and tree rings) is that, in the perspective of the past 1000 years, the earlier part of this century, from about 1910 to 1960, was the most unusual fifty-year run of weather in the entire millennium.

From 1910 to 1940 the global climate warmed up by about 0·5°C (0·9°F), but then

THE LEGEND OF SANTA CLAUS

The Victorian idea of Santa Claus may have originated from the traditions of tribes that once lived in Siberia, whose life-style goes back centuries, perhaps to the end of the last Ice Age. Tales of these people, the Koryak, Chuckchee and Kamchadel tribes, have been related by travellers since the early eighteenth century. The generally accepted European Father Christmas myth, of a team of aerial reindeer that were a little merry, may have evolved from the intrinsic part played by reindeer in the culture of these tribes and their renowned fondness for the local fly agaric mushroom, which has hallucinogenic properties.

it began to fall back from the peak levels. During this half-century of equable weather, harvests were good, rainfall reliable and climatic zones of the world as a whole shifted slightly towards the poles. The overall effect contributed to the explosive improvement in agricultural yields in the twentieth century. Scientific farming and mechanization played an equally significant part; but as the agricultural failures of the 1970s have shown, scientific farming and mechanization are not enough to maintain the record when the climate turns against us.

From 1880 to 1938, air temperatures in the Northern Hemisphere rose by about 0·6°C (1°F), bringing with it associated changes in rainfall and agriculture. Since about 1950 the fall in temperature has been about 0.3°C (0.5°F), half-way back to nineteenth-century conditions. If the trend continues for two decades, the weather will once again be as harsh as it was when Napoleon marched on Russia and Charles Dickens was playing in the snow in England. Ironically, it seems that the weather conditions we think of as "normal", the middle decades of the twentieth century, were in fact part of the most abnormal half-century of weather the world has experienced during the past 1000 years. The simplest way to make a guess of what weather will be like in the next 50 years is to guess that conditions will return to the true "normal" state of the past millennium – the Little Ice Age. But a better forecast of future weather prospects can be gained by finding out why the climate changes on a timescale of decades.

It is apparent that over the past 1000 years, continental drift has played no part in changing our climate, and the Milankovitch cycles have only had time to tilt us a tiny way farther towards the next ice age. One reason why the climate varies from century to century is simply that the weather on Earth is such a delicately balanced system that variations are bound to occur simply by the random workings of chance; just as one day is bright and sunny at one location, another day may be cloudy and wet.

A few meteorologists believe that this is the only explanation needed to account for the difference between the Little Ice Age of the seventeenth century and the warmth of the 1940s. But to predict the climate of the next 50 years we have to consider the details of the two or three most plausible ideas put forward to explain the changing climate rather than merely assuming it to be due to the blind workings of chance. It seems most likely that more than one process is at work

and the constant fluctuations of the climate represent a shifting point of balance between several forces, which are either in synchronization or in opposition, rather like the interacting cycles of the Milankovitch Model.

There are three main natural candidates involved in this tug of war. The first possibility, which would obviously affect the climate on Earth, is that the amount of heat being given by the Sun itself varies. The second, an equally straightforward possibility, is that changes in the atmosphere of the Earth affect its transparency, so that even if the same amount of heat arrives from the Sun at the top of the atmosphere, the amount getting through to the ground may vary. The third possibility, only recently recognized and much harder to understand, is that changes in the Earth's magnetic field influence the climate. Besides these three factors, there are two additional conflicting ones created by human activities, particularly during the twentieth century: as a result of burning fossil fuels, the amount of carbon dioxide in the atmosphere has increased. This is accentuated by the growing tendency to burn trees for fuel or to clear land for agriculture; the carbon stored in their trunks is converted to atmospheric carbon dioxide.

The last of the ice on the River Thames at Tower Bridge as the Little Ice Age waned in the 1890s. This time the ice was too rough and chunky and never froze hard enough for any amusements to take place on it.

Atmospheric Transparency

The Sun certainly does vary over the centuries, although it is far from clear whether these variations affect its temperature. Over a cycle which is roughly 11 years long, the Sun changes in appearance from being almost featureless to being dotted with dark spots, and then reverting back to the featureless state again. The spots give this cycle its name, the "sunspot cycle", and although sunspots had long been known to Chinese astronomers, and to the Ancient Greeks, their rediscovery by Galileo in the early seventeenth century marked the beginning of modern astronomical interest.

Astronomers now know that the spots are only a symptom of much more fundamental changes in the whole level of solar activity. When more spots are present, the Sun is more active and the stream of particles it sends across space, the "solar wind" of cosmic rays, blows strong and gusty. When there are few spots, the Sun is quiet and the solar wind is calmer. Besides the regular sunspot cycle itself, there is a longer-term pattern of solar changes. Sometimes there are relatively few sunspots even in the year of maximum activity in the cycle; in other cycles, the peak activity reaches dramatic heights. It has been suggested that in decades when the Sun is in an overall quiet phase, when even the peak sunspot activity reached is relatively low, the Earth is colder. The best evidence for this comes from the Little Ice Age itself. The second half of the seventeenth century was the coldest half-century of the Little Ice Age, and coincided with the quietest period of solar activity observed since the sunspot cycle first began to be recorded. This could just be a coincidence, but more substantial

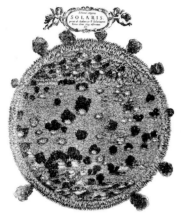

The Sun first began to be scrutinized by early seventeenth-century astronomers – this representation drawn in 1635 was one of the first to acknowledge the existence of sunspots.

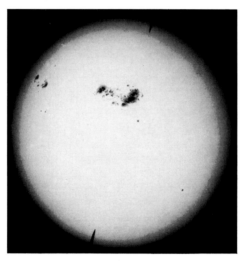

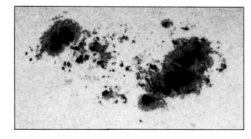

Solar activity was peaking when this photograph of the Sun and an individual sunspot was taken by the Hale Observatories in America on 7 April 1947.

Visible sunspots recorded between 1750 and 1980 show an obvious 11-year cycle and a more subtle 80-year cycle. Periods of high sunspot activity strongly correlate with warm epochs on Earth and may be associated with the effect of sunspots on the Earth's magnetic field.

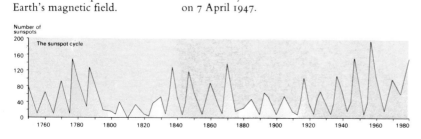

Number of sunspots

The sunspot cycle

200 | 160 | 120 | 80 | 40

1760 1780 1800 1820 1840 1860 1880 1900 1920 1940 1960 1980

evidence is provided by further observations that show that from 1800 to 1820, when the cold returned, the Sun was relatively quiet again. During the middle of the twentieth century, when the world was unusually warm, the Sun was more strongly active.

Using a variety of techniques, including the old Chinese records and the way the cosmic ray particles of the solar wind produce radioactive carbon-14 in the atmosphere, astronomers and meteorologists have pushed the correlation back for 2000 years. The link remains: when the Sun is less active, the Earth is colder. Perhaps the Sun itself is cooler when it is less active or perhaps it is less active because it is cooler. The latest evidence suggests that the changing activity of the Sun affects the transparency of the atmosphere, through the influence of the solar wind. This last possibility emerged in the late 1970s, from

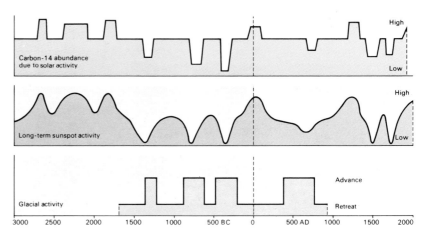

Changes in solar luminosity deduced by the abundance of carbon-14 in tree rings can be perfectly correlated with climatic changes on the Earth since the Bronze Age. Glacial advance and the onset of the Little Ice Age matches a decrease in solar activity, whereas the Medieval solar maximum corresponds to a warm epoch, when temperatures were comparatively warmer than today's.

Bristlecone pine trees, *Pinus aristata,* that grow in California's White Mountains survive for more than 4000 years – holding the current world record for all living things. The carbon preserved in each tree ring tells us the proportion of carbon-14 that was present in the atmosphere that year, and indicates how active the Sun was – an ingenious method of tracing the history of solar luminosity.

163

The explosion of the hydrogen bomb in 1952 completely destroyed the test island of Elugelab, and, at that time, the resulting fireball was the largest ever produced. This picture, taken from a height of 3640 metres (12,000 feet) and 80 kilometres (50 miles) from the detonation site, shows the familiar mushroom cloud. Two minutes after Zero Hour the cloud rose to 12,120 metres (40,000 feet) and ten minutes later the cloud stem had pushed 40 kilometres (25 miles) upwards, deep into the stratosphere.

A balloon-borne instrument being launched – at the Ural Aerological station at Dubrovo in Russia – to investigate the composition of the upper stratosphere.

a variety of studies. The most convincing single piece of evidence comes from a series of balloon fights launched by Soviet scientists in the 1960s. They sent instruments 30 kilometres (19 miles) above the ground to monitor the Sun's output without interference from the Earth's atmosphere. Their first results, published in 1970, seemed to imply that the Sun's heat does vary in line with the changing sunspot activity.

However, in the early 1960s it gradually became apparent that nuclear bomb tests have an effect on these kinds of measurements. Nitrogen oxides produced by the fireball of a nuclear explosion rise so high into the stratosphere that they affect its transparency, even in the tenuous layers above 30 kilometres. In 1961 and 1962, just before the partial test ban treaty came into force, the superpowers detonated more than 300 megatons of nuclear explosive. In response, the same Russian team reanalysed their balloon data and in 1979 arrived at a different conclusion. The data showed that there was a reduction of 2·5 per cent in the amount of solar heat penetrating the lower atmosphere because the nitrogen oxides, produced by the explosives, absorbed solar radiation high in the stratosphere. The overall effect was that the stratosphere was warmed while the ground below was cooled. It now seems that

this may explain why the winter of 1962–63, which was the worst of the century in many parts of the Northern Hemisphere, was so severe. This was a dramatic discovery, completely reversing the traditional meteorologist's dismissal of the idea that "The Bomb" causes bad weather. It may also explain why the Earth's temperature is low when the Sun is inactive.

Besides being showered with particles from the Sun, the Earth is bombarded with energetic particles, or cosmic rays, from deep space. One effect of these is to encourage nitrogen oxides to form in the atmosphere. If the nitrogen oxides block solar heat, as the Russian study suggests, then the Earth should be cool when the Sun is quiet, for when the solar wind is weak it cannot shield the Earth from galactic cosmic rays. As far as ground temperatures are concerned, the effect would still be as if the Sun's heat output changed. This could explain the results of another study carried out in the late 1970s by Stephen Schneider and Clifford Mass of the US National Center for Atmospheric Research.

Schneider and Mass assumed that the heat received from the Sun is 2 per cent lower when there are no sunspots than when the monthly sunspot number is between 80 and 100. As they were interested in long-term effects that occur over centuries rather than decades, they concentrated only on the broad trends of the Earth's surface temperature. The Earth's weather systems cannot respond immediately to a change in the Sun's output, because the oceans store heat and so "remember" the average climate of the past few years, which means that the data is bound to give a more spiky graph, with an unreal 11-year cycle, than the temperature trends in the real world. But besides analysing the varying sunspot number since 1600, the American team also took into account an estimate of the amount of dust incorporated into the atmosphere each year due to volcanic eruptions. There is little doubt that big volcanic eruptions like Krakatoa in 1883 or Mt St Helens in 1980 cool the globe, because the dust they blow into the stratosphere blocks the Sun's heat. Once again, the stratosphere warms while the ground cools. The typical aftermath of a major volcanic eruption is a wet summer, as was experienced across North America and Europe in 1980. The records of volcanic activity are good enough to make a reasonable estimate of the size of the volcanic sunshield effect each year since 1600.

By combining the changing solar heat index with the volcanic dust index, Schneider and Mass produced a "forecast" of temperature fluctuations since 1600 that precisely match the observed historical pattern. The dominant features are the cold of the late seventeenth and early nineteenth centuries, and the warmth of the middle of the twentieth century. It appears as if this combination of factors – sunspots and volcanic dust – does explain past climatic changes. But unfortunately, to use the combination to predict future climatic trends one needs to be able to forecast the changing level of solar activity plus the occurrence of volcanic eruptions, and it has not yet been possible to achieve this. In the past, solar activity reached unusual heights in the middle of the twentieth century, while the volcanoes were unusually quiet. If "normal service" is resumed, the Earth should cool off over the next 50–100 years.

It is worth stressing that both solar and volcanic activity have the same fundamental effect, which is to change the atmospheric sunshield. The Sun does not, as far as we know, vary in brightness over the sunspot cycle. Rather, the changes in the solar wind affect the production of nitrogen oxides in the atmosphere, and when the stratosphere contains more nitrogen oxides it allows less heat to reach the ground, just as it does when it contains more volcanic dust. In both cases the atmosphere acts like a reflective screen, a barrier to incoming heat.

The cataclysmic eruption of Krakatoa in 1883 – the most massive volcanic explosion of recent times – poured volcanic ash into the stratosphere which formed a world-wide sun filter, reducing the intensity of the Sun's heat by 20–30 per cent.

Dust and ash being belched into the upper atmosphere in 1831 during the formation of Julian Island – a new volcanic island off the coast of Sicily.

165

The volcanic dust warmed the high atmosphere. It was spread by stratospheric winds and subsequently cooled the whole world, because the dust absorbed solar heat that would otherwise have reached the ground.

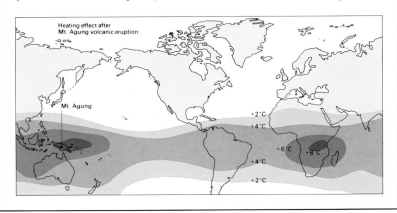

The sky in Europe (*right*) was clear on 7 May 1980, before the eruption of Mt St Helens. The inset photograph of the same part of the sky on 5 June 1980 was taken soon after the event, and shows the haziness of the atmosphere, now filled with volcanic dust, reflecting the Sun's rays back into space. The pictures were taken during stratospheric balloon observations, and the camera recorded that after the explosion the stratosphere was three times as bright as normal.

The eruption of Mt St Helens on 18 May 1980, in Washington State, USA. The northern flank of the mountain was completely blown off and volcanic dust was hurled 14 kilometres (9 miles) into the air.

The lava produced by the eruption of Karkar volcano on Karkar Island in Papua New Guinea in 1978 completely devastated all local vegetation.

When volcanoes erupt they throw an enormous amount of dust into the atmosphere and the dust that settles in the upper layers plays an important role in moulding our climate on a year-to-year basis. The dust reflects the heat from the Sun back into space, acting as a sunshield.

The connection between volcanic eruptions and cool weather first became apparent after the eruption of Tambora in Indonesia in 1816. That year was the coolest on record and months of blazing red sunsets were seen as far afield as London in England. The greatest and most spectacular eruption of this century was that of Krakatoa, an island between Java and Sumatra in the Pacific Ocean. Within a month of the explosion the dust it produced had encompassed the whole world, again creating blazing red sunsets of most unusual brilliance. Astronomers of the time estimated that the dense cloud of dust cut the Sun's heating effect by one-fifth. The energy derived from Krakatoa's one great explosion was equivalent to a total of twenty-six of the most powerful H-bombs ever tested.

Using a combination of fossil evidence, rocks and historical records, climatologists have linked the Earth's distinctly cool decades to episodes of exceptional volcanic activity. During the seventeenth and twentieth centuries excess volcanic dust in the atmosphere coincided with the worst summers and coolest winters felt in America, Japan and Britain. In contrast, during the middle part of the twentieth century, the world was remark-

ably free from volcanic activity and these decades coincided with periods of mild and stable weather. However, the situation has changed recently, with volcanic activity picking up again during the 1970s, releasing more dust into the atmosphere – the trend of the decade culminating on 18 May 1980 with the unexpected major eruption of a dormant volcano, Mt St Helens, in Washington State, USA. As a result the summer of 1980 saw 25 per cent more rainfall than usual, 15 per cent less sunshine and an average drop in temperature of 1°C (1·8°F).

These effects are felt more intensely in higher-latitude regions – not because the volcano is sited at 65°N but because sunlight takes a near vertical path through the atmosphere in the tropics, whereas in the higher latitudes sunlight enters the atmosphere at an angle and so takes a longer path through the atmosphere. If the atmosphere is dusty the sunlight has a longer path through the dust and is diminished all along the way.

A single volcano must erupt on a massive scale to produce a noticeable impact on the weather and huge eruptions such as those of Krakatoa and Mt St Helens are rare: a comparable impact is only produced during geologically active periods in the Earth's history which show a close correlation with cold epochs and advancing ice-sheets at high latitudes. Volcanism is either associated with normal events in Earth evolution, such as continental collision, or more subtle events, such as the impact of a meteorite.

Magnetism

Magnetic effects, the least comprehensible of the three factors, curiously provide a much better prospect for long-range forecasting, although the discovery of the link between magnetism and climate is still relatively new and the details have yet to be verified.

The work has been done by Dr Wollin and his colleagues at the Lamont-Doherty Geological Observatory in Palisades, New York. They began investigating relatively long-term climatic changes on a timescale of tens of thousands of years, the period that corresponds to the Milankovitch cycles. They found a curious effect whereby the magnetic changes strengthen the influence of the longest Milankovitch cycle, the 100,000-year rhythm in which the Earth's orbit stretches from being elliptical to circular and back again.

The Earth possesses a magnetic field which changes both in strength and direction within this period of time. The magnetic north pole is located a few kilometres from the geographical north pole, but its position and strength vary from year to year. Without knowing exactly how the magnetic field is produced, by studying the Earth's rocks scientists have managed to build up a remarkably detailed picture of the Earth's magnetism. Over a period of a few thousand years, the magnetic field dies away entirely and then it gradually builds up again in completely the opposite direction, so that over millions of years the north magnetic pole and the south magnetic pole reverse in position. This does not mean, as some doom-mongers have mistakenly assumed, that the Earth itself flips over in space, bringing havoc to all life on the surface. The Earth stays spinning on its axis as it travels around the Sun as usual, and only the direction of the magnetic field reverses.

The direction of the magnetic field of the past is revealed from the record that it leaves in the Earth's rocks. When molten rock from volcanic eruptions sets, magnetic particles within the rock align in the same direction as the Earth's magnetic field. The alignment of the magnetic particles is set within the rock as it hardens and when the Earth's magnetic field periodically reverses, the magnetic par-

Dr Goesta Wollin linked the Earth's magnetism with climate in the early 1970s.

The Earth's magnetic field (below) not only varies with time but also periodically reverses. The reversals take place in a surprisingly short time – within one or two thousand years.

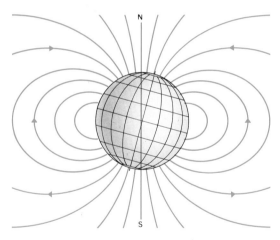

Iron filings around a bar magnet assume the same pattern as the Earth's magnetic field and, if pivoted, the magnet will align with it.

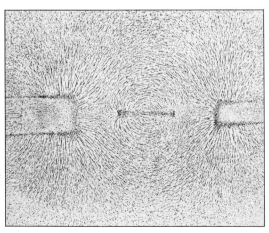

Photomicrographs of basaltic rock (*below*), or any rock that contains magnetic minerals, show black grains of magnetite aligned in the same direction as the Earth's magnetic field at the time the rock was formed.

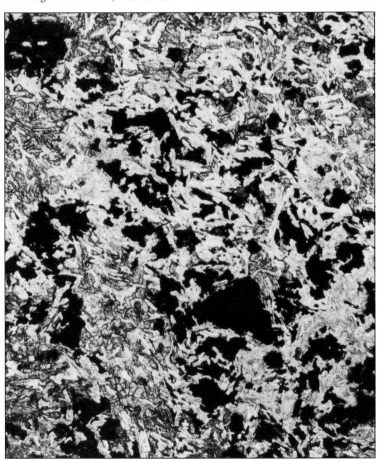

ticles retain their original direction. This property of retaining the direction of the magnetic field is called remanent magnetism. Geological techniques can determine the age of the rocks, and the strength and direction of the Earth's magnetic field at the time the rocks were being laid down. The most obvious discovery that comes from this kind of analysis is that during a geomagnetic reversal, when there is no magnetic field, the Earth is colder, and many species of plants and animals become extinct. This is one of the theories put forward to explain the demise of the dinosaurs, 65 million years ago, and it also fits with the latest work produced by Russian meteorologists on the changing transparency of the upper atmosphere.

One of the many effects of the magnetic field is that it helps to shield the Earth from galactic cosmic rays; the shield is not perfect, but it does block some of the rays.

When the shield is removed there should be more cosmic rays in the atmosphere, making more nitrogen oxides and blocking out more of the Sun's heat. This fits with the idea that a weaker magnetic field creates a colder Earth. The Earth's magnetic field is at present weakening, perhaps building towards the next geomagnetic reversal, which is another factor that points towards colder times ahead.

The link with the Milankovitch rhythms comes in a more roundabout way. Although the details of how the Earth's magnetic field is generated are still a mystery, and nobody knows just how or why it reverses, there is little doubt that the field is generated by electric currents flowing in the molten material that makes up the Earth's core. Electric currents generate magnetic fields, and changing magnetic fields produce electric currents in nearby conductors, whether the conductor is a copper wire, an iron-rich fluid rock or even sea-water. When the flow of the fluid inside the Earth is smooth, the field ought to be strong and steady, but when the flow is disturbed, the field ought to be weaker and more erratic, with the Earth consequently cooler.

The changes in the Earth's orbit which stretch it from a circular to an elliptical shape and back again are caused by the gravitational tug of the Sun and the planets in the solar system all pulling in different directions but with a regular rhythm. The same forces tug with the same rhythm on the fluid core of the Earth, altering the way the fluid flows, and thereby changing the strength of the geomagnetic field. Wollin has found that the long-term magnetic effect is exactly in step with the long-term Milankovitch effect,

enhancing its influence on temperature. This is a welcome discovery, since the only real objection anyone had to the Milankovitch Model as an explanation of recent climatic cycles was that the 100,000-year cycle revealed by the sea-bed samples seemed to imply much stronger forces at work than the Milankovitch cycle alone could account for.

The different climatic influences can be seen to interweave. Magnetic and solar changes both affect the transparency of the atmosphere, just as volcanic dust does. But the magnetic changes also interweave with the environment in another way, on a much shorter timescale. After establishing the reality of these long-term effects, Wollin's team moved on to look at the changes in the temperature of the Northern Hemisphere from year to year, hoping to find a relationship that correlated with the year-to-year fluctuations in the magnetic field. In the beginning of the 1980s they made a breakthrough. By investigating the influence of temperature change on the circulation of the Pacific Ocean, they explained the way these

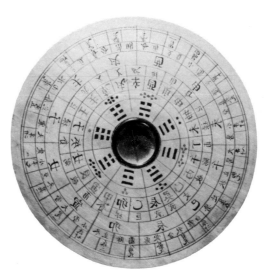

The Chinese had invented a simple compass which was traditionally used for astrological purposes by the first century AD, but they did not realize that the reason that the bar points north to south is due to the influence of a magnetic field produced by the Earth itself.

fluctuations seemed to follow precisely two years after magnetic fluctuations.

The Pacific Ocean is the greatest circulating water mass on Earth. A great slow-moving current, or gyre, carries warm tropical water northwards up the western Pacific and across towards Alaska, from where the now cool water returns to the equator down the eastern edge of the ocean. Seawater is a conductor of electricity – not as good as a copper wire, but not entirely negligible, and in effect this ocean current is also an electric current. As the magnetic field and the ocean currents are tied together by electrical forces, whenever the magnetic field

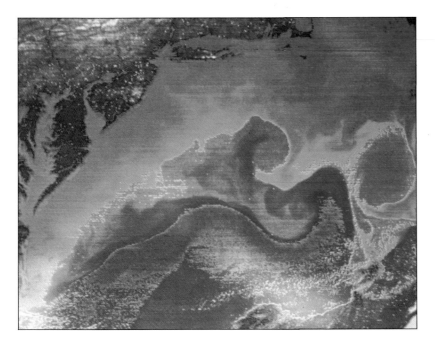

Infra-red satellite pictures of the Gulf Stream, which transports warm water from the tropics to the Arctic circle, show how the Earth's heat is transported by the oceans; warm water appears purple ranging to red, and cool water appears blue.

undergoes a sharp temporary increase, the electric grip on the ocean current tightens, and it moves more slowly. Warm water from the tropics takes longer to move northwards, and loses more of its heat along the way, so cooling the high latitudes. This does not only affect the Pacific – the Pacific Ocean is such a huge reservoir of heat – it also affects the surface temperature of the whole planet. The net result of a sudden upsurge in the strength of the magnetic field is that the world experiences cooler temperatures. Conversely, when the field weakens its electromagnetic grip on the ocean, the Pacific gyre speeds up. Warm water is carried vigorously northwards and the whole hemisphere benefits.

This discovery is of only marginal interest in climatic terms. Fluctuations from year to year are too rapid to be of concern in assessing long-term climatic trends. But if the relationship is valid, it does mean that Wollin and his colleagues have discovered a way of forecasting, two years ahead, the likely temperature changes from year to year. (The two-year delay is simply because it takes that amount of time for the slow-moving ocean currents to play their part in altering the circulation of the atmosphere and the temperature of the whole Northern Hemisphere.)

Leaving aside these short-term fluctuations, every identifiable natural influence on climate points to a cooling in the immediate future – back to the Little Ice Age within a century and back to a full ice age within a few thousand years at the most. But, in the last quarter of the twentieth century, a new factor came into play. Since we are all pro-

ducts of the terrestrial environment, any influence of mankind on the climate is, in the deepest sense, also "natural". But these anthropogenic influences are certainly unique in the long history of our planet. Man is the joker in the pack that may throw out all predictions that are based on what has happened before.

Human Activities

There are two main theories of how Man's activities are affecting the climate. One idea is that by increasing the dust content of the atmosphere through pollution from factory chimneys and wind-blown soil from agricultural land we are acting as a "human volcano", building up a sunshield which blocks out some of the heat from the Sun and causes the Earth below to cool. The alternative idea is that there is a build-up of carbon dioxide in the atmosphere, due to burning fossil fuels and simultaneously destroying forests, so that trees are prevented from absorbing the extra carbon dioxide. This acts like a blanket around the Earth and causes it to warm up. It has been argued by a few optimists that the two effects might cancel each other out, but this is extremely unlikely.

The chief proponent of the "human volcano" idea is Professor Reid Bryson of the University of Wisconsin-Madison, in the United States. His argument is based on the firm evidence that great volcanic eruptions do cause the Earth to cool, and quotes the classic example of the eruption of Tambora, in Indonesia, in 1815. As a result of that one eruption, the summer of 1816 was so bad that it has gone down in history as "the year without a summer" and more graphically in the folklore of the American pioneers as "eighteen hundred and starve to death". Temperatures were a full 1°C (1·8°F) below normal across the Northern Hemisphere, and 3°C (5·4°F) below normal in much of Britain. New England and eastern Canada had snow in June and frosts in every month of 1816. Bryson argues that volcanic dust produces cooling; since the 1940s there has been a dramatic increase in dust production by humans, and since the 1940s the world has cooled; so human dust is responsible.

Volcanic eruptions were more common in the nineteenth century than the first half of the twentieth century, which according to Bryson explains why the world warmed up until the 1940s. Many climatologists agree with this hypothesis, but very few of them agree that the subsequent cooling is due to anthropogenic dust. Indeed, some calculations suggest that the kind of dust particles

Forest trees are either burned to make room for agriculture or felled and their wood burned. The carbon that was once locked up in the trees is converted to carbon dioxide in the atmosphere and acts like a gigantic insulation jacket, warming the planet by storing heat that would otherwise escape.

produced by Man's activities can help to warm the globe, reflecting back to the ground heat that would otherwise be lost to space. The majority view today (although science, being undemocratic, does not always prove the majority view to be eventually right) is that mankind is indeed causing global warming, perhaps through the dust effect and certainly through the influence of the amount of carbon dioxide in the atmosphere.

The Greenhouse Effect

Most of the energy radiated by the Sun is at frequencies near those of visible light. This is no coincidence, since our eyes have evolved to use those frequencies because they are the ones radiated by the Sun. Solar radiation warms the ground and sea, which in turn radiates energy back outwards, but at the lower frequencies of infra-red radiation. Some of the outgoing infra-red heat is in turn absorbed by molecules of water vapour and carbon dioxide in the air, and reradiated back to the ground, keeping the Earth warmer than it would be if it had no blanket of air around it. This is the greenhouse effect. By burning coal and oil, we are rapidly increasing the concentration of carbon dioxide in the air, and by cutting down the great forests of the world we prevent them from absorbing the extra carbon dioxide and storing it as wood. The result is that the greenhouse effect is gaining strength, and may soon overwhelm the natural climatic processes on Earth.

Looking ahead over the next 50 years or so, this carbon dioxide greenhouse effect is seen by many people as the key issue of environmental concern facing mankind and is sometimes regarded as even more important than the risks of radiation leakage from nuclear power plants. Indeed, one of the strongest arguments in favour of a switch to nuclear power is that since nuclear power stations produce no carbon dioxide they would not add to the greenhouse effect. But it is still too early for the climatologists to be able to predict exactly how the climate will change if unrestricted use of fossil fuel continues.

In a greenhouse the short-wave radiation from the Sun penetrates the glass and is absorbed and used by the plants. In turn, they give out long-wave radiation, which cannot penetrate glass, and so heat is trapped.

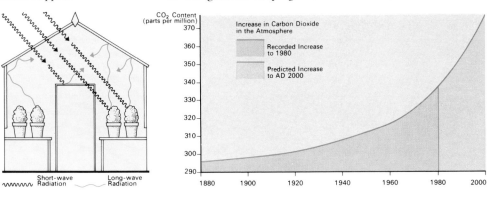

Short-wave Radiation   Long-wave Radiation

CO₂ Content (parts per million)

Increase in Carbon Dioxide in the Atmosphere

Recorded Increase to 1980

Predicted Increase to AD 2000

The concentration of carbon dioxide in the atmosphere has recently been increasing at a rate which corresponds to the increasing rate at which Man is burning fossil fuels – oil, natural gas and coal. As the concentration increases, more of the Earth's heat is trapped, and this may lead to a profound long-term alteration of the Earth's climate.

HUMAN THREAT

The destruction of trees, in this case by the south Vietnamese authorities to prevent camouflage being provided for the Vietcong, creates another factor influencing the climate. Many people believe that chemicals enlisted during wartime situations specifically to destroy the natural vegetation balance could create climatic changes with far-reaching adverse consequences.

All there is left of the natural tropical forest covering is the foliage on the river bank in the background of the picture.

They need more time to observe how the atmosphere actually does respond to increasing levels of carbon dioxide before they can refine their theories enough to produce accurate detailed forecasts.

The present estimate is that a doubling of the natural level of carbon dioxide in the atmosphere will produce a rise in temperature of about 2°C (3·6°F) overall, with perhaps three times this increase at the more sensitive high latitudes around the poles. If no brake is put on the growing use of fossil fuel around the world, this level will be reached in about 50 years' time. And although a naïve guess might suggest that a warmer world would be an easier place to live in, this is not necessarily the case. Besides temperature changes, there would be rainfall changes. Both temperature and rainfall would change unevenly around the globe – some regions will be hotter, a few actually cooler, some wetter, some drier. All of these changes could have a dramatic impact on agriculture at a time of rapidly increasing population and a world food shortage.

This is particularly significant because of the dramatic changes in agriculture that have occurred during the twentieth century. More "scientifically" orientated farming has meant, in many cases, a dependence on a single crop, intensively fertilized and irrigated. Any climatic shift is bound to be beneficial for some crops and detrimental for others; but it happens that today virtually the only region of the world exporting food on a large scale is North America. Everybody else depends, in the bad years, on the surplus of grain produced by the United States and Canada – even the USSR is a frequent and large purchaser of grain on the world market.

So when we attempt to peer into the cloudy crystal ball and predict how the climate will vary in our own lifetimes, this is what we must keep in mind. A century ago, if the climate changed, a farmer would lose some crops but others would do well; today, vast areas are devoted to a single crop, and if that fails all is lost. Every other consideration – coastal flooding, effects on energy demand or transport – fades into insignificance beside the key question. How will the changing climate affect world agriculture in general, and the grainlands of North America in particular?

Impacts of Future Weather

To understand how future climatic changes are likely to affect mankind, it is important to examine some details of the impact of climatic extremes on human activity in the historical past.

In the longer term, we know that a new ice age is due, and the evidence of cyclic variations from analysis of the Greenland ice-cores suggests that a little ice age may be imminent, assuming the natural patterns continue to hold true. Of course, European civilization survived the extremes of the seventeenth century without the aid of our modern technology, and so from that point of view we are far better equipped to cope with a return to those conditions. But the world today is more densely populated than the world of the seventeenth century, and in global terms any disruption of the patterns of climate – the patterns of the mid-twentieth century that are regarded as normal, but are now known to be the most unusual climatic decades of the past millennium – is bound to disrupt a world agricultural system that is

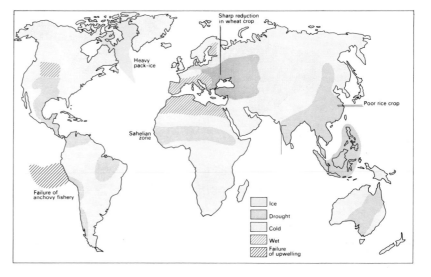

delicately tuned to make use of these so-called "normal" conditions. Indeed, we have to look no farther back than the year 1972 to see just how much mankind is still at the mercy of the weather.

The year 1972 seemed to be a freak period of climatic extremes. In the USSR, the Moscow region experienced the worst drought for 300 years, and overall Soviet food production fell by 8 per cent. In Africa, the Sahel drought reached a peak, and in India a failure of the monsoon brought an 8 per cent drop in rice production. Besides droughts in Australia and South America, there was a failure of the vital anchovy crop off the Peruvian coast of South America, caused by changes in the oceanic circulation patterns of Pacific waters.

Since 1972 it has become clear that this "freak" year was more a harbinger of climatic extremes to come rather than a uniquely bad year. Throughout the 1970s there have been

The unusual weather during 1972 produced bad harvests in Australia, Asia, Africa and North America, which meant that there was no extra grain available for famine relief. Some experts believe that the excess production of carbon dioxide by Man upsets the natural atmospheric balance and so similar extremes of weather will be more common in the near future.

more extreme fluctuations of climate and weather from year to year. The record-breaking droughts and record-breaking blizzards in the United States, floods in 1976 in parts of the USSR, coinciding with the worst drought on record in parts of Europe, and the "unseasonable" frosts affecting the coffee crop in Brazil are just a few of the recorded calamities of that decade.

Such outbreaks of "unusual" weather would not be so catastrophic if our global society were organized to make the most efficient use of farmlands to feed the growing population. Using official United Nations figures, agricultural economists have calculated that by using modern farming techniques and existing available land effectively, twice the present population of the world could be adequately fed. People starve in the world today not because the Earth is "over-populated" in an absolute sense, but because of economic and political factors. In a nutshell, poor people in poor countries starve because, as individuals and countries, they have no money to buy food on world markets. As far as climatic studies are concerned, it is a fact of life that the world food system is balanced on a knife edge, and that virtually all of the "trade" in food is the surplus grain produced by North America.

Whether it is the USSR that needs to purchase grain to make up deficits in the five-year plan or the nomads of the Sahel that need food aid from relief agencies, the ultimate source of the extra food to plug the gap is the North American grain surplus. Thus any change in climate is likely to be initially detrimental to world food production because modern agribusiness takes longer to adjust than small-scale, unmechanized farming. Even if the change brought better conditions in the long term, millions could starve in a year or two while agribusiness adjusted to the new pattern – which is the real threat of the changing climate today.

The naïve guess that a planetary cooling could cause crop failure in temperate latitudes, whereas a warming could create a beneficial effect, cannot be used as a guide to forecast how changes in climate would affect mankind. The vital question – whether the globe is warming or cooling – still remains, and any future trends that might occur in our lifetime are unforeseeable.

The Influence of the Planets
The reliability of the forecast of a cooling trend, based on the 80-year and 180-year cycles from the Greenland ice-cores, was strengthened in 1980 when two Chinese

scientists published a study of how planetary alignments have affected the weather on Earth over the past 3000 years.

Similar ideas have been put forward before, but have largely been dismissed · by the present scientific community, which is generally reluctant to accept any new theories on forecasting that are based on astrology. But the Chinese explanation of these influences owes nothing at all to astrology. At the same time, it neatly explains the rhythms of warming and cooling found in the isotope record of the Greenland ice-cores and similar isotope records from other sites. All in all, although it cannot be taken as established scientific fact as yet, it is an idea which is currently being investigated by many scientists, and which offers both an explanation of past patterns of warming and cooling over the centuries and a clear forecast for the decades ahead.

Ren Zhenqiu of the Peking Academy of Meteorological Sciences and Li Zhisen of Peking Astronomical Observatory initially compared Chinese weather data for the past 1000 years (the Chinese have more detailed and more accurate historical records than any Western country, having been civilized for longer) with the alignments of the nine planets in the solar system. Each planet in its orbit around the Sun takes a different time to complete one circuit, with the planets nearest the Sun (Mercury, Venus, Earth and Mars)

The highly mechanized strip-farming system used in the wheat triangle of Montana, USA, where most of the world's extra grain is produced (*far left*).

A synod occurs only once every 180 years, when the planets are grouped on one side of the Sun with the Earth on the other. The planets are all within 60 degrees of each other during the synod of October 1982, which is represented on the left. According to Ancient Chinese records each of the past five synods can be linked with unusually cold decades on Earth and Chinese astronomers predict that the 1982 synod may be initiating a cold spell of 30–50 years in length.

♓ Pisces	♍ Virgo
♒ Aquarius	♌ Leo
♑ Capricorn	♋ Cancer
♐ Sagittarius	♊ Gemini
♏ Scorpio	♉ Taurus
♎ Libra	♈ Aries

175

cycle found by some astronomers in variations of solar activity, including sunspots. The coincidence has encouraged many people to try to develop explanations of how the planetary alignment could affect the weather on Earth. None of these ideas appeared to be as plausible as the new Chinese theory.

The records that the Chinese have examined show that one particular type of synod seems to be important in terms of climate on Earth. The weather on Earth is colder when there is an alignment of the planets with the Earth alone on one side of the Sun and the other planets grouped together on the other side of the Sun. From 1300 BC to the present day, this kind of synod has always been associated with cold decades on Earth. The statistics are convincing – but why should the effect occur?

The explanation put forward by the Chinese team involves changes in the Earth's orbit around the Sun, but much more subtle changes than those responsible for the Milankovitch cycles. Although the planets orbit the Sun, both the Sun and planets also orbit around the centre of mass of the whole solar system, equivalent to the point of balance between two ice-skaters that are pirouetting around each other. Just as their point of balance is always nearer to the heavier partner rather than being equidistant from both of them, so the centre of mass of the solar system is very close to the Sun – indeed, for much of the time it is actually inside the Sun. But as it is tugged in different directions by the gravity of the planets, the Sun undergoes a stately dance around the centre of mass, a dance which has a regular, repeating cycle of 179 years. As far as the Earth is concerned, the effect is that during a synod, with all the other planets pulling together, the Earth's orbit is effectively "stretched" by 1·5 million kilometres (0·9 million miles), 1 per cent of its average distance from the Sun.

This is a significant change, reducing the amount of heat arriving at the surface of the Earth and effectively lengthening the winter. And, because the outer giant planets move so slowly in their orbits compared with the Earth, the pattern will persist for several years, giving the subtle change in heating time to work.

Since the year AD 1000 there have been five intervals of low temperature in China: in the first half of the twelfth century, in the fourteenth century, at the end of the fifteenth century, in the seventeenth century (the Little Ice Age) and in the nineteenth century. In the same period there were just five planetary synods – in 1126, 1304, 1483, 1665

Early Chinese astronomers surveyed the heavens amazingly accurately and their records – particularly records of planetary alignments during the past 3000 years – are a valuable resource for modern climatologists.

orbiting more quickly than those farther out (Jupiter, Saturn, Uranus, Neptune and Pluto).

Usually, the nine planets are scattered around their orbits in no noticeable pattern, with the faster inner "runners" repeatedly lapping their slower outer counterparts. But inevitably, from time to time all of the planets happen to lie on the same side of the Sun, grouped in the same part of the sky as viewed from Earth, although still, of course, at great distances from one another along the line of sight. It just happens that, because of the regular motion of each planet in its own orbit, this kind of pattern – which the Chinese call a "synod" – occurs regularly, at intervals of almost exactly 179 years. This regular cycle matches the roughly 180-year

and 1844. If this is "just a coincidence" it is a very remarkable one indeed. The method gives a clear and unambiguous forecast for the decades ahead, backing up the "forecast" obtained by extending the cycles found in the isotope record.

The next synod is due late in 1982, with approximate synods following in the next few years. By calculating the extent of the associated stretch in the Earth's orbit, the Chinese came up with a forecast that over the next few decades average temperatures in the Northern Hemisphere will fall by about 1·5°C (2·7°F), compared with the warm peak of the 1950s. This trend has already set in, judging from the world-wide measurements of temperature made during the 1960s and 1970s, and over the next 20 years, if the Chinese prove to be right, the trend will take us back, not quite to the full rigours of the Little Ice Age, but at least to the white Christmases and associated climatic extremes of Dickens's day.

All in all, there seems very little reason to doubt the many forecasts that the natural climatic trend today marks a retreat from the unusual warmth of the mid-twentieth century and a return towards Little Ice Age

conditions. But there is yet another joker in the pack – the build-up of carbon dioxide due to human activities. That joker may well turn out to be the most important climatic card in our lifetime.

Life in the Greenhouse
The carbon dioxide greenhouse effect could either become noticeable in the immediate future, and overwhelm the expected cooling of the next 20 years, or else we may be destined for decades of cold before the warmer climate becomes established. The fundamental problem is to predict how these changes will affect world agriculture.

The key to the build-up of carbon dioxide in the atmosphere today is the rate at which demand for fossil fuels, mainly coal, is growing. Up until about 1950, the main effect of mankind's activities on the atmosphere was the rate at which forests were cleared and trees burnt to make room for agriculture; but since 1950 the burning of oil, natural gas and especially coal has rapidly overtaken deforestation as a source of "anthropogenic" carbon dioxide.

Today, about 5 thousand million tonnes of carbon in the form of fossil fuel (5 gigatonnes,

The results of famine – peasants taking thatch from roofs to feed cattle in Russia.

177

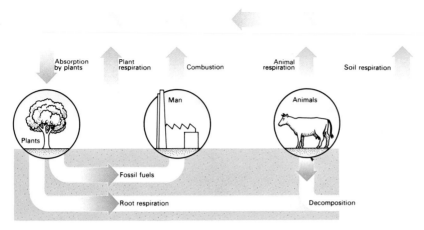

Absorption by plants Plant respiration Combustion Animal respiration Soil respiration

Plants Man Animals

Fossil fuels

Root respiration Decomposition

A balance of carbon dioxide normally results from the natural processes that produce it being in equilibrium.

Burning coal for power pumps extra carbon dioxide into the atmosphere, creating an imbalanced situation.

or 5 gts) are burnt each year. As it combines with oxygen to make carbon dioxide, each tonne of carbon becomes about 20 tonnes of carbon dioxide and is absorbed into the atmosphere to form part of the global carbon cycle. This does not, however, pose any threat to the oxygen in the air. About 23 per cent of the atmosphere today is oxygen, such a huge amount that we could burn all the fossil fuel on Earth without running short of oxygen to breathe. But not all of the carbon dioxide remains in the atmosphere.

If all of the coal on Earth were burnt very slowly, over a period of thousands of years, then all of the extra carbon dioxide produced would slowly dissolve in the oceans. The problem is that we are burning fuel today faster than the oceans can dissolve carbon dioxide. The result is that roughly half of the carbon dioxide produced each year by Man stays in the atmosphere.

Before the industrial revolution of the nineteenth century, the proportion of carbon dioxide in the air was a tiny 280 parts per million – tiny compared with the 23 parts per hundred, or 23 per cent, of oxygen. In 1980, the concentration reached 335 parts per million, and the rate at which it is building up is increasing. Since 1957 alone, when accurate monitoring of carbon dioxide began at the Mauna Loa Observatory in Hawaii, which is isolated, as far as possible, from any industrial pollution, the concentration has increased by about 7 per cent, from just over 310 parts per million.

Even if present consumption of fuel continued at 5 gts of carbon per year, it would not pose any great threat of a dramatic greenhouse warming. In the developed world (sometimes called the "rich North"), demand for energy has levelled off as population growth has remained static and people have achieved an affluent way of life. But in the Third World (the "poor South"), economic growth is essential to catch up with the North, and that growth requires energy, which can most easily be obtained from coal.

The result is that global use of fossil fuel is increasing at about 4 per cent per year, which means a doubling of the amount of fuel burnt per year every 16 years. This poses a real greenhouse effect threat, and also changes the pattern of regional producers of carbon dioxide. If "business as usual" continues at the same rate, the concentration of carbon dioxide in the atmosphere will reach double the pre-industrial level by about AD 2025 – a disturbing fact for most climatologists: many believe that the increase in carbon dioxide could have far-reaching consequences.

178

Clues from the Past

Going beyond the simple forecast that a doubling of carbon dioxide concentration would raise mean temperatures by 2–3°C (3·6–5·4°F), the best modern computer models predict that there would be very little change in temperature in the tropics but an increase of 6–9°C (11–16°F) at high latitudes, near the poles. But the computers cannot give more detail on regional changes in temperature, nor on changes in rainfall patterns, which will be crucial for agriculture. To assess those details, the climatologists turn back to the real world and the study of past climatic extremes, but use the information in a slightly different way.

Accurate records of temperature and rainfall covering most of the landmass of the Northern Hemisphere go back only to 1925, but by picking out warm and cold years from the period since 1925, and using data from the warmest and coldest few years to build up composite pictures of the weather of the world at each extreme of the natural range of fluctuations, climatologists can discern how a "warm Earth" differs from a "cold Earth". These composites cannot be used as a prediction of what will happen if and when the world warms up.

The climatologists who developed the techniques are careful to call their reconstructions "scenarios" rather than "forecasts", but the picture they paint is suggestive. For the interval between 1925 and 1974, the differences between a composite of the five coldest years (1964, 1965, 1966, 1968 and 1972) and the five warmest years (1937, 1938, 1943, 1944 and 1953) show the same latitudinal pattern of temperature changes that the computer models predict for the greenhouse effect. Although the overall average temperature difference between the warm and cold composites is only 0·6°C (1°F) (just a quarter of the expected greenhouse effect warming for a doubling of carbon dioxide), the region above 65°N warms by 1·6°C (2·9°F), while the tropics hardly warm at all. But these "real Earth" composites go far beyond the computer models in picking out subtle changes in the regional distribution of both temperature and rainfall.

While a region from Finland across the USSR eastwards to 90°E warms by more than 3°C (5·4°F), the United States warms by only 1–2°C (1·8–3·6°F) and parts of the world, including Japan, India, Turkey and Spain, actually show a small decrease in temperature. At the same time, although the warm composite shows almost 2 per cent more rainfall over land than the cold composite, this

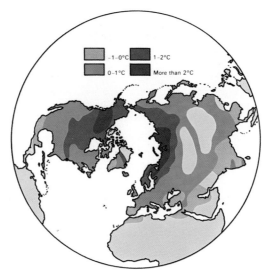

A suggestive map, produced by a computer, comparing the especially warm years with especially cold years since 1925, indicates what the effects of a global warming might be; subarctic areas would warm most, subtropical areas least.

Legend:
−1–0°C
0–1°C
1–2°C
More than 2°C

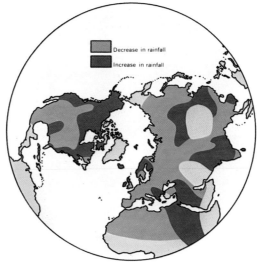

By analysing the patterns of rainfall during the warm years since 1925 one can envisage what a warmer world may be like. The US and USSR grain belts would receive less total rain, whereas India, western Asia and most of China would receive more. In terms of food production, this suggestive forecast indicates how a global warming may be beneficial to some nations but detrimental to others.

Legend:
Decrease in rainfall
Increase in rainfall

The observatory set on the peaks of the Hawaiian islands in the Pacific ocean is a perfect site for monitoring the amount of global atmospheric carbon dioxide produced.

pattern is unevenly distributed. India and the Middle East experience a much bigger than average increase, but, most significantly, the United States, Europe and the grain-growing regions of the USSR all suffer a decline in rainfall, and higher temperatures.

This is, potentially, a recipe for disaster. A combination of higher temperatures and less rainfall is the formula for drought and perhaps dust bowl conditions – certainly the harbinger of reduced grain yields in these key areas of the globe. If this pattern of climatic changes actually occurs, then the North American grain surplus on which so much of the world depends would certainly disappear, while at the same time the USSR would be seeking sources of grain to make up its deficits. This is not something any politician – or anyone at all – in the world today can face with equanimity, and it is this disturbing agricultural and political scenario that is making the carbon dioxide "threat" an important part of debate on energy policy today.

The problems that the politicians face can be imagined by considering two "obvious" ways to reduce the size of the threat. Should the developed world supply nuclear power stations to the developing countries of the Third World so that they do not need to rely on coal for development? Or should the developed world "de-develop", reducing its use of fossil fuel to compensate for the growth of the Third World, eventually meeting the developing countries half-way? Neither possibility looks realistic. But unless some such drastic action is taken, it will be "business as usual" and the greenhouse effect will be overwhelming the cooling trend by the early twenty-first century, with all its implications. We have no more than 20 years to come to grips with the problem and some climatologists believe it may already be too late.

The transition from a natural cooling trend to an unnatural warming is hardly likely to be smooth. The weather machine, like any other machine, is not likely to respond smoothly to a sudden change of gear from reverse to forward, or to having an anthropogenic spanner thrown in its works. While the weather machine is adjusting to the changed conditions, the first noticeable response ought to be an increase in weather variability around the globe, with more extreme conditions of all kinds recurring from year to year. This means there will be more droughts and floods and more severe winters and scorching summers.

This is exactly the pattern of the 1970s, the pattern ushered in by what now seems not a freak year but an archetype, the year 1972. In

Nuclear power is one way of generating energy without adding to the amount of carbon dioxide in the air.

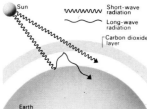

The global warming that might result from an excess of atmospheric carbon dioxide would produce a dank, murky environment with a wealth of tropical trees, usually surrounded by stagnant water. The situation would be similar to that of the Everglades in Florida today, where mean temperatures are between 17–28°C (63–82°F).

Carbon dioxide creates a barrier that allows light in but traps the Earth's heat.

such conditions, the best long-range predictions can be no more than crude guide-lines to what we might expect, and planning from year to year becomes much harder for both agriculture and industry. Short-range forecasting, the ability to predict the weather a few weeks or even a few months ahead, becomes increasingly important as the weather becomes more variable. Fortunately, the art of forecasting is rapidly becoming a precise science.

Artificial Climate Modification

A few years ago, when climatologists began to be worried about the imminent natural global cooling, one team of United States scientists pointed out that we have the technological capability to prevent the "next" ice age happening.

It seems that it is very easy, in principle, to tilt the climatic balance of the world today away from ice age conditions. The trick depends on the way in which ice and snow cover reflect away incoming solar heat – the same property which is so important in establishing the Milkankovitch ice age cycles. If the thin cap of ice over the Arctic Ocean were black instead of white, it would absorb solar heat, warm up and melt. Once it melted, it would be very difficult for a new

ice age to start, because the exposed ocean water is itself less reflective than snow or ice (it has a lower albedo) and would continue to absorb heat from the Sun. To end the present pattern of Milkankovitch cycles, it seems that all we have to do is paint the Arctic.

The idea is not quite as crazy as it sounds, and two practical ways of achieving it have been suggested. One is to scatter millions of small, black plastic discs on the ice from aircraft. The black plastic would absorb solar heat and melt the ice, but there would then remain the rather large problem of clearing up the "litter" afterwards. A slightly more realistic idea involves modifying the engines of giant transport aircraft – the big jets usually used to ferry troops and their equipment around the world – so that one or more of them pours out a sooty trail. A fleet of such aircraft flying low over the ice-cap would be able to sufficiently blacken the snow below to melt it by solar heating alone – and the more ice-cap that melts, the more dark sea water is exposed to help the warming along.

Of course, no one is seriously proposing such action today. As it is impossible to be sure of or cope with the many environmental consequences, the Arctic is likely to be left to its own natural rhythms at least for the foreseeable future.

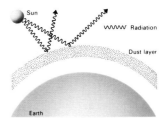

Dust in the atmosphere creates a barrier that acts as a reflector covering the Earth.

If excess dust lingers in the atmosphere, the Earth might cool and the world could be encompassed by ice, making the landscape similar to that of Mt Blanc today.

FORECASTING

"Yesterday it thundered, last night it lightened, and at three this morning I saw the sky as red as a city in flames could have made it. I have a leech in a bottle, my dear, that foretells all these prodigies and convulsions of nature: no, not as you will naturally conjecture by articulate utterance of oracular notices, but by a variety of gesticulations, which here I have not room to give an account of. Suffice it to say, that no change of weather surprises him, and that in point of the earliest and most accurate intelligence, he is worth all the barometers in the world."

William Cowper – *Letter to Lady Hesketh,*
10 November 1787

Weather forecasts have been attempted for as long as Man has planned ahead. With its beginnings immersed in the crude guesses of the Stone Age hunter, forecasting took on the semblance of a science in the Classical period, became enveloped by myth and magic during the Middle Ages and resumed its status as a science in the eighteenth and nineteenth centuries. More recently it has become transformed by the technologies of space and micro-electronics and has become a multimillion-dollar international business that affects the security of nations and the world's economic future.

Meteorological outposts are located in all parts of the globe – even in the frigid wastes of the Arctic – to help unravel future weather.

The zodiac ceiling in the ancient Egyptian temple at Dendera was orientated towards the Dog Star, Sirius, which after the year 3200 BC rose just before dawn, marking the beginning of the Egyptian new year and the rising of the Nile. As the flooding of the Nile was the most important event in the lives of Egyptian farmers, the Dog Star became the god of the rising waters.

The Pre-Scientific Era

The study of weather forecasting reflects the development of people's beliefs, ideas and skills through the ages. Gradually the art of forecasting has changed from its dim beginnings immersed in mythology to being based on scientific methods using modern technology. As a science, meteorology is relatively young when compared with classical mathematics or astronomy, but simply as a branch of human consciousness it is extremely old. Just how early in Palaeolithic times mankind first began to formulate rules for predicting the weather will probably never be known.

The prehistoric hunting and food-gathering way of life was closely dependent upon the vagaries of the weather and people gradually developed an almost intuitive feeling for atmospheric conditions. This "weather sense" has largely been lost by modern Man, whose livelihood does not usually depend upon the weather and who lives insulated from the natural world by his urbanized environment; weather sense is retained only by people whose lives still depend upon the weather.

However, recent weather extremes, together with increasing social and economic pressures, are reminding even the urban dweller of his inherent vulnerability to atmospheric conditions.

Ancient knowledge concerning the nature and regularity of celestial cycles, used in formulating the first calendars, was correlated with cyclic changes on Earth and became related to the study of weather and natural phenomena. For example, in Mesopotamia the annual cycle of the seasons was defined by astronomical and meteorological observations. Similarly, in Egypt, where material prosperity has always depended upon the annual rise and fall of the River Nile, the periodic appearance of stars in certain constellations, such as the rising of Sirius, the Dog Star, indicated the recurring seasons of flood and drought. One of the earliest and most famous long-range forecasts was made in Egypt when, according to the book of Genesis, Joseph interpreted one of the Pharaoh's dreams as a prediction that seven years of famine were to follow seven years of feast; a prediction that might well have been based on the 14-year cycle of the flooding of the River Nile that had been discovered by Egyptian astronomer-priests.

However, a knowledge of the broad pattern of the annual cycle of the seasons was not the whole story and the need arose to predict short-term weather fluctuations and unseasonable spells of cold, warm, wet or dry conditions. One of the first advances in meteorology was the observation that certain kinds of weather often follow particular types of phenomena. This "sign" meteorology appears to have been independently developed in the different parts of the ancient world – the lower Tigris and Euphrates valleys, the valley of the Nile, the Indus Valley, the Yellow River and the shores surrounding the Mediterranean Sea.

Thus collections of weather omens, proverbs and folk sayings, which were easily committed to memory, gradually evolved about various signs, which were regarded as indicators of coming weather. Although some were based on superstition and mythology, many others reflected a considerable volume of empirical weather wisdom that had been built up from actual observations of natural phenomena – appearance of the sky, winds, optical conditions, the carry of sound, phenological events such as leafing of trees or the first appearance of migratory birds, and many other effects that are significant of atmospheric conditions and are related to coming weather.

This early weather lore embodied the collective experience of countless and nameless past generations of prehistoric hunters, herdsmen, farmers, mariners and others who all led outdoor lives. It became an integral part of the oral traditions of early societies and cultures and was transmitted and augmented from one generation to another. Weather lore eventually became preserved in a literary form following the invention of writing, in about 3000 BC.

Epic poems and philosophical writings of ancient civilizations are particularly rich in weather lore. Babylonian epic poems date as far back as 2000 BC and contain graphic accounts of the Creation and the Flood, in which the power of the gods over the weather is invoked. In particular, the Babylonian "Gilgamesh" epic includes a reference to a violent storm and a description of the subsequent hurricane-force winds, torrential rain and disastrous floods that predates the Old Testament version by a thousand years.

For many centuries before the Christian era, historical documents in the form of clay tablets were kept by the Babylonians living in the fertile river valleys of the Tigris and Euphrates. They indicate that weather prediction was practised extensively as early as the seventh century BC. Babylonian astrologers, or Chaldeans, were public functionaries, charged with the task of predicting terrestrial and astronomical phenomena: droughts, floods, thunderstorms, earthquakes, locust plagues, comets and eclipses. Their predictions were based on "omens" of many kinds, including observations of planetary motion, optical phenomena and the appearance of the sky. They particularly used solar and lunar haloes and were even able to distinguish between the two different types that occur – the small halo of 22 degrees, called "tarbasu" (so named because its radius subtends an angle of 22° from the eye of the observer), and the larger one of 46 degrees, called "supuru". It appears that the Babylonians were trying to discover recurrent

The biblical story of the Deluge, in which the hero Noah received a divine warning of the impending disastrous flood and built an ark to house all animal species, has close affinities with early Babylonian traditions.

Clay tablets from the cuneiform library of the Assyrian King Ashurbanipal (668–627 BC) are now preserved in the British Museum and illustrate how the Babylonians predicted the weather from the appearance of the sky: "When a dark halo surrounds the Moon, the month will bring rain or will gather clouds. When a halo surrounds the Moon and Mars stands within it, there will be a destruction of cattle. When a small halo surrounds the Sun, rain will fall. . . ." They believed that celestial conditions and cycles governed all earthly events.

THE CHINESE CALENDAR
By the third century BC the Chinese had divided their year into months of 30 days and as part of their concern for establishing an accurate calendar, one man was appointed as chief astrologer and recorder of celestial events. Since the chief occupation of the people was agriculture, a cycle of meteorological events was incorporated into the calendar, dividing the year into 24 consecutively named festivals. The name of each festival told people the right time to carry out various farming practices, such as sowing or reaping.

Symbols for two of the four seasons, originally depicted on a Chinese compass, are shown (right).

立夏 Beginning of Summer
小滿 Grain Filling a Little
芒種 Grain in Ear
夏至 Summer Solstice
小暑 Slight Heat
大暑 Great Heat

立冬 Beginning of Winter
小雪 Little Snow
大雪 Heavy Snow
冬至 Winter Solstice
小寒 Little Cold
大寒 Severe Cold

cycles in terrestrial phenomena similar to those they had used so ingeniously and successfully in celestial forecasting and on which they had based their calendar: but no cyclical pattern was ever observed. However, old ideas die hard and many centuries later medieval thunder almanacs or brontologies were still listing "signa tonitrui" – a scheme for predicting weather events that had been developed by the Chaldeans and was based on the belief that weather and harvests could be predicted from thunderclaps heard on specific days.

More than 3000 years ago the Chinese, clustered along the fertile banks of the Yellow River, were able to foretell the coming of the seasons by the stars. By the third century BC, they had established an agricultural calendar or meteorological cycle based on phenological and weather events, with the year divided into 24 consecutively named "festivals". Each festival had its own particular type of weather; earliness or lateness in the occurrence of certain phenological and meteorological events, characteristic of each festival, would have indicated whether certain farming activities, such as the sowing of crops, should have been delayed or advanced.

Crop fertility was ritualized to resurrect the Egyptian Earth goddess, Osiris (*above*).

Neptunalia was a festival to worship Neptune, shown here with his son Triton (*right*), the Roman god of water.

The findings of Roman science were combined with those of Babylonia, Egypt and Greece in the *Historia Naturalis* (*below*) by Pliny (AD 23–79).

In India attempts to predict major events, such as the summer monsoon by noting various weather effects during the preceding months, date back to ancient times. An Indian astronomer, Varāha-mihira, of the sixth century AD, grouped these signs according to the Hindu lunar months, so that major events could be forecast if specific features were observed in the sky in the appropriate month.

In general, peoples of the ancient world regarded natural phenomena as being manifestations of a divine power, and the mythological personification and deification of nature was established in many early societies and cultures. Religious rites were performed by priests to obtain the goodwill of the gods, and in times of crop failure and famine, sacrificial offerings were made to placate the wrath of the deity.

The various kinds of divine agencies who were believed to control the physical world included the Vedic gods of the Indians, Marduk of the Babylonians, Osiris of the Egyptians, Jahweh of the Hebrews and many of the Olympian deities, such as Zeus and Poseidon. Any attempts to explain atmospheric phenomena by natural causes were disapproved of and led to a conflict between religion and science that was to continue for many centuries.

Thus, at the time of the emergence of the ancient Greek civilization, weather knowledge was a curious mixture of mythology and astrology, together with a fair measure of sound empirical knowledge based on actual observations of natural phenomena. The initial shift in attitude from an acceptance that the weather elements were under the personal control of the gods to a more rational and common-sense approach based on observational experience can be detected in some of the epic poems and philosophical works of the ancient Greeks. The earliest Greek poems, such as Homer's *Iliad* and *Odyssey*, which date from about the ninth century BC, still designated certain elements of the weather to personal control of the gods – Zeus being in charge of the air and Poseidon of the sea. But gradually, in later philosophical works, a more rational approach based on observational experience began to emerge.

By the time of Aristotle, who lived between 384 and 322 BC, the scientific approach to meteorology had firmly taken root. Most of the weather elements were objectively discussed in Aristotle's treatise *Meteorologica*, which was to remain the unquestioned authority on all aspects of theoretical meteorology for the next 2000 years. However, then, as now, the general public was far more interested in knowing what the weather was going to do rather than understanding the how and why of it.

In Aristotle's time, weather calendars recording the normal succession of weather events throughout the year – prototypes of modern climatic statistics – were being produced. Such calendars, known as "parapegmata", or peg calendars, were displayed on public buildings in Greek cities. But their value, both then, as indicators of coming weather, and now, as documents of historical weather, is much impaired by the fact that the data used in their compilation were often derived from climatically dissimilar places scattered over the shores and islands of the Mediterranean Sea.

Interest in meteorology continued with the Romans, who began the tradition of compiling encyclopedias of the natural sciences. The best known of these are Pliny's *Historia Naturalis*, which was compiled from some 2000 works by Roman and Greek authors, and Ptolemy's *Tetrabiblos*, which includes a summary of weather signs and became the basic authority for weather prediction by astrology in the Middle Ages.

A fresco, by Raphael, of the Greek philosophers Aristotle and Plato, who were among the first to advocate a more scientific approach to meteorology. Aristotle's pupil Theophrastus (380–285 BC) wrote a treatise, *On weather signs*, which comprised a large collection of forecasting rules and became a major source of weather lore.

Astrometeorology

The decline and fall of the Roman Empire after about AD 400 did not provide a particularly favourable intellectual climate for the progress of knowledge. Although the study of meteorology never completely ceased in Europe, no new ideas emerged on the subject of predicting the weather during the first few centuries of the Christian era. It was not until after the seventh century, following the death of Muhammed in AD 632, that Graeco-Roman, Persian and Indian knowledge became preserved, fused and enriched by the work of a host of Muslim philosophers and scientists that flourished in the early Middle Ages, between the eighth century and the end of the eleventh century AD. Thus Islam rose to become the centre of the civilized world.

The Arabian approach to meteorology through astronomical observations encouraged the traditional belief that the weather could be predicted from studying the motion of heavenly bodies. The inherent Arabian curiosity about astronomy well prepared the ground for the great upsurge of interest in the applied pseudo-science of weather prediction by astrology that was about to occur in the Western World.

Apart from dissident ideas put forward by individuals such as Roger Bacon, who lived between 1214 and 1294, and advocated an experimental approach to science based on actual observations of natural phenomena, Aristotelian theory prevailed. It was regarded as gospel – complete and infallible – by medieval scholars and became incorporated into the doctrine of the Latin Church. This formed an absolute block to all further progress in meteorology, and practical men who wished to apply any new-found knowledge to forecast the weather had to turn to other authorities for guidance. Unfortunately, this led to some false trails, which were followed until the seventeenth century and beyond. Although many of these paths have been proved invalid, they deserve some attention in order to understand the development of modern weather forecasting.

Books claiming to predict Man's destiny, the weather and other natural events from the motions of the stars, planets, Sun, and Moon were enthusiastically received as novel and promising. The new astrological theories held out hope that it might be possible to make longer-range weather predictions rather than simply forecasting the weather for a short period ahead by using "sign" meteorology. Couched in pseudo-scientific terminology and requiring a knowledge of mathematics and astronomy, the literature on astrology was regarded in awe by the populace.

One of the first astrological weather prophecies which attracted much attention and alarmed the whole of the Western World was the "Toledo Letter", of 1185. A certain astronomer called Johannes of Toledo predicted that in September of the following year all the known planets would be in conjunction, which, besides causing a treacherous wind that would destroy almost all buildings,

Astrolabes provided the Arabs with the means to make more accurate astronomical observations and encouraged them to extend the traditional belief that the weather could be predicted by studying the motion of heavenly bodies.

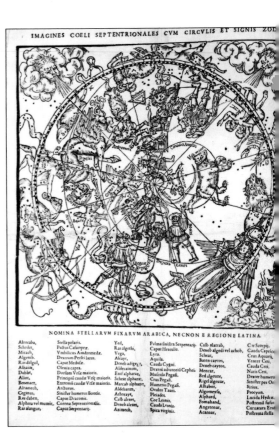

would also bring about a famine and many other disasters. People were so frightened by the prediction that they took all kinds of precautions and even made underground houses for protection. Although the prediction turned out to be entirely false, further "Toledan Letters" were published and circulated during the next two centuries with accompanying portents and calamities such as comets, extraordinary planetary conjunctions and earthquakes.

The great interest in astrometeorology during the Middle Ages is exemplified by the large numbers of tracts on weather prediction in European archives. Astrometeorology even came to enjoy the patronage of rulers and the Church, and even Johannes Kepler, Tycho Brahe and other notable figures in the history of science practised astrology and published weather prognostications.

However, not all scholars in the Middle Ages were convinced of the validity of making weather forecasts based on astrology. One such doubter was Nicole Oresme, who lived between 1323 and 1382 and who recognized the great problems involved in weather prediction. He had little regard for his contemporary astrometeorologists and believed that weather forecasting would only become possible when the proper rules had been discovered – a far-sighted objective

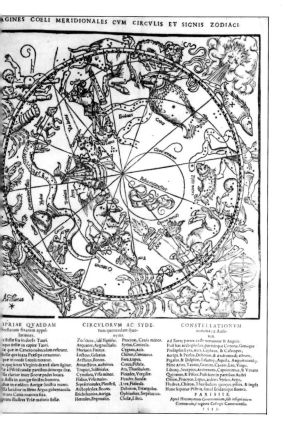

An Arabian painting (*left*) of the zodiac and the constellations with Arabian star names.

Tycho Brahe (1546–1601) with the instruments he used to compile his astrological predictions.

which is still not completely within the grasp of our contemporary twentieth-century meteorologists and forecasters.

The bonus for current research into past climates that emerges from these early attempts to predict the weather by astrological methods is the wealth of daily meteorological observations made available to us by many individuals throughout Europe during the Middle Ages. The manner of making the entries – in the margins of astronomical tables and almanacs – appears to suggest that initially people were not concerned with keeping a detailed record of the weather in its own right, but rather in trying to establish links between certain astronomical phenomena, such as eclipses, planetary conjunctions and phases of the Moon, with particular types of weather. Compiling meteorological statistics to assess the success or failure of previous astrometeorological predictions was also a popular occupation.

During the period between the thirteenth and seventeenth centuries, a gradual change-over can be seen in these records, with astrological entries becoming less frequent and meteorological observations becoming more continuous and orderly. The best of medieval meteorology is exemplified by the work of the English meteorologist William Merle, who has the distinction of being the author of

the earliest known systematic weather record – extending from January 1337 to January 1344. Besides this, he wrote a comprehensive treatise on predicting the weather using an amalgamation of sources – ranging from Aristotle, Virgil, Pliny and Ptolemy to ancient English weather lore.

The heyday of astrometeorology began in the closing years of the Middle Ages and lasted until the birth of scientific meteorology in the seventeenth century. A new style of literature came into vogue, consisting of small tracts known as "prognostica", most of them written in Latin, each containing a prediction of the weather for a single year, prepared in accordance with the rules of astrology. These predecessors of almanacs appeared in astonishing numbers, particularly after advances in the printing industry in the mid-fifteenth century made large-scale multiplication of books possible. In the sixteenth century, 3000 publications of this type were issued by about 600 different prognosticators.

At first only particularly prominent astronomical events, such as extraordinary planetary conjunctions, gave rise to these astrological predictions. One such occurrence, the prognosis made by Justus Stöffler in 1499 for the month of February 1524, created a great sensation. This prognosis, which forecast unusually heavy rainfall for that month, gave rise to an extensive controversy, with authorities being divided as to whether there was to be a universal deluge, like the Noachian one, or merely an exceptionally rainy spell, with local inundations. But in the scores of works published on the subject in Europe, the fact that the three planets Saturn, Jupiter and Mars would all be in the constellation of Pisces at one time during February 1524 was declared to be a sure sign of tremendous downpours. These announcements caused general consternation. Many people left their homes and took refuge on hill tops, where they remained until the fatal month had passed. However, on the day of the predicted event, the weather proved to be unexceptional, the rains failed to appear and no large-scale inundation occurred. From similar past experiences, such as the failure of the "Toledo Letter" prediction over two centuries earlier, one would have thought that this type of forecast would have discouraged astrologers and made the public distrustful. Not at all, the faith in the infallibility of astrological

New printing techniques that were developed in the fifteenth century enabled notable scientists of the time, such as Johann Müller (1436–76), to publish numerous and prolific weather predictions.

predictions continued unabated.

In the sixteenth century the popularity enjoyed by these prognostications for particular years was overtaken by works of a more general character, containing rules for weather predictions which were supposed to be applicable at any time. On the Continent, the most famous popular compendium of this kind was *Die Bauern-Praktik*, which was first published in German in 1508 and became one of the most widely disseminated general works on the weather. It was subsequently translated into all the principal languages of Europe, the English version being known as *The Husbandman's Practice*.

Justus Stöffler's (1452–1531) astrological prediction for the year 1524 did not hold true.

By the eighteenth and nineteenth centuries pocket-sized, paper-bound almanacs became very popular. Besides containing information about the tides, astronomical features and religious festivals, they also contained weather predictions based on astrology – which were always read with great interest. The method adopted in writing these forecasts was to avoid definite statements, especially with regard to time and place, and to let the changeable behaviour of typical mid-latitude weather do the rest. In America, Benjamin Franklin annually wrote and published his own version, *Poor Richard's Almanac*, in which he predicted the weather for 25 years from 1732. While ridiculing the whole subject of astrological prediction in every issue, Franklin knew that popular superstition would cause his almanac to sell well. In fact his average annual sale was as many as 10,000 copies.

On occasions, of course, it has happened that an almanac weather prophet who ventured to make a definite and explicit prediction has turned out to be right on target. The classic example is Patrick Murphy's forecast for 20 January 1838. In his *Weather Almanac* for that year, published in London, England, he noted opposite the date in question: "Fair. Prob. lowest deg. of winter temperature." Amazingly, the day of 20 January proved to be not only the coldest day of the year but was also described as the coldest day of the century in London. The temperature fell to $-20°C$ ($-4°F$) at Greenwich and $-25°C$ ($-13°F$) at Beckenham; the cold was so intense at Doncaster that the River Don froze hard enough for sheep to be roasted on it. This one lucky prediction made its author famous; copies of his almanac were quickly sold out, and in order to satisfy public demand, the work underwent more than 50 reprintings. From the sale of that year's almanac alone Murphy made a profit of over £3000, and the winter of 1837–38 became famous and known in England as "Murphy's Winter".

From earliest times it has been believed that the Moon exerted a control over the behaviour of the atmosphere, and many systems for predicting the weather have been based on this idea. In France, Jean Baptiste Lamarck issued long-range weather predictions based on lunar data in his *Annuaire Météorologique* from 1800 to 1811, and in Germany, Rudolf Falb, who lived between 1838 and 1903, became known as a "lunar prophet". Falb coined the expression "critical days" for dates when the Earth, Moon and Sun occupied certain relative positions, which were supposed, according to his views, to be associated with various types of weather anomalies. Similarly, in Russia, Demchinskii issued long-range weather forecasts, from 1901 to 1903, based on supposed lunar effects for a number of places in Russia and Europe, and later published information even for locations as far afield as the United States, Japan and India. Although his forecasts were severely criticized by contemporary official meteorologists, they were eagerly received by the general public and published in the British newspaper the *Daily Mail*. Like all other past and present amateur weather prophets, Demchinskii presented a challenge to the professional meteorological establishment to provide a service of long-range weather forecasting, which was very much in demand at the time, especially by workers in agriculture, industry and commerce, whose livelihoods depended on the weather.

The late nineteenth century was a period when astrological weather prophets made some even more extraordinary speculations than usual. Forces exerted by bodies such as an invisible Moon revolving around the Earth, or a series of Saturn-like rings surrounding the Earth, or even an elusive planet called Vulcan were said to be influencing our atmosphere. The supposed existence of Vulcan, inside the orbit of Mercury, at one time even received quasi-recognition in standard works on astronomy.

However, the pendulum of scientific inquiry swings to and fro, and despite some earlier ill-conceived beliefs, astrometeorology still flourishes today with the fascinating theory that certain planetary alignments might indirectly affect the weather and seasons by causing a shift in the centre of mass of the solar system.

Birth of Scientific Meteorology

With Leonardo da Vinci as one of its principal precursors, the Scientific Revolution freed science from its medieval constraints. It was inaugurated in 1543 with the publication of the heliocentric theory of the solar system by Nicolaus Copernicus. Although the Copernican theory spread very slowly at

The French naturalist Jean Baptiste Lamarck (1744–1829) became interested in meteorology while studying in Paris.

Members of the Accademia del Cimento demonstrating their new meteorological instruments at a meeting that was attended by Galileo Galilei himself.

WINDS

The important relationship between wind direction and the coming weather was recognized from early times. In Mesopotamia the Babylonians had devised a windrose of eight thumbs, counting the four cardinal points in the order south, north, east and west (sutu, iltanu, sadu, amurra). They formed the intermediate directions by a combination of these. By the beginning of the Christian era wind vanes were being constructed and used to make regular observations and Pliny (AD 23–79) even described the expected wind patterns of the Mediterranean. In the Middle Ages, mankind was subject to the winds of the greater world – fire, water, earth and air – of which Man and the universe were thought to be composed.

Otto von Guericke
(1602–86) was one of the first people to use the barometer for forecasting the weather. The height of the water column in his barometer was indicated on a graduated scale by the outstretched arm of a small wooden figure of a man floating on the water surface.

first, the ancient concept of predicting the weather by the motions of heavenly bodies began to be questioned as it became generally accepted that the annual cycle of the seasons was controlled not by the stars but by the movements of the Earth around the Sun.

Even before meteorological instruments came into general use, sixteenth- and early seventeenth-century astronomers and men of science laid the foundation of meteorology as an exact science by making systematic weather observations. Instrumental meteorological observations began in the seventeenth century with the invention of the thermometer by Galileo Galilei in about 1600 and the barometer by Galileo's pupil Evangelista Torricelli in 1643. Great interest was shown in the new meteorological instruments, which appeared to provide a means of predicting the weather using the scientific method that had been advocated in the 1620s and 1630s by a new brand of philosophers such as Francis Bacon and René Descartes.

International Networks

People realized that the value of meteorological observations would be greatly increased if simultaneous reports made at several different places could be compared. The earliest documented instrumental meteorological observations made in concert were recorded, in Paris and Clermont Ferrand, in France, and Stockholm, in Sweden, between 1649 and 1651. The first attempt at establishing an international network of meteorological observing stations was made in 1653 under the patronage of the

Grand Duke Ferdinand II of Tuscany, who founded the Accademia del Cimento (Academy of Experiments) four years later. Standard instruments were constructed and sent to observers in Florence, Pisa, Bologna, Vallombrosa, Curtigliano, Milan and Parma and later to locations outside Italy as far afield as Paris, Warsaw and Innsbruck. A uniform procedure was devised for making the observations, which included pressure, temperature, humidity, wind direction and state of sky. The reports were entered on special forms and subsequently sent to the Academy for comparison. Although this activity ceased with the closing of the Academy in 1667, it did provide a model for later efforts that were carried out in the eighteenth and nineteenth centuries.

Following the invention of the barometer, a term first introduced by Robert Boyle in 1665, it was recognized that variations in the height of the liquid column were usually followed by certain changes in the weather, such as rain, wind or frost. Before the introduction of the weather map, the barometer, or "weather glass", was the most important tool in weather forecasting. The first documented forecast based on the behaviour of a barometer was made by Otto von Guericke at Magdeburg in Prussia in 1660. He predicted a severe storm from a rapid and large fall of pressure that had occurred on his water barometer two hours before the storm.

With reference to Francis Bacon's earlier project to compile a history of the weather, in 1663 Robert Hooke proposed a scheme for

192

recording daily instrumental and eye observation, "A Method for Making a History of the Weather", which was to be kept in meteorological registers by members of the newly founded Royal Society of London. Two years later Hooke invented the wheel barometer, the first mercury barometer to have various weather terms on its scale.

In France, the Académie Royale des Sciences, founded in 1666, also began to make systematic instrumental observations at its observatory in Paris and similar observations were made in Germany at Hanover in 1678 and Kiel from 1679 to 1714. These were initially instigated by the mathematician and philosopher Gottfried Leibniz, to test the capacity of Hooke's wheel barometer for weather forecasting.

In the eighteenth century further attempts were made to establish international networks of meteorological observing stations. In 1723, James Jurin, Secretary of the Royal Society of London, published an invitation for meteorological observations to be sent annually to the Society. Included in his request were instructions on how these observations were to be made and recorded. For a time, the response was rewarding, with observations being received from England and on the Continent, and in North America and India.

From an investigation of some of these records the English scientists William Derham and George Hadley found that pressure changes did not always occur simultaneously at different places. In a similar experiment with meteorological observations made simultaneously at a number of stations in France, the physicist J. de Borda further found that pressure changes were propagated with a direction and speed that was closely related to the wind velocity. Thus the first steps towards appreciating the concept of travelling pressure systems – so important in present synoptic weather forecasting – were being taken. In the early 1730s a network of meteorological observing stations was established in Siberia by scientists taking part in the Great Northern Expedition led by Vitus Bering, and in 1759 Mikhail Lomonosov also proposed setting up a network of stations in Russia in order to forecast the weather for farmers and mariners.

Despite the early promise and the masses of quantitative data collected since the introduction of the barometer and thermometer at the beginning of the Scientific Revolution, the progress towards finding a satisfactory method of weather forecasting was slow. The German astronomer Tobias Mayer must have voiced the opinion of many of his contemporaries when he suggested that if the

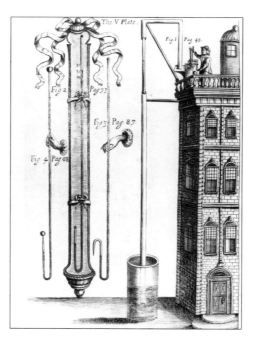

Robert Boyle (1627–91) published a manuscript, *Continuation of New Experiments*, in 1669, which included descriptions of a water barometer (left) and a new siphon barometer (far left); the Royal Society was particularly impressed by the portability of this instrument.

Scientists from all over Europe met at the Académie Royale des Sciences in Paris, to discuss their new ideas.

The tragic death of Vitus Bering on Bering Island in December 1741 marked an end to his expeditions. His reports of Arctic weather and geography later proved to be a valuable contribution to eighteenth-century meteorology.

Benjamin Franklin (1706–90) proved lightning was a form of electricity in an experiment using a kite made of a silk handkerchief, as shown in this painting in the Museum of Philadelphia. Being a statesman as well as a scientist, he arranged for lightning conductors to be fitted to two local public buildings.

atmosphere could be computed in a similar way to that of the motion of the stars, then at least the major effects and perhaps their causes could be identified.

In contrast, examples from the writings of the American Benjamin Franklin illustrate that he appreciated some of the factors involved in attempting to forecast the weather, both in the short and long term, and that this could only be achieved from a well-established observational data base.

On 21 October 1743, he was puzzled by a storm which affected Philadelphia and obscured an eclipse of the Moon, predicted for about 9 p.m., whereas he heard from his brother later that there had been a good sighting of the eclipse on the east coast of America at Boston, 640 kilometres (384 miles) to the northeast, and that the stormy weather had not begun there until nearly 11 p.m. After collecting material from newspaper reports of the event at other places in the colonies, Franklin determined that the storm and its associated northeasterly winds and rain had moved northeast from Georgia to New England. He thus made the first synoptic weather study in America.

Writing later at Passy, near Paris, in 1784, he suggested that the severe winter of 1783–84 might have been due to the dry fog or haze that had been prevalent during the previous summer. He proposed that the turbidity had been caused by particles introduced into the Earth's upper atmosphere either by severe volcanic activity in Iceland during the previous summer or by the disintegration of

meteorites, which had been frequently observed in 1783. Two years later he predicted that the winter of 1786–87 would also be severe in New England, illustrating his pioneering efforts in long-range forecasting.

In France and Germany concerted efforts in making and collecting meteorological observations were being made on an increasingly ambitious scale in the latter part of the eighteenth century. Following the lead of the Dutch physician Hermann Boerhaave, the medical profession became interested in the possibility of finding a relationship between weather and diseases. In 1778 the Société Royale de Médecine was set up in France under the patronage of Louis XVI to maintain detailed and regular correspondence on medical and meteorological matters with doctors throughout the kingdom. In particular, the French meteorologist Louis Cotte was actively involved with establishing and maintaining an extensive network of observing stations for the Society.

Detailed instructions were issued on instrumental operation and exposure and observational procedure, with the request that standard observations of pressure, temperature, wind, humidity, rainfall, evaporation, state of sky and any other significant weather phenomena should be made three times a day at specified times. The correspondents of the Society were also issued with specially printed forms for recording the daily observations during each month. These forms were sent at regular intervals to Paris for perusal and analysis. By 1784 the network

De Borda (1733–99) presented new theories on the dynamics of meteorology to the Academy of Sciences.

Weather lore, recorded in letters, diaries and paintings such as this one (*left*) by Hodges – a rare sighting in 1773 of a waterspout off Cape Stephens in New Zealand – provided valuable information about weather at sea.

comprised over 70 stations and had been extended beyond France to include correspondents in Holland, Germany, Austria, the United States and Persia (now Iran).

Struck by de Borda's experiments made with simultaneous observations earlier in the century, Antoine Lavoisier pressed for the establishment of a network of stations all over Europe, and even over the whole Earth. With all this information Lavoisier believed it should be possible to forecast the weather one or two days ahead. He also advocated that a weather forecast bulletin published every morning would be of great value to society. However, the means to transmit the information quickly to a collecting centre and then to analyse the data in a meaningful way were lacking in Lavoisier's time and had to await developments in communications and meteorology which were to take place later in the nineteenth and twentieth centuries.

During the eighteenth century, Mannheim, in Germany, the capital of the Palatinate of the Rhine, developed into an influential centre of the arts and sciences under its Elector Karl Theodor. In 1780 he founded the Societas Meteorologica Palatina with Johann Hemmer as its director. Again, standard instruments were supplied to correspondents of the Society with instructions on instrumental operation and observational procedure. Like the Société Royale de Médecine, correspondents were requested to make full meteorological observations three times a day. Records were dispatched to Mannheim for collation and publication in the annual *Ephemerides* of the Society. From a nucleus of about a dozen stations, mostly located in central Europe, the network spread extensively from the beginning of 1781 so as to include over 50 observatories from Russia across Europe to Greenland and North America during the next five years. From the entries in these publications it can be seen that the Mannheim Meteorological Society was using a system of weather symbols that owed something of its origins to earlier schemes devised by Pieter van Musschenbroek and Johann Lambert; traces still survive in the present international synoptic weather code.

Besides the officially organized networks of stations, a large number of individuals, such as Thomas Barker of Lyndon Hall, Rutland, and Gilbert White at Selborne, Hampshire, both in England, were making and recording their own meteorological observations during the eighteenth century. Besides these, similar efforts were being made in America by individuals such as Thomas Jefferson at Charlottesville, Virginia. These show that in general people directly or indirectly appreciated the need to build up a good series of actual daily observations so that they could gain a more complete knowledge of atmospheric behaviour in the hope of being able to forecast the weather on a scientific basis. Another valuable source of historical weather data from the seventeenth and eighteenth centuries can be derived from ships' logs.

Nautical Weather Lore
Based on the behaviour of the sea, winds and state of the sky, nautical weather lore has been handed down by countless unknown mariners from the first use of sails on sea-going vessels, dating back to 2000 BC. Since lives were at stake, it is an outstandingly reliable branch of empirical knowledge.

Some of the earliest recorded information about seafaring in antiquity originated from the Mediterranean region during the first millennium BC. For example, in *Works and Days,* written in about 800 BC by Hesiod, advice is given about the best time for sailing, together with warnings about unkind interventions by the weather gods. Major geographical differences of winds and weather were later experienced on more distant voyages; knowledge about large-scale

Assyrian boat tablets give some of the earliest recorded information about seafaring in the Mediterranean region during the first millennium BC and give advice about the best time for sailing, together with warnings about unkind interventions from the gods.

Edmund Halley (1656–1742) published the first map showing the general circulation of the winds, and in 1700 a world map of magnetism (*below*).

Robert Fitzroy (1805–65), captain of HMS *Beagle*, found that his logbooks were vital in obtaining weather details of the world's oceans.

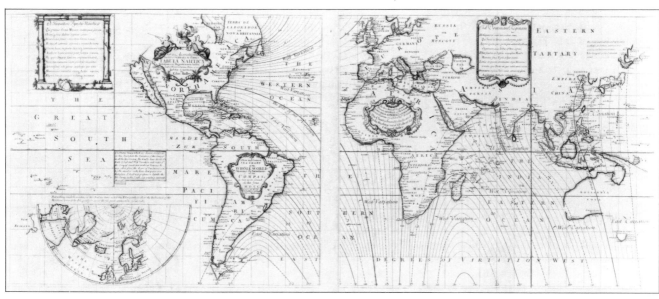

196

weather patterns such as those of the North Atlantic Ocean and wind systems such as the monsoon of the Indian Ocean began to be collected and recorded by the Phoenicians, Norsemen and Arabs.

During the fifteenth and sixteenth centuries, the search for sea routes to India and Cathay by early explorers such as Christopher Columbus, Vasco da Gama and Ferdinand Magellan, and the long voyages of discovery made by explorers such as William Dampier, Edmond Halley and James Cook resulted in a much wider knowledge being gained of the geographical distribution of wind and sea-current circulation patterns and the general weather conditions over the Earth's surface.

Besides his celebrated memoir on winds, Edmond Halley made a further practical contribution to marine meteorology by taking command of the ship *Paramour* from 1698 to 1700. This was for a special voyage to the South Atlantic, and was the first of its kind undertaken for purely scientific purposes. As an ordinary barometer was not suitable at sea because the motion of the ship caused the mercury to pump violently up and down, Halley took a "marine barometer" – a combination of an air and spirit thermometer designed by Robert Hooke.

Although Halley reported that his personal barometer of Hooke's design had never failed to give advance warning of bad weather, it does not appear to have been generally accepted for use at sea; apart from on ships that were specially commissioned for scientific duties, like those of Edmond Halley and James Cook, mariners on ordinary naval vessels and merchantmen in the seventeenth and eighteenth centuries continued to rely on ancient nautical lore for guidance about the coming weather. Like farmers, they practised the art of single-observer weather prediction. For observers on land, this had been considerably improved with the use of mercury barometers, which, by the end of the seventeenth century, had become generally available from instrument-makers in London, England. The publication of collections of rules based on barometric pressure readings also facilitated forecasting the weather on land.

It was not until the nineteenth century that a satisfactory method of making pressure observations at sea was obtained. From the beginning people realized that the barometer inscriptions introduced by Robert Hooke in the latter half of the seventeenth century were misleading. The original inscriptions related particular weather terms such as "much rain", "changeable", "very dry",

with certain heights of the mercury column, which did after all only suggest the experience of people in London, and mariners, whose knowledge of the weather comes from all parts of the world, could never have set much store by them. This was not rectified until the 1850s, when Admiral Robert Fitzroy, as head of the newly established Meteorological Department of the Board of Trade, authorized that the inscriptions should be omitted on marine barometers; he realized that it was more important to note changes in the height of the mercury column over a known period in order to forecast the weather than by simply noting the actual height at any particular time.

However, forecasting methods were to change quickly due to the use of synoptic weather maps, which were first developed during the early 1800s in central Europe.

Beginnings of Synoptic Meteorology

Despite a greater understanding of the formation, shape and movement of hurricanes and depressions that had been gained from specific investigations into their nature, meteorologists of the 1830s and 1840s felt frustrated because it was still not possible for them to forecast the weather a day or so ahead; there continued to be no means by which actual observations could be collected quickly enough to produce a synoptic picture of the current weather situation that could then be analysed. The idea of synoptic weather mapping was not followed up immediately because of this problem of communications. H. W. Brandes, professor of mathematics and physics at the University of Breslau (now Wroclaw in Poland), was the first to have developed the idea of synoptic weather mapping by comparing meteorological observations made simultaneously over a wide area. But then, by one of those remarkable coincidences that makes the history of science such a fascinating subject, a technological development occurred which matched the theoretical achievements that had already been made.

Samuel Morse first conceived the idea of the telegraph in 1832 and by about 1840 he had made it possible for it to be used as a workable system for rapid communications. This, together with its almost immediate application by meteorologists, revolutionized meteorology as dramatically as the invention of the thermometer and barometer had done some 200 years before. From 1840 onwards, rapid advances were made in the field of weather forecasting.

In 1842, Carl Kreil of the Prague Observa-

Robert Hooke (1635–1703) designed the first sea-going barometer in 1667. It was composed of an air thermometer mounted alongside a spirit thermometer; the difference in their readings was converted into pressure units by a sliding scale.

tory suggested that meteorological observations should be collected by telegraphy as a basis of forecasting. This plan was put into practice at almost the same time in both the United States and Great Britain. From then on developments took place simultaneously on both sides of the Atlantic. In 1847 Joseph Henry, Secretary of the Smithsonian Institution in America, proposed to organize a network of meteorological observational stations across the United States. He envisaged that telegraphic links between the eastern States and the recently opened-up western territories would provide a ready means of giving warning to observers in the eastern States of storms approaching from the west.

The following year in England, the *Daily News* commissioned the balloonist James Glaisher to organize the collecting of standardized meteorological observations from a network of stations in the British Isles. The observations were made daily at 9 a.m. and telegraphed to London so that they could be published in that day's issue of the newspaper. The first of these "Daily Weather Reports" appeared on 31 August 1848. Although daily weather maps were not printed in the paper, it does appear that Glaisher was preparing manuscript charts. To demonstrate the new invention, the English Electric Telegraph Company, again with the aid of Glaisher, exhibited a "Register

Map indicating conditions of the atmosphere on the same day in several parts of Great Britain'', at the Great Exhibition held in London in 1851.

Meanwhile, in America, Henry had negotiated a series of agreements with telegraph companies whereby operators signalled weather reports to the Smithsonian Institution in return for the provision of meteorological instruments. In 1849, over 200 observers were making daily weather reports for the Smithsonian, where, for the interest of visitors, the collected observations were displayed on a large map. Daily reports were also tabulated and supplied to the *Washington Evening Post* for publication. However, between 1861 and 1865 these activities were temporarily abandoned because of the American Civil War. The telegraphic links diligently forged by Henry in setting up a nationwide network of meteorological stations were broken and the system was sadly closed down in 1862. After hostilities had ended, the Smithsonian network was re-established, but never on the same scale as before.

In contrast, the development of weather forecasting in Europe was brought forward by a wartime disaster – this time wrought by nature rather than by man; the losses suffered by the Anglo–French Fleet in the severe storm of 14 November 1854 at Balaclava during the Crimean War stimulated official

The first synoptic chart was prepared by Elias Loomis (1811–81) and showed a storm which affected the eastern US in 1842 (*below*). He used arrows of different lengths to represent the direction and force of the wind; regions of clear and cloudy weather, rainfall, snowfall and fog were coloured blue, brown, yellow, green and red respectively.

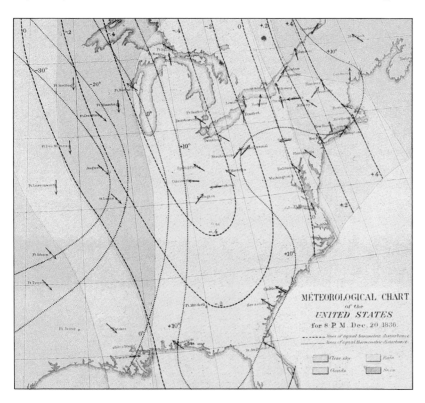

interest in the synoptic study of weather systems. Urbain Le Verrier, Director of the Paris Observatory, later collected weather data to prove that this storm had travelled eastwards across Europe. In France, this led to the establishment of the first national storm-warning service, based on the collection of telegraphic weather reports. The response in Britain was to appoint Robert Fitzroy, an Admiral of the Royal Navy, as Head of the Meteorological Department of the Board of Trade – the first official meteorological post in the United Kingdom.

The Department began by preparing a series of daily weather maps based on simultaneous observations made at a number of stations on land as well as at sea within the area 40°N to 70°N and 10°E to 30°W. Besides the established observatories, ships' captains, lighthouse keepers and private individuals were later invited to assist in a trial scheme of preparing daily weather maps over a larger area by sending their daily registers at monthly or quarterly intervals to Fitzroy in London. The United States co-operated with this plan by arranging for observations to be made, collected and sent to Fitzroy.

Receiving daily telegraphic weather reports from 15 British stations plus telegraphic reports via Paris from European stations, Fitzroy began publishing generalized three-day forecasts of the weather in April 1861. But, unfortunately, other scien-tists advising the Board of Trade felt that Fitzroy had exceeded his brief in issuing forecasts instead of merely giving warnings of actual storms that had already been reported at outlying stations. As a result, after his tragic death by suicide in 1865, forecasts were temporarily discontinued.

Fearing the kind of criticism that had been levelled at Fitzroy, the new Meteorological Office, which had been transferred from the Board of Trade to the Royal Society in 1867, attempted to continue the forecasting service by simply using empirical rules. As these attempts proved to be rather unsuccessful, synoptic charts and a "daily weather report" began to be prepared again by 1872. At first forecasts were only issued from one event to another, but became more systematic as time went by, with daily forecasts eventually being resumed for government offices, newspapers and many other subscribers. Fitzroy's original system of transmitting storm warnings by telegraphy to coastal stations, where "cautionary signals" were hoisted, was also resumed in February 1874.

At the Paris Observatory Le Verrier, originator of international weather telegraphy, began to issue regular weather forecasts in 1863, based on some of the earliest known actual synoptic weather maps for western Europe, which were published in the *Bulletin International de l'Observatoire de Paris*. Whereas Fitzroy had abstrusely indi-

Daily weather maps (*below*) were compiled from a variety of sources besides established observatories; ships' captains, lighthouse keepers and private individuals sent daily registers at monthly or quarterly intervals to Fitzroy as part of his experiment in synoptic mapping during 1860.

James Glaisher (1809–1903) made numerous risky meteorological hot-air balloon ascents (*left*), and on one flight, while testing the composition of the air at 8840 metres (29,000 feet), was almost asphyxiated. He was the last of the scientific balloon pioneers.

In the Great Exhibition of 1851 (*above*), daily weather maps were among the popular items that were sold for the price of one penny. They were collated using balloon data and telegraphy and denoted pressure, wind and the general state of the weather.

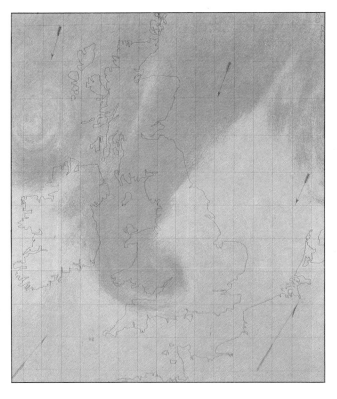

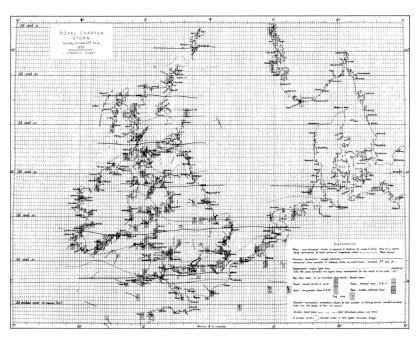

Fitzroy's synoptic chart of the eastern North Atlantic region (*above*), published soon after the "*Royal Charter* Storm" of 29 October 1859, illustrates early techniques of mapping.

The sinking of ships like the *Great Eastern* (*right*) in September 1861 and the loss of numerous lives at sea encouraged the issue of regular gale warnings using telegraphy.

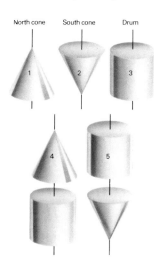

Cautionary signals were issued by Fitzroy in 1861 to coastguard stations so that, from information received by telegraphy, ships could be warned of oncoming bad weather. The system used cones and drums and the various signals were: a cone (1), indicating an approaching gale from the north; an inverted cone (2), indicating an approaching gale from the south and a drum (3), indicating successive gales. A cone and drum (4 and 5) predicted severe gales.

cated pressure by lines drawn vertically from the parallels of latitude on his charts of the "*Royal Charter* Storm" of October 1859, in which over 400 people were drowned off the coast of Anglesey, the adoption, by Le Verrier, of isobars to represent the pressure field was far more satisfactory for analysis and has been used ever since.

The French introduced many important innovations to synoptic weather mapping, and during the 1860s and 1870s the service became one of the best in Europe; by 1864 information was being received from 50 stations in Europe, and in its Bulletin, the Paris Observatory also published a large number of observations made in America, Africa and over the Atlantic.

After 1865 the idea of establishing a national weather service also occurred to many people in America. In 1869, Cleveland Abbe, Director of the Cincinnati Observatory, Ohio, founded an unofficial system of telegraphic weather stations with the help of the Western Union Telegraphic Company and regular bulletins and weather maps soon began to be published. In 1870, the Federal Meteorological Service was established by the United States Government as a division of the Army Signal Service under the direction of General Albert Myer. As with the original British and French meteorological organizations, this service was nominally created for

the purpose of giving warnings of storms on the Great Lakes and the sea coasts rather than for the issue of general weather predictions.

However, because of public demand, regular weather predictions were begun in 1871 and immediately became the most popular feature of the service. A "Study Room" group of the country's leading meteorologists was formed with Abbe as their chief. The predictions were known as "probabilities" until 1876, when the term "indications" was substituted. This was finally changed to "forecasts" in 1889. In the following year the Signal Service was reorganized under civilian control and became known as the US Weather Bureau.

Advances in synoptic studies were also being made in the rest of Europe. A German department of weather telegraphy was set up under the leadership of W. Köppen and a Norwegian Meteorological Institute was established by H. Mohn in 1866. During the 1890s the first upper-air soundings using meteorgraphs (the forerunners of radiosonde instruments) that were carried aloft by balloons or kites were made in both Europe and America. Instrumental data from these ascents gave a better understanding of the vertical structure of weather systems in the troposphere and led to the discovery of the stratosphere, where, to the astonishment of nineteenth-century physicists, the tempera-

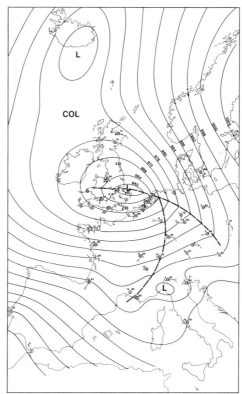

Early synoptic maps, such as those made by Brandes (1777–1834), who realized the value of plotting observations made simultaneously from different locations, are being painstakingly reconstructed (*left*) so that modern methods of analysis using isobars and fronts can be used to evaluate climates of the historical past.

ture remains constant with height.

A new type of synoptic chart depicting how pressure changes with time was introduced in Russia by Miller of the St. Petersburg Observatory in 1864. Lines of equal pressure change, later termed isallobars, were drawn through places where the rise and fall in height of the barometer over a given interval of time, usually three hours, was the same. These isallobaric charts were used in conjunction with ordinary synoptic weather maps to detect the formation and movement of pressure systems. This novel approach became an accepted and widely used technique in forecasting.

In 1913, the Norwegian meteorologist V. Bjerknes became the Director of the Leipzig Geophysical Institute, where he continued to develop his ideas on the dynamics and physics of meteorology. However, due to increasingly difficult working conditions during the First World War, Bjerknes returned to Norway in July 1917, accompanied by his son Jakob and his assistant H. Solberg. Because of the hostilities, neutral Norway had become cut off from meteorological data by the combatants and weather forecasting was made virtually impossible. But this was to be the spur for action, and during the latter part of the First World War Bjerknes established the Bergen Geophysical Institute in Norway with the major objective of improving the nation's weather forecasting service. A very dense network of observing stations was established, especially over southern Norway, using "indirect aerology" – a method based on detailed cloud reports – to make up for the lack of upper-air measurements and soundings.

Analysis of the synoptic weather maps that began to be constructed at Bergen from 1918 revealed the fine structure of weather that had been mostly overlooked by meteorologists in the nineteenth century. The major contribution of meteorology of the Bergen Geophysical Institute was in developing a specific method of analysis that helped to reduce the subjective element in weather forecasting. Bjerknes and his colleagues produced synoptic models of fronts which made it possible to integrate observations made over wide areas into comprehensive weather patterns. The identification of a definite life-cycle in the development of frontal low pressure systems, from youth through maturity to old age, provided the means to predict cyclonic activity – an important advance on merely extrapolating their future movement. A further important contribution to weather analysis and forecasting was made by the Swedish meteorologist Tor Bergeron, also a member of the Bergen School, who identified and classified air masses according to their thermal properties and moisture conditions.

Helium-filled balloons (*far right*) are used to lift apparatus for investigating the upper atmosphere to altitudes of 35–40 kilometres (20–25 miles) above the Earth's surface.

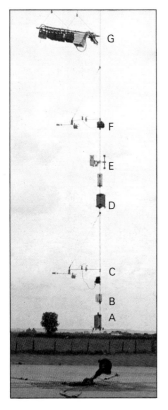

The lowest layer of the atmosphere – the boundary layer – is investigated by instruments tethered to balloons (*above*). Attached to a line is a radio transmitter (A), a pressure sensor (B), a radiometer to measure radiation (C), a radio transmitter (D) to send turbulence probe data to a ground receiver, the turbulence probe itself (E), a radiometer to measure net incoming and outgoing radiation (F) and, finally, (G) nearest to the balloon and at the highest point, are instruments which measure water droplet size in cloud and fog.

The Upper Air

With the introduction of balloon soundings in the 1920s, speculations about the behaviour of the upper air could be compared with actual observations, and although many of the ideas about the structure of storms, inferred from the Bergen "indirect aerology" studies, were confirmed, fronts in the upper air appeared to be transition zones rather than the sharp discontinuities depicted on surface maps.

Balloon-borne radio-sonde instruments which could transmit measurements of pressure, temperature and humidity to a receiving station on the ground first became practicable in the late 1930s. This initiated the establishment of hemisphere-wide networks of upper-air stations during and soon after the Second World War, enabling upper-level charts for the entire Northern Hemisphere to be constructed for the first time.

Today, meteorological observations, both from the surface and from the upper air, are made simultaneously at regular intervals at thousands of stations all over the world. They are rapidly exchanged by an international communications system using radio, cable and satellite links to central forecasting offices, where the observations are analysed and redistributed at national level in the form of weather charts and forecasts.

Up to the 1950s weather forecasts were almost entirely produced by synoptic methods; the current weather situation was analysed on surface maps by drawing isobars and fronts together with distinguishing areas of significant weather, such as rain, thunderstorms and fog, and on upper-air charts by drawing pressure contours and thickness lines. Radio-sonde ascents, plotted on aerological diagrams, were also studied to obtain information about the variation of temperature and humidity with height. After examination of the depicted circulation patterns, in relation to those drawn on earlier maps, the movement and development of pressure and weather systems, for example lows, highs, areas of precipitation and fine weather, were extrapolated to produce similar charts for the future, 24 hours ahead.

For all this, the forecaster required a knowledge of synoptic models and rules, an experience of the way similar situations had developed in the past, an understanding of the physics and dynamics of the processes involved and, not least, an indefinable grasp of the different ways in which the atmosphere behaves. This impressive combination of experience, skill and judgement was developed to a fine degree by many forecasters of

this era. By their efforts, forecasting gradually developed a higher degree of accuracy during the first half of the twentieth century than ever before, but there was always an element of subjectivity which continued to make forecasting as much an art as a science.

From a historical point of view, the level of forecasting skill in the 1950s had probably reached a limiting value in terms of human capacity. It became an increasingly difficult task to assemble, assimilate and interpret the huge amount of data in time to keep pace with the weather.

With the innovation of high-speed electronic computers that have the capacity to handle large quantities of data and to perform complex calculations very speedily, it was only natural that meteorological services should begin to turn to this new technology in order to achieve a more objective method of weather prediction.

Numerical Forecasting

Bjerknes made a pioneering effort in numerical forecasting and numerical prediction methods that have transformed weather forecasting over the past three decades. To put their development into perspective, one must look back to the early part of the twentieth century. Although the name of Bjerknes is usually connected with the Polar Front theory that was introduced during the First World War, it was an earlier concept – the idea of applying hydrodynamical principles to the synoptic map, presented by Bjerknes in 1904 – that was to have a far greater impact on weather forecasting in the long run. Bjerknes's farsighted research programme was funded by the Carnegie Foundation from 1905 until 1941, which enabled him to engage a number of talented assistants who became internationally known as the "Bergen School".

Influenced by the work of Bjerknes and his co-workers in Norway, the British mathematician L. F. Richardson began to formulate a new approach to the problem of predicting the weather by numerical methods in 1911. During the First World War Richardson continued to pursue his ideas while serving with a Quaker ambulance unit in France. In the confusion of a battle in 1917 his manuscript was lost, but, happily, was found again some months later under a heap of coal. Five years later he published his results in *Weather Prediction by Numerical Process* – a prophetic work which has become a classic in the history of forecasting. Richardson also had a vivid imagination – his fantasy: "A Forecast-Factory", of 64,000 human computers,

equipped with desk calculators, to keep ahead of the weather on a global basis was unfortunately not a practicable proposition; the computational work involved in such a programme would have been impossible to carry out with the comparatively unsophisticated technology available in 1922.

After the Second World War, interest in numerical weather prediction was revived with the development of high-speed electronic computers, together with the expansion of meteorological observing networks, both at the Earth's surface and in the upper air.

In 1950 a model of large-scale atmospheric behaviour was used to make the first successful numerical forecast, and by the mid-1950s forecasts based on numerical methods began to be issued in the United States. Electronic computers were later acquired by other national meteorological services and an increasing number of daily weather predictions based on three different levels of the atmosphere were being made in the 1960s.

However, it was soon realized that, although the models were giving fairly satisfactory predictions of the larger-scale weather systems, it was not possible to obtain commensurate forecasts of smaller-scale disturbances, such as small depressions, fronts and jet-streams. Consequently, with the increasing capacity of computers, far more sophisticated prediction models using up to ten atmospheric levels were developed. In 1980, plans were in hand for introducing a new model with yet more levels, which would allow an improved analysis of the surface and jet-stream levels as well as a representation of the stratosphere.

Despite all these technological developments, predictions produced by numerical methods from automatically processed data still ultimately depend upon human forecasters. Meteorologists continued to have an important role to play in forecasting by monitoring the numerical processes and modifying the products in the light of their experience of atmospheric behaviour. Their basic understanding of the numerical analysis and forecast models is important in case there are any errors in the data being used; also

The main computer in the Richardson's Wing of the Meteorological Office at Bracknell, England, stores a mathematical model of the atmosphere. It amalgamates all incoming data to produce a numerical forecast on a video screen at a computer terminal which is rapidly evaluated by an expert forecaster (*below*).

new observations which have been received after processing have to be taken into account, together with data derived from the latest satellite pictures. The final responsibility for the interpretation and presentation of weather information and forecasts to industry, commerce and the general public remains in the hands of human forecasters.

Long-range Forecasts

The history of scientific long-range forecasting began in 1784, when Benjamin Franklin suggested that the cold winter of 1783–4 was related to a reduction of insolation – the amount of sunlight received by the Earth. He thought this may have been caused by extensive dust veils thrown up by the violent volcanic eruptions in Iceland and Japan the previous summer. However, it was nearly a century later before the next major advance was made.

The discovery by de Bort in 1881 of the existence of large semi-permanent areas of high and low pressure, which he termed "great centres of action", was an important step forward in long-range predictions. It soon became clear that meteorological conditions over wide areas and for extended periods were determined by these large-scale features of the general circulation and that the prediction of their varying extent and position would be of great value. But since no physical theory was available to explain the evolution of these features, a number of investigations were carried out using statistical techniques. This was the beginning of the study of teleconnections, whereby atmospheric events in areas remote from each other were analysed and compared by long-range forecasters.

Organized research into long-range forecasting began in India following a disastrous famine in 1877 caused by the failure of the monsoon rains that year. Six years later the first long-range scientific forecast of the Indian monsoon was made. It was based on a relationship that had been established between the incidence of summer drought in the Indian plains and snowfall accumulation during the preceding winter and spring over the Himalayan mountains.

By the beginning of the twentieth century the success of the national meteorological services in short-range forecasting had encouraged the general public to hope that it might become possible to predict the weather for the coming month or season. Although meteorologists of the time knew that it was impossible to meet this wish, demands from agricultural, commercial and maritime in-

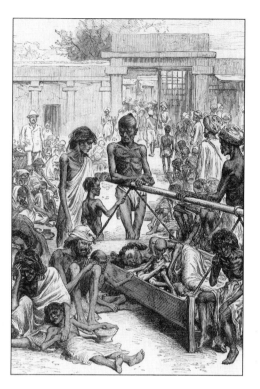

The famine in India in 1877, caused by the failure of the monsoon, led to more organized research into long-range forecasting. Attempts were made to forecast future Indian monsoons and to correlate them with other factors such as the amount of snowfall in the Himalayas.

terests were pressing. Eventually, in 1908, in response to public pressure, the US Weather Bureau began experimenting with the preparation of generalized weekly forecasts based on experimental methods, and two years later, on the basis of this research, they began issuing them regularly.

A concerted attack by the Massachusetts Institute of Technology and the US Weather Bureau under C.-G. Rossby was begun in 1935 to determine a more scientific basis for long-range forecasting. This led to the important discovery that the evolution of the "centres of action" were closely related to correspondingly large-scale and slow-evolving systems in the upper air. This concept provided J. Namias, from the Chicago School of Meteorology, with the much sought-after rationale for developing an objective procedure for long-range predictions and led to the idea of issuing "30-day forecasts". After several years of experimenting, using a combination of statistical, synoptic and physical techniques, the US Weather Bureau began issuing such forecasts to the public in 1948, together with charts of the Northern Hemisphere showing areas that were expected to be warmer or cooler, wetter or drier than average during the forthcoming 30-day period.

Meanwhile a different approach had been made in Russia. In 1912 the Institute of Long-Range Weather Forecasts was established at the Central Geophysical Observatory in St.

Petersburg with B. P. Multanovsky as its head. He began a study of long-range forecasting using synoptic methods. Within a few years he had developed a system of classifying weather systems based on the mean tracks of anticyclones. He also developed the concept of "natural synoptic periods", during which certain well-defined regions became affected, either by a series of lows or a series of anticyclones. On the basis of these ideas the first regular long-range forecasts, initially for between five to seven days and then for whole seasons, were issued in the USSR in 1922. The methods established by the Multanovsky School were to remain more or less in continuous use for long-range forecasting in Russia up to the present day.

In Germany a Research Institute of Long-Range Weather Forecasting was established by F. Baur in 1929. Besides the issue of 10-day

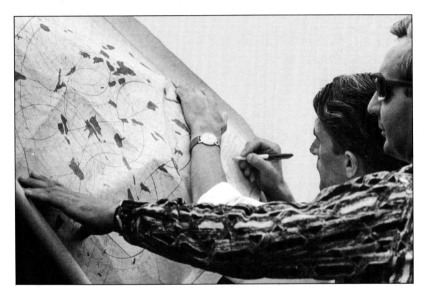

Forecasting hailstorm clouds so that they can be dispersed artificially using anti-hail guns has prevented extensive damage to crops in the northern Caucasus, and the Armenian and Georgian areas of Russia.

forecasts during the summer months of the 1930s, experimental monthly and seasonal forecasts were prepared by the Institute. In the early stages of his research, Baur tried to resolve the problem of long-range forecasting by correlation methods, with the main objective being to establish a link between the atmospheric circulation over the Atlantic and subsequent weather conditions in central Europe. Although many persistencies and recurrent processes were identified, Baur later attempted to improve the accuracy of the forecasts by introducing synoptic methods. Following the lead of de Bort and Multanovsky, he recognized that lows and highs are steered along fairly definite paths by certain large-scale features of the general circulation which he termed

"Grosswetterlagen".

As the weather of the British Isles is affected at different times by maritime, continental, polar and tropical characteristics it is far more difficult to forecast – even for a few days ahead let alone on a longer time scale – than it is in continental regions such as North America and Eurasia. It was only after pressure from both public and press following the severe winter of 1962–3 that the UK Meteorological Office were stimulated to issue their first monthly forecast.

The method that came to be adopted, under the direction of R. C. Sutcliffe, was mainly based on analogues and physical reasoning and at the end of each monthly period the previous month's weather was reviewed by a team of forecasters. Thermal charts depicting mean isotherm patterns between the 1000 and 500 millibar pressure levels were used in conjunction with charts showing mean sea-level pressure patterns, together with maps of their anomalies. This examination was combined with an analysis of the circulation patterns and the large-scale synoptic situation over the British Isles and adjacent areas, using established catalogues of weather types that were first devised by Professor H. H. Lamb and Professor Baur and synoptic indices devised by R. Murray. This process was followed by a computer search through the long-range data bank for analogues, that is comparable periods in previous years during which the weather pattern bore a close resemblance to that of the month under review. The forecast was then prepared on the basis of developments that occurred in the analogous situations. The confidence of the prediction depended on the degree of agreement in the analogues selected. This approach was supplemented with a study of any anomalies that might have occurred in the sequence of weather patterns of the month under review.

However, by the late 1970s, monthly forecasting in the Meteorological Office had reached an impasse comparable to that which had faced short-range forecasting before the advent of the electronic computer in about 1950. Only a modest level of success had been achieved and a fresh approach was required before there could be any hope of improvement. Owing to economic measures the service was suspended at the end of 1980, but the practical experience and theoretical knowledge gained over an operational period of 17 years was of great value.

One of the main objectives of the current Global Atmospheric Research Programme (GARP) and the European Centre for

Medium-Range Weather Forecasts, established in the United Kingdom, is to produce extended-range forecasts for four to ten days ahead. The Centre was officially opened on 15 June 1979, and operational forecasting began in the same year. Programming is more complex and demands more powerful computing facilities than those needed for short-range forecasting. This is because the prediction model has to include information about the physical and dynamical processes that determine the formation and life-cycle of low-pressure systems and anticyclones yet to appear on the synoptic scene. For predicting the development and movement of existing weather systems, the model also has to include details of the initial atmospheric state.

For this, and for long-range forecasting in general, it is vitally important that a better understanding of the large-scale anticyclonic behaviour that occurs at times in the westerly flow of air in mid-latitudes is obtained. These anticyclonic developments create a "blocking" action which impedes the zonal movement of low-pressure systems. Once established this situation is self-maintaining and can persist for many days or weeks, giving rise to anomalous spells of extreme weather – cold or hot, wet or dry. At present blocking patterns are being studied intensively so that a numerical model may be designed for their prediction.

The Effect of the Oceans

In 1969, during the latter part of a life-long study of weather forecasting, J. Bjerknes pioneered the investigation of air-sea interactions at the University of California in Los Angeles, America. He showed that large-scale changes of atmospheric circulation over the equatorial part of the Pacific Ocean are associated with a local warm water current –

The anchovy fishing industry off the Peruvian coast (*above*), which depends on coastal upwelling of cold, deep water bringing nutrients to the surface, is seriously affected in years when the tropical El Niño current extends farther south than usual, preventing the upwelling from reaching the surface. The Niño current is associated with severe weather conditions farther afield in North America.

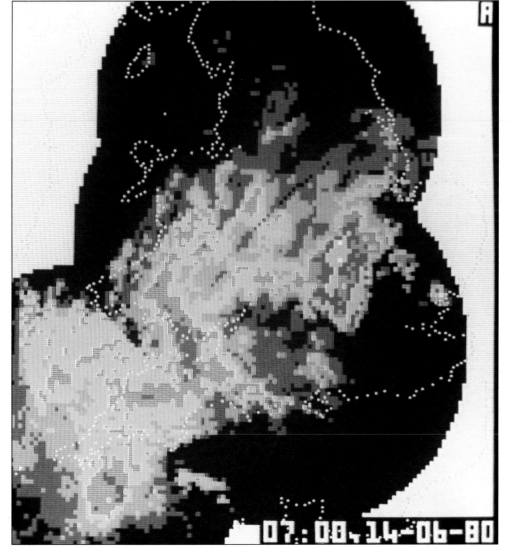

Radar echoes of falling rain from several stations are processed by computer and displayed on a coloured television set; the varying intensities of rain are indicated by coded colours. This system allows information to become available almost instantaneously and to be updated several times an hour for accurate rain and snow forecasts.

Meteostat 1, the geostationary weather satellite launched by the European Space Agency on 9 December 1977, remains fixed in space at a height of 36,000 kilometres (22,370 miles) above a point on the equator. It continuously scans one large area of the Earth and every 30 minutes it transmits global cloud pictures. The photograph (*right*), is its first raw image.

International co-operation is important in meteorology so that cloud pictures, such as those taken by the Soviet Meteor satellite (*below*) of the Southern and Northern Hemispheres can be compiled and used to provide vital information on areas where few conventional ground-based observations are made.

"El Niño" – which occurs off the coast of South America in certain years, causing disastrous effects on Peruvian marine and bird life. It was further demonstrated by Namias that "El Niño"-type anomalies are associated with and may explain the occurrence of some of the more severe North American winters. Also, in 1970 similar connections were found by Ratcliffe and Murray between circulation patterns over the British Isles and preceding sea-surface temperature anomalies in the North Atlantic, south of Newfoundland.

Because they remain stable for a long time, sea-surface temperature anomalies can be regarded as part of a long-term "memory" of the combined ocean–atmosphere system and need to be fully integrated into numerical prediction models in order to produce more successful long-range forecasts on monthly and seasonal time-scales.

Global Weather Programmes

The launching of Sputnik 1 in 1957 by the USSR made the idea of obtaining a global view of weather from space a practical proposition, and in 1960 the first fully equipped meteorological satellite, TIROS 1, was launched by the USA. Acting in response to President Kennedy's 1961 proposal for an international weather prediction programme, the United Nations requested the World Meteorological Organization (WMO) and the International Council of Scientific Unions (ICSU) to develop a world meteorological system. The United Nations resolution led to the formation of two major programmes: a global meteorological system undertaken by the WMO and a global atmospheric research programme jointly undertaken by the WMO and the ICSU.

In 1963 the new global meteorological system, in which actual and potential developments in satellites, computers, automatic weather stations and telecommunication techniques would be incorporated, was endorsed by the Fourth Congress of the WMO at Geneva under the name of World Weather Watch (WWW). Implementation of the programme began in 1968.

WWW is a global meteorological system which comprises the facilities and operations of the national weather services of all 150 members of the WMO. In the basic WWW observation system, simultaneous surface-based observations are made at standard times every day by about 9200 land stations and about 7000 ships at sea, and upper-air observations are made by about 850 stations. Global observations from space are made by five geostationary and five polar-orbiting satellites.

World Meteorological Centres, located at Moscow and Washington in the Northern Hemisphere and at Melbourne in the Southern Hemisphere, collect, process and disseminate these observations and prepare analyses and forecasts on a global basis. Regional centres prepare predictions for more limited areas, while national centres are responsible for weather services in their own countries.

The formation of WWW focused attention on the two outstanding problems in weather forecasting: inadequate data from the Southern Hemisphere and incomplete understanding of tropical weather systems (which, in many respects, behave differently from those in mid-latitudes). When dealing with periods of more than just a few days ahead these deficiencies in data and knowledge have an important bearing on weather forecasting in temperate latitudes. In response, co-operative efforts by WMO members have been made to overcome these problems in a number of experimental global research programmes.

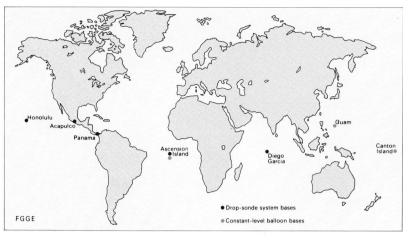

FGGE

● Drop-sonde system bases
● Constant-level balloon bases

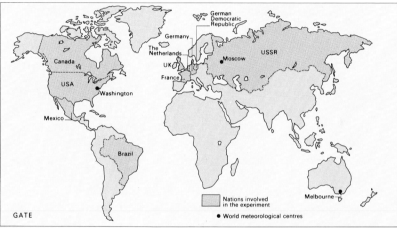

GATE

Nations involved in the experiment

● World meteorological centres

The Global Atmospheric Research Programme (GARP), jointly undertaken by the WMO and ICSU, was the first international project entirely centred on meteorology. It was primarily designed to develop the study of global atmospheric behaviour in order to extend the time-scale of numerical weather forecasting to its theoretical limit.

The GARP Atlantic Tropical Experiment (GATE), the first major observational project of GARP, took place in the summer of 1974, from 15 June to 30 September. It was probably the largest and most complex scientific experiment ever undertaken up to that time, involving some 5000 personnel from ten nations – Brazil, Canada, France, West Germany, East Germany, Mexico, The Netherlands, UK, USA and USSR.

It incorporated 39 specially equipped ships, 13 research aircraft and several meteorological satellites, together with land-based weather stations in over 50 African and South American countries. These observations were collected over a region covering one-third of the Earth's tropical belt, centred on the Atlantic, off Dakar on the west coast of Africa, the field headquarters of the experi-

In the First Garp Global Experiment (FGGE) in 1979, packages of instruments attached to parachutes were dropped from aircraft based at Panama, Acapulco, Honolulu, Diego Garcia and Ascension Island to collect data on the wind, temperature and humidity of the atmosphere. Further data was collected by over 200 balloons that were released from Canton Island, Guam and Ascension Island.

The long nose found on meteorological research aircraft is specially designed to house sensitive instruments as far away from any air disturbances as possible. The radar equipment is located above the cockpit.

ment. One of the primary objectives of the programme was to study the behaviour of "cloud clusters" in relation to larger-scale tropical weather systems, which are thought to have an important role in the energetics of the general circulation.

Building on the experience of earlier research projects with more limited aims, the first GARP Global Experiment (FGGE) was designed on a grand scale, with the objective of providing a more complete and comprehensive set of global data, at least for a limited period, than previously had been available. Virtually all 150 WMO members participated in the experiment, in which the most up-to-date data-observing systems were employed to subject the entire atmosphere to the most intensive surveillance ever made. The operational phase lasted for one year (from 1 December 1978 to 30 November 1979) with two separate periods of two months (5 January to 5 March and 1 May to 30 June 1979) for special observations in the tropics and Southern Hemisphere.

In addition to five geostationary satellites, which continuously monitored areas north and south of the equator to about 50°–55° latitude, and five polar-orbiting satellites, special efforts were made to supplement the data of areas where the observational network was otherwise inadequate. For example, during the two special observing periods, about 40 ships, stationed in tropical oceans, made surface observations and balloon soundings up to the stratosphere; also an aircraft "drop-sonde system" was used to

measure temperature, wind velocity and humidity from the flight level of the aircraft to the Earth's surface.

During the whole experiment over 200 constant-level balloons were released in the tropics which were to float at an altitude of about 15 kilometres (9 miles), measuring pressure and temperature. A satellite-borne data-collection and location system received this data; wind velocities were computed by monitoring the balloon tracks.

From the vast, mostly data-absent, southern oceans, measurements of surface pressure and temperature from floating buoys were again collected by the satellite system. Out of a total 368 buoys launched, 130 were still in operation at the end of the experiment and continued to provide additional data for the normal WWW network. Finally, much information was collected from commercial airlines; an integrated data system was installed on about 80 aircraft to automatically record pressure, temperature and wind velocity at intervals of about 200 kilometres (120 miles) along their flight paths. On average this resulted in 1800 observations being recorded per day over the entire globe.

The large amount of observational material collected during the operational year of the experiment has been processed and is catalogued on magnetic tape and housed at the World Data Centres in Moscow and Washington. Current research based on this material is being carried out by national meteorological services, institutes and universities, with greatest attention being given to the major problem of how to improve weather forecasts.

The availability of a comprehensive set of global data provides meteorologists with a means of testing and improving prediction models so as to determine whether or not it is possible to forecast the weather for more than just a few days ahead using the numerical methods first conceived in the early decades of the twentieth century.

Modern Forecasts and Services

Forecasts are based on the concept that at any moment in time there is a coherent pattern of weather covering the Earth which can be determined from a global network of stations making simultaneous observations, the data being collected and plotted on maps for synoptic analysis.

The 150 WMO member nations co-operate with the preparation and exchange of weather information by means of the WWW – the global meteorological system

which comprises the facilities and operations of the individual national weather services. This system is basically centred round the four main synoptic hours – 00, 06, 12, and 18 Greenwich Mean Time (GMT). Several hundred upper-air stations all around the world, including the ocean weather ships, make soundings twice daily, at 00 and 12 GMT; intermediate wind-finding flights which regularly reach altitudes of 30,000 metres (100,000 feet) or more are also made at 06 and 18 GMT. In addition, large numbers of reports are received from aircraft giving temperature and wind velocity at flight level as well as information about meteorological conditions which can be hazardous to air travel, such as icing, turbulence and storms.

The most noteworthy advance in meteorological observing during recent years has been the introduction of weather satellites, which view the Earth's atmosphere on a grand scale. Cloud pictures, transmitted back to Earth both by day and night, show the position and structure of a wide range of weather systems. Satellite photographs are particularly useful in providing information from areas where there are few conventional observations, for example in detecting hurricanes over tropical oceans. The speed and direction of upper winds can be determined by measuring the movement of clouds between successive photographs. By measuring the radiation emitted by atmospheric gases, such as carbon dioxide and water vapour, satellites also provide information about the vertical distribution of temperature

View-data systems have been installed in meteorological offices (*above*) so that a computer data bank, connected to a modified domestic television set and telephone, can be used to distribute weather information.

Tiros (*left*) was until recently a polar-orbiting satellite, circling the Earth once every two hours at heights varying between 700 and 1500 kilometres (420 and 900 miles). It sent back high-definition pictures that revealed the formation and distribution of clouds and the extent of snow cover.

211

A CODED MESSAGE

A meteorological code has been established which presents data in groups of five figures. For example the message shown here, transmitted in the form 03534 23025 59158 07507 22401 02108 82818, contains details of a typical hourly observation which can be decoded by a meteorologist at any national meteorological centre.

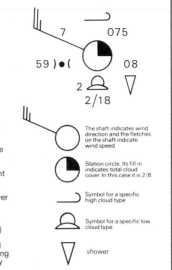

03524	International index number 03 – British Isles, 534 – name of station in UK
23025	2 – total amount of cloud (2/8) 30 – surface wind direction (300°) 25 – wind speed in knots
59158	59 – visibility (9 kilometres) 15 – present weather (precipitation) 8 – past weather (showers)
07507	075 – atmospheric pressure (1007.5 millibars) 07 – air temperature (7°C)
22401	Decode the different types of cloud grouping present, their extent of cover and height
02108	02 – dew point temperature (2°C) 108 – pressure characteristic and tendency, indicating rise of pressure by 0.8 millibars

The shaft indicates wind direction and the fletches on the shaft indicate wind speed

Station circle. Its fill in indicates total cloud cover. In this case it is 2/8

Symbol for a specific high cloud type

Symbol for a specific low cloud type

shower

Vital meteorological statistics are collected at the Chilean Base, King George Island, on the lifeless and frozen wastelands of Antarctica. The continent holds important clues to long-term global weather patterns.

and humidity in the atmosphere.

So that this large amount of information is made available to forecast centres around the world with the minimum of delay, it is essential that all the national meteorological services are linked by an efficient global telecommunication system. The various categories of meteorological observations are prepared for transmission by making use of internationally agreed specifications and codes which can carry a large amount of information in a condensed and concise form, a kind of weather language.

Regional meteorological centres such as Bracknell in England, Montreal in Canada and Rome in Italy are responsible for collecting synoptic observations from meteorological centres and for transmitting total regional compilation of coded weather messages to one of the three world meteorological centres in Washington, Moscow and Melbourne. The information is then processed by computer into global data sets. Analyses and forecasts are issued to the other 21 regional meteorological centres throughout the world, where in turn more detailed analyses and forecasts are prepared for their respective regions and distribution to the national meteorological centres.

Upper-air data from radio-sonde ascents are also synoptically analysed by drawing the maps at the standard pressure levels – 850, 700, 500, 300, 200 and 100 millibars. Because of the fewer radio-sonde stations compared with surface stations, the information they produce is less complete and so is augmented mathematically by computer.

Twice daily, following the collection of observations for 00 and 12 GMT, numerical forecasts are produced of the weather over most of the Northern Hemisphere for 24 hours ahead at Bracknell; the programme is continued to give a medium-range forecast for the next 72 hours and once a day a six-day prediction is produced. A further forecast model is run to predict the weather in more detail over the British Isles and western Europe for the following 36 hours. Thus Richardson's dream of 60 years ago that perhaps some day in the future it would be possible to advance the computations faster than the weather, has now become a reality – 24-hour numerical forecasts involving ten thousand million arithmetical calculations can be accomplished in about half an hour, and there are prospects for further advances in the 1980s with more powerful computers.

Hemispheric charts are plotted for the main synoptic hours at central forecasting offices; when all the observations for a given time have been plotted, the synoptic situation is analysed by drawing isobars to indicate the distribution of pressure, and fronts to demarcate the regions being affected by warm and cold air masses. Areas of precipitation and fog are sometimes emphasized by being shaded in green and yellow, respectively.

Weather maps drawn manually and by computer are used in combination to prepare weather forecasts for international and internal dissemination by the central forecasting offices. Forecasts are regularly issued for the next 24 hours and are also prepared for the 24- to 72-hour period, although not in so much detail. These form the basis of forecast services for aviation, shipping, agriculture, industry and the general public. Central fore-

casting offices also issue warnings of hazardous weather conditions, such as gales, fog, snow, heavy rain, frost, icy roads, thaw and thunderstorms. Forecasts and warnings are generally disseminated by radio, television, telephone and the press, although some specialized forecasts are issued direct to public institutions.

The world's first television weather chart was broadcast by the BBC from Alexandra Palace, London, in 1936, but, as with all other forms of weather forecasts issued to the general public, this service was suspended for security reasons during the Second World War and was recommenced as a regular feature in 1949. The first live television presentation by professional weather men was begun in 1954 in the United Kingdom.

A DAILY FORECAST
Issuing daily weather maps is among the tasks undertaken at all meteorological offices throughout the world. Maps similar to the ones shown for the United States are issued by the Meteorological Office at Suitland, Maryland.

Map A, made on August 26, 1981, shows the 48-hour forecast of the weather situation for 0000 GMT on Friday, 28 August, 1981. Note the low-pressure system centred over eastern Illinois and the weather fronts from below the great lakes to the lower Mississippi valley, which were expected to produce thundershowers throughout much of the region.

Map B shows the actual weather situation as it appeared 48 hours later on Friday, 28 August, 1981. Note the position of the low-pressure system and its associated fronts centred near the Iowa-Missouri border, only slightly west of the forecast position on Map A. Actual weather maps are larger than illustrated here and also show station information as explained at the top of page 212 for each station in the area covered by the map

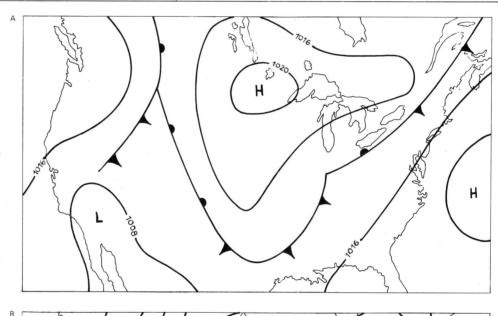

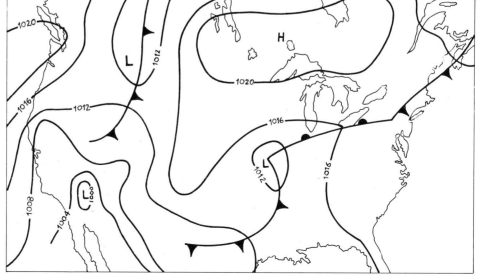

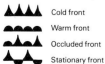

Cold front

Warm front

Occluded front

Stationary front

Amateur meteorology

In the 1820s, artists, inspired by the new cloud classifications of the time, became interested in meteorology, and their paintings, such as those of Turner (*centre, right*), show detailed and intricate studies of cloud formations.

The flowering of the horse chestnut tree is an important internationally recognized phenological event heralding spring and is officially used in some countries to predict grain harvests.

For much of its history meteorology has owed its development and progress to the studies of amateur scientists – in fact our knowledge of climatic conditions in the seventeenth, eighteenth and early nineteenth centuries is mostly drawn from records kept by amateur observers. However, since the establishment of the first national weather services in the 1850s, meteorology has become an increasingly complex science with professional meteorologists now having vast instrumental and technical resources at their command.

Nevertheless, there is still room for the amateur meteorologist today. Indeed, apart from the fact that amateur observations may become accepted into the network of official meteorological stations, watching the weather is rewarding in its own right by providing an absorbing and growing scientific interest in the natural environment. Contact with other meteorologists, both amateur and professional, can be made through membership of meteorological societies, such as the Royal Meteorological Society and the American Meteorological Society; their regular meetings, field study courses and publications provide forums for the discussion and exchange of ideas about weather and climate.

One of the chief charms of meteorology for the amateur is that it can be pursued at different levels of commitment, with or without instruments, according to the means and inclination of the individual, the all-important common factor being a lively curiosity about the weather. But how and where to begin? An early task must be to develop your powers of scientific observation by carefully watching the sky. With an unobstructed skyline it is possible to see high clouds above the horizon at a distance of 240 kilometres (150 miles).

Present and approaching weather is indicated by the appearance of the sky and the various forms of clouds provide visual guides to the physical and dynamical processes at work in the atmosphere.

Cloud forms and related features can be recorded daily in a weather diary. By relating these observations to subsequent weather conditions you will discover that most of the well-known weather sayings involving clouds are not infallible, for example mackerel skies indicated by *cirrocumulus*

clouds do not always herald rain. After a while you should be able to formulate a number of general relationships between clouds and future weather, as well as the exceptions to the rules. By analysing these deviations you may be able to evolve an improved set of forecast rules based on your cloud observations and thus complete a useful piece of original research.

Amateurs can also make valuable contributions to meteorology by observing and recording optical phenomena such as coronas, haloes, rainbows and mirages; thunderstorms, lightning and tornadoes; and the effects of local topography on wind flow and temperature distribution, such as katabatic winds and frost hollows. The editors of weather magazines always welcome accurate eye-witness accounts of notable atmospheric events, illustrated, if possible, with sketches, photographs and maps.

The study of phenology is another interesting activity which can be inexpensively pursued by the amateur. This involves observing and recording annually recurring events in nature such as the leafing and flowering of plants, migration of birds and behaviour of insects. Being manifestations of prevailing climatic conditions, phenological events generally occur in a seasonal order that is substantially constant. However, the individual dates from year to year can vary widely according to vicissitudes of weather. By providing natural indicators of atmo-

By accurately recording unusual forms of lightning and other natural phenomena which illustrate the behaviour of light and colour in nature, amateurs can provide a valuable service to the professional meteorologist.

Amateur meteorologists in the United Kingdom send monthly observations, of the kind shown below, to the National Meteorological Office at Bracknell. The only stipulations the office makes are that the individual possesses a set of standard instruments – thermometers housed in a Stevenson Screen and a barometer – and makes daily observations, 365 days per year. The observations are written in abbreviated form. Specific code letters such as "b" and "c" denote fine and cloudy conditions respectively.

spheric conditions, phenological observations can be applied to studies relating agriculture to weather and climate. Plants are generally easiest to observe and a good long-period record for half a dozen plants and trees growing in one's locality provides a real contribution to science.

If resources permit, the addition of instruments such as a barometer, a set of thermometers, a wind vane and a rain gauge can provide the type of extra information which will transform your descriptive weather diary into a more fully quantitative meteorological register. Apart from the barometer, which should be kept indoors in a room where temperature variations are minimal, the ideal site for an amateur weather station is a level plot of lawn, approximately 9 metres by 6 metres (30 feet by 20 feet), situated away from any obstructions such as trees and buildings, the thermometers being housed in a wooden shelter or screen standing about 1·2 metres (4 feet) above the ground.

The large-scale laboratory in which we all live – the atmosphere – is free and open to all, and although you may be less well endowed with instrumental and technical facilities than professional colleagues, you may, nevertheless, owing to circumstances of time and space, sometimes be favoured with witnessing rare or important atmospheric phenomena which escape the open network of official meteorological stations and the broad viewpoint of the weather satellites.

STATION NAME.. *NEWTON RIGG*.... MONTH.. *MAY*.... YEAR *1981*

Date	Pressure	Temperature before 0900 hours		Weather diary after 0900 hours (midnight to midnight)
01	2934	63	Sunny	b.c. fine cold, sunny periods, ex. visibility
02	2942	63	Sunny	b. fine, sunny, cold
03	2892	61	Rain	c. mod. inter. rain, calm, occ. sun even
04	2883	62	Little sun	c. dull v. cold, morn. sunny, a'noon sl. rain at intervals & sunny periods.
05	2910	62	Severe o'night frost	b. fine, sunny, v. cold, rain later
06	2910	61	Sunny periods	c. fine, sunny, clouding 16.00 hrs
07	2920	62	Little sun	c. fine, sunny periods, heavy rain o'night
08	2914	64	Little sun	c. fine, dull, warmer, occ. hazy sun
09	2941	65	Little sun early	c. fine, dull, rain o'night
10	2920	65	Heavy rain	c. heavy inter. rain, clearing later
11	2918	64	Sunny	b. fine, sunny, hot
12	2905	63	Sunny	b. fine, sunny, hot, calm, hazy, little thunder
13	2919	66	Some sun	b.c. fine, sunny periods, warm
14	2915	65	Little sun	c. fine, long sunny periods, rain o'night

GLOSSARY

adiabatic   Literally, without direct heating; adiabatic changes in temperature occur within air masses as a result of pressure changes, which cause them to expand or contract.

albedo   The proportion of incident radiation directly reflected by a particular surface; it is usually expressed as a percentage.

anemometer   An instrument for determining the speed of the wind.

anticyclone   The circulation of air around a central area of high pressure that is usually associated with settled weather; pressure rises steadily when an anticyclone is developing and falls when it is declining.

aphelion   The point at which the orbit of a planet is at its farthest point from the Sun; in the case of the Earth it occurs in early July.

bar   The unit of atmospheric pressure that is equal to the pressure of 750·062 millimetres of mercury (or 29·530 inches of mercury).

barometer   An instrument for measuring atmospheric pressure.

Beaufort Scale   Series of numbers devised by Admiral Beaufort in 1806 to denote the strength of wind from 0 to 12, hurricane force – "That which no canvas can stand". The scale has been revised to 0–17.

black body   A surface which absorbs all of the electromagnetic radiation striking it and radiates the maximum possible at any temperature.

black body radiation   The electromagnetic radiation emitted by an ideal black body. It is the theoretical maximum amount of radiant energy at all wavelengths which can be emitted by a body at a given temperature.

blocking high   Any high-pressure centre that remains stationary, effectively blocking the more usual eastward progression of weather systems in middle latitudes for several days.

Buys Ballot's Law   A rule which states that if an observer stands with his back to the wind in the Northern Hemisphere, atmospheric pressure will be lower to his left than to his right, and if he stands with his back to the wind in the Southern Hemisphere, lower pressure will be on his right.

centre of mass   The point at which all the mass of a body or system of bodies may be considered to be concentrated for the purpose of calculating the gravitational effect when a force is applied.

Coriolis force   The apparent force that deflects a wind or moving object, causing it to curve in relation to the rotating Earth.

cut-off low   A low-pressure centre which has been displaced out of the basic westerly current so that it lies on the current's equatorial side.

cyclone   The circulation of air around a central area of low pressure that is usually associated with unsettled weather. In tropical latitudes it can refer to an intense storm that does not attain the status of a full hurricane.

depression   An area of low pressure and often unsettled weather.

dew point   The temperature to which air, at constant pressure and moisture content, must be cooled for saturation to occur.

dry adiabatic lapse rate   The rate at which dry air cools with height when it is forced to rise into regions of lower pressure: 1°C per 100 metres (5·4°F per 1000 feet) rise. Dry, sinking air warms at the same rate.

ecliptic   The plane in which the Earth's orbit traces an elliptical path round the Sun.

electromagnetic radiation   The energy from the Sun that travels through the vacuum of space to reach the Earth as electromagnetic waves.

evaporation   The transformation of liquid to gas.

eye   The central portion of a tropical hurricane or typhoon; a roughly circular area of relatively light winds and fair weather.

front   The transition zone between two air masses of different properties.

geostationary satellite   A satellite which orbits above a particular point on the Earth's surface at the equator. The satellites are always stationed at a height of 36,000 kilometres (21,600 miles), at which altitude they orbit at the same angular speed with which the Earth rotates.

geostrophic wind   The horizontal wind resulting when only atmospheric pressure differences and the deflecting Coriolis force are taken into account.

greenhouse effect   The global heating effect due to the atmosphere being more transparent to incoming short-wave solar radiation than it is to outgoing long-wave radiation.

Hadley cell   A system of atmospheric circulation that ultimately distributes air from the tropics to the poles. It is sustained by large-scale convection currents in which hot air is replaced by cooled air.

high   An area of high atmospheric pressure with a closed circulation – an anticyclone.

hygrometer   An instrument for measuring the humidity of the air.

insolation   Solar radiation received at the Earth's surface; the word is a contraction of "incoming solar radiation".

Intertropical Convergence Zone   The axis along which the northeast trade winds of the Northern Hemisphere meet the southeast trade winds of the Southern Hemisphere.

isobar   A line joining places of equal pressure.

jet-stream   Relatively strong winds concentrated within a narrow belt that is usually found in the tropopause.

Kelvin temperature scale   The scale which begins at the point, in theory, that all molecular action ceases. (−273·16°C).

kinetic energy   The energy that a moving body possesses as a consequence of its motion.

knot   One nautical mile per hour, the unit of speed in the nautical system. A nautical mile is equivalent to one-sixtieth of a degree or one minute of arc. The international nautical mile is 1852 metres long.

latent heat   Heat absorbed when a solid changes to a liquid or a liquid to a gas with no change in temperature or heat released in the reverse transformations.

lapse rate   The decrease of an atmospheric variable (usually temperature unless otherwise specified) with height.

low   An area of low atmospheric pressure – a cyclone or a depression.

magnetosphere   The region of the Earth's high atmosphere in which the Earth's magnetic field controls the motion of ionized particles.

mesosphere   Region of the Earth's atmosphere between the stratosphere and thermosphere. It extends from about 40 to 80 kilometres (24 to 48 miles) above the Earth's surface.

micron   Unit of measurement equivalent to one-thousandth of a millimetre.

millibar   A unit of atmospheric pressure that is equivalent to one-thousandth of a bar (*see* bar).

nautical mile   A distance unit in the nautical system, defined internationally as 1852 metres (1·15 statute miles) or the length of one minute of arc along any great circle.

numerical forecasting   Forecasting the behaviour of the atmosphere using mathematical models.

occlusion   The boundary that is formed when warm air behind a warm front is lifted above the surface by an overtaking cold front.

ozone   A form of oxygen whose chemical symbol is O_3. It is a highly unstable gas found in trace quantities in the atmosphere, primarily in a layer above the tropopause.

perihelion   The point at which the orbit of a planet is at its nearest to the Sun. In the case of the Earth, it occurs in early January.

phenology   The study of the times of recurring natural phenomena in relation to climatic conditions.

polar-orbiting satellite   A satellite which circles the Earth over the poles – at right angles to the equator. As the Earth rotates in relation to the satellite's orbit, the satellite passes over a succession of north-south bands. The interval between the bands for meteorological satellites is usually about 30 degrees of longitude, depending on the height of the orbit above the Earth, which is typically between 700 and 1500 kilometres (435 and 923 miles).

radiation   The process by which energy from the Sun is propagated through the vacuum of space as electromagnetic waves and is a method, along with conduction and convection, of transporting heat.

radiosonde   A balloon-borne instrument for the simultaneous measurement and transmission of meteorological data.

relative humidity   The ratio of the amount of moisture in the air to the amount which the air would hold at the same temperature and pressure if it were saturated; it is usually expressed as a percentage.

ridge   An elongated area of relatively high pressure extending from the centre of a high-pressure region.

saturated air   Air that contains the maximum amount of water vapour it can hold at a given pressure and temperature. Saturated air has a relative humidity of 100 per cent.

saturated adiabatic lapse rate   The rate at which a parcel of saturated air decreases in temperature as it rises vertically and cloud droplets form.

solar wind   An outflow of particles from the Sun which represents the expansion of the corona.

solstices   These occur twice a year at the times when the distance of the Sun from the equator is at its greatest. As the direction of the Earth's axis remains fixed in space, the Sun appears to move northwards and southwards during our yearly path around it and the summer solstice occurs when the Sun appears to be at its most northerly position, on 22 June. The Sun is then directly overhead at a latitude of 23°27′N and the line joining all points with this latitude is called the Tropic of Cancer. Six months later the winter solstice occurs, on 22 December, when the Sun is at its most southerly point and directly overhead at a latitude of 23°27′S, along the Tropic of Capricorn.

stratosphere   Upper layer of the atmosphere that is said to be "above the weather": it lies between the troposphere and the mesosphere at a height of 25 to 50 kilometres (15 to 30 miles) above the Earth's surface. The air in this layer is usually stable and temperatures are generally constant or increase slowly with height.

sublimation   A process by which a gas is changed to a solid or a solid is changed to a gas without going through the liquid state.

supercooling   The cooling of a liquid below its freezing point without it becoming a solid.

supersaturation   The condition of air having a relative humidity greater than 100 per cent.

synod   The alignment of the Sun, planets and their accompanying moons.

synoptic weather mapping   The analysis of weather observations made simultaneously at many points over a large geographical area.

temperature inversion   A layer of the atmosphere in which the temperature increases with altitude as opposed to the normal tendency for temperature to decrease with altitude.

thermosphere   The outermost layer of the atmosphere in which the temperature increases regularly with height.

tropopause   The boundary between the troposphere and the stratosphere; it is usually marked by an abrupt change in lapse rate to a more stable pattern.

trough   An elongated area of low atmospheric pressure, usually extending from the centre of a low-pressure system.

upper air   In synoptic meteorology and weather observing, the atmosphere above the lowest 1000 metres (3280 feet) within which surface friction has an influence. No distinct lower limit is set, but the term is normally applied at pressures of around 850 millibars.

Van Allen belts   Regions of high-energy particles trapped by the magnetic field of the Earth.

virga   Wisps or streaks of water or ice particles which fall from clouds and evaporate before reaching the Earth's surface.

warm front   The boundary of an advancing current of relatively warm air which is displacing a retreating colder air mass.

warm sector   Warm air between the retreating warm front and an approaching cold front.

INDEX

Numbers in *italics* refer to
illustrations and their captions

Index compiled by Helen Baz

BIBLIOGRAPHY

Atkinson, B. W., *The Weather Business,* Aldus Books (London, 1968).
Barry, R. G. & Chorley, R. J., *Atmosphere, Weather and Climate,* Methuen (London, 1976).
Calder, N., *The Weather Machine,* BBC (London, 1974).
Frisinger, H. Howard, *The History of Meteorology: to 1800,* Science History Publications (New York, 1977)
Gribbin, J., *Weather Force,* Hamlyn (London, 1979).
Kkrgian, A. Kh., *Meteorology – A Historical Survey,* Israel Program for Scientific Translations (Jerusalem, 1970).
Lockwood, J. G., *Causes of Climate,* Edward Arnold (London, 1979).
Minnaert, M., *The Nature of Light and Colour in the Open Air,* Dover Publications (1954).
Observer's Handbook, HMSO (London, 1969).
Schneider-Carius, K., *Wetterkunde Wetterforschung,* Karl Alber (Freiburg/Munich, 1955).
Shaw, Sir N., *The Drama of Weather,* University Press (Cambridge, 1934).
Thompson, P. D. & O'Brien, R., *Weather,* Time-Life International (Nederland, 1966).
Trewartha, G. T. & Horn, L. H., *An Introduction to Climate,* McGraw-Hill (New York, 1980).
White, G. W., *Outlook: Weather Maps and Elementary Forecasting,* Stanford Maritime (London, 1967).
Young, L. B., *Earth's Aura,* Penguin Books (London, 1980).

ACKNOWLEDGEMENTS

Harrow House Editions would like to thank
Celia Dearing, Jane Greening, Martyn
Bramwell, Bryan Sage and the Meteoro-
logical Office for their assistance.

Editor Zuza Vrbova
Designer John Pallot
Picture Researcher Anne-Marie Erhlich
Production Manager Kenneth Cowan
Production Editor Fred Gill

Artists

All maps by **Eugene Fleurey**
All diagrams by **Richard Lewis**, excepting
pages 30, 33 by Terry Allen Design;
page 109 by Nigel Partridge;
page 200 by Jeremy Banks

Picture Credits

A: Above **B**: Below **L**: Left **R**: Right
C: Centre

10/11 Bildarkivet! 13 (R): NASA 14/(CR):
Laboratory for Planetary Atmospheres, UCL
15 (CR): B. Sagel/Ardea 16 (BL): Dr Ray
Clark/Science Photo Library 17 (AR): ZEFA
19 (AR): Christian Bonnington (BL):
Marion Morrison (BR): Jon Gardey/Robert
Harding 20 (CL): The Mansell Collection
(BR): ZEFA 22 (AL): NASA 23 (L):
Michael Maunder 24 (BR): NOAA/Met
Office 26 (CL): Peter Parks/Oxford Scientific
Films 26/27 (A): Robert Harding 29 (BR):
Colin Molyneuz 30/31 (B): K. Pilsbury 32/
33 (A): J. Allen Cash 34/35 (L): Peter
Loughran 36 (CL): British Antarctic Survey
(BL): Reproduced by permission of the
Director, IGS NERC 36/37 (B): Heather
Angel 38 (AR): Seaphot (B): A. Low/
Daily Telegraph Colour Library 39 (AL):
Chris Bonnington/Daily Telegraph Colour
Library (B): Alan Hutchison Library 40 (A):
Popperfoto (BR): Sunday Telegraph/Met.
Office 41 (B): Mary Evans Picture Library
42 (BR): WFA/National Museum of Anthro-
pology, Mexico 43 (L): ZEFA (CR): Paul
Brierley 44 (AL): Paul Brierley 45 (BR):
Archiv fur Kunst und Geschichte 46 (BL):
Mary Evans Picture Library (BR): NASA
47 (BL): Frank Lane 48: Heather Angel 49
(A): Peter Loughran (B): Mary Evans
Picture Library (BR): K. Pilsbury 50: G. R.
Roberts 52: John Cleare 53 (A): John Simms/
Oxford Scientific Films 53 (B): G. R.
Roberts 54 (A): G. R. Roberts 54/55 (B): Jon
Gardey/Robert Harding 55 (A): Ian Dundas/
Frank Lane (C): David Hoadley/Frank Lane
(B): G. R. Roberts 56 (C): K. Pilsbury 57
(A): John Shelton 57 (B): CSIRO Division
of Cloud Physics 58: Explorer 59 (A): Mark
Newman/ES/Oxford Scientific Films (B): L.
West/Frank Lane 60 (AL): O. Peterson/Met.
Office 60/61 (AR): Picturepoint 61 (A):
BBC Hulton Picture Library 62 (BL): Harry
Miller/Camera Press 62/63 (BR): R. J.
Marsch/Image Bank 63 (BR): Werner For-
man Archive 64 (AL): Ann Ronan Picture
Library (BL): From the MGM release
"SINGIN' IN THE RAIN" 1952 Loew's Inc.
Copyright renewed 1979 by MGM Inc. 65
(AL): Mansell Collection (AR, CR, BR):

Ann Ronan Picture Library 66/67 (A): Kol
Bhatia/Image Bank 67 (AR): C. M. Dixon
(BL): Ann Ronan Picture Library 68 (AR):
Mansell Collection (B): Popperfoto 69
(AL, BL): Popperfoto 70/71 (A): Malcolm
Aird 71 (AR): Ulf Blomberg 72 (BR):
ZEFA 73 (AL): Mansell Collection (AR):
Keystone Press (B): Jerry Cooke/ES/Oxford
Scientific Films 74: Ulf Blomberg 75 (BL):
Ulf Blomberg 76: Dr T. Kobayashi 77 (A):
Bill Noonan (B): John Noble 78 (A):
Heather Angel (B): Ann Ronan Picture
Library 79 'CR): Frank Lane 80 (AR):
Joseph Larson/USDA 81 (A): Frank Lane
(BL): Mary Evans Picture Library (BR):
Novosti 82/83: Mark Newman/ES/Oxford
Scientific Films 83: Werner Forman Archive
84: Ken Pilsbury 85 (A): AG Siemans (B):
Frank Lane 86: Mary Evans Picture Library
87 (A): Peter Loughran (BL): Mary Evans
(BR): Roy Jennings/Frank Lane 88 (L):
Frank Lane (R): Mary Evans Picture Library
89 (A): Phil Krider/Frank Lane (B): General
Electric/Frank Lane 90: Exploerer 92 (AR):
G. R. Roberts (CL): Ray Gardner/British
Library 93 (AL): CEGB 94/95 (B): ES/
Oxford Scientific Films 95 (AL): Ardea (AR,
CR, BR): Alistair Black 96 (AL): Keystone
Press (B): CEGB 97 (AR): Peter Loughran
98 (CR): G. R. Roberts 99 (AL): NASA
(BR): Alan Hutchison Library 100 (A):
KLM/Frank Labe (B): GLC Public Relations
101 (AL): by courtesy of the Royal Nether-
lands Embassy 102 (AR): Alan Hutchison
Library (BR): NASA/Frank Lane 105 (AL):
American Red Cross/Frank Lane (BR): US
Air Force/NOAA 106 (BL, BR): NOAA
106/107 (A): Space Frontiers 107 (BL):
NOAA 108 (AL): NOAA 108/9: Frank
Lane 110 (BR): J. C. Allen/Frank Lane 111
(L): Michael Maunder (CR): Dinsmore/
Frank Lane 112 (AR): US Weather Bureau/
Frank Lane 113 (A): D. Bergquist/Frank
Lane 114 (AR): Paul Huffman/Frank Lane
(B): Nat. Severe Storms Lab./NOAA 115
(BL): Nat. Severe Storms Lab./NOAA 116/
117 (B): ZEFA 117 (BR): Mary Evans
Picture Library 118 (CL): Frank Lane (R):
Ardea 119 (B): G. R. Roberts 120 (AR):
Ricardo Maranges/Frank Lane 121 (B):
Popperfoto 122/123: ZEFA 126 (B): Chris
Bonnington/Daily Telegraph 127 (A, B): J.
& D. Bartlett/Bruce Coleman 129 (AL): J.
Allan Cash (AR): Iren Vandermolen/Frank
Lane (B): Richard Waller/Ardea 130 (A):
Paolo Koch/Vision International (B): Robert
Harding 131 (A): John Cleare (B): Robert
Harding 132 (B): Nicholas Devore/Bruce
Coleman 133 (A): G. R. Roberts (B):
Popperfoto 134: Robert Harding 135 (A):
Robert Harding (B): Christine Osborne/
Topham 136 (BR): Frank Lane 137 (AR):
G. R. Roberts (B): Alan Hutchinson 138 (A,
B): Alan Hutchinson Library 139: Robert
Harding 140 (A): J. Allan Cash (B): John
Topham Picture Library 141: J. Allan Cash
142 (L): Alan Hutchison 142/143 (C): Alan
Hutchison 143 (R): J. G. Mason 144 (CR):
Hawker Sideley Dynamics Ltd/Science Photo
Library 145 (A): Harry Smith Collection
(B): G. R. Roberts 146/147: Peter Loughran

149 (AR): Heather Angel (CR): C. M.
Dixon (BR): G. R. Roberts 150 (CL):
Picturepoint 151 (AL, B): G. R. Roberts 153
(A): John Marmaras/Daily Telegraph Colour
Library 154 (A): Paul Brierley (B): Oxford
Scientific Films 155 (CR): Ardea 156 (CL):
H. Lamb Climatic Research Unit, University
of E. Anglia/Met. Office 156/157 (A): Statens
Historiska Museen 157 (AR): Museum of
Nat. Antiquities, Stockholm/Weidenfelt &
Nicolson (B): National Museum Copen-
hagen/WFA 158/159: E. T. Archive 159:
Eileen Tweedy 160 (A): Bib. Nat. Paris/
Giraudon (BL, BR): Mansell Collection
161: © Royal Met. Society/Met. Office 162
(CL): Mount Wilson and Las Campanas
Observatories, Carnegie Institution of Wash-
inton (CR): M. A. Chappell/ES/Oxford
Scientific Films 164 (L): Novosti (R):
Popperfoto 165 (A, B): Mary Evans Picture
Library 166 (A): Rex Features (B): Helena
Vrbova 167: Dr Marcel Ackerman/Nature
168 (A): John Gribbin (BL): Courtesy of
The Royal Institution (BR): Reproduced by
permission of the Director IGS NERC ©
169 (B): Michael Holford/Science Museum
170 (A): World Data Center/Goddard Space
Flight Center 171: Walter Rawlings/Robert
Harding 172 (B): Nigel Watt/Camera Press
174: Bruce Coleman Ltd 176 (AL): re-
produced by permission of the British Library
177 (A): Mansell Collection 178 (BL): Peter
Loughran 179 (BR): D. P. Cruikshank 180
(BL): CEGB (BR): Frank Lane 181 (B):
John Noble 182/183 Derek Fordham/Arctic
Camera 184 (A): Photo Science Museum,
London 185 (AR): Mansell Collection (C):
by permission of the Trustees of the British
Museum 186 (AL): Michael Holford/Louvre
Paris (AR): Michael Holford/V & A 187 (C):
Mansell Collection 188: Photo Science mu-
seum, London 188/189: Ray Gardner 189
(AR): Ann Ronan Picture Library 190 (CL):
Crown Copyright, Victoria & Albert Mu-
seum, London (BL): Ann Ronan Picture
Library 191 (AR): Ann Ronan Picture Lib-
rary (B): Museo della Specola/Scala 192
(AR): Mansell Collection (CL): Ray Gardner
193 (A): Ray Gardner (B): A. C. Cooper/
Royal Astronomical Society 194 (AL):
Philadelphia Museum of Art: the Mr & Mrs
Wharton Sinkler Collection (AR): The
National Maritime Museum, London 195
(AC): Michael Holford/NMM (AR): Roger
Viollet 196 (CL): by permission of the
Trustees of the British Museum (CR): The
National Maritime Museum, London 197
(R): Museum of the History of Science,
Oxford 198 (BR): Ray Gardner 199 (BL):
E. T. Archive 200 (AL): Photo Science
Museum, London 200/201 (A): The National
Martitime Museum, London 202 (L): Cour-
tesy MOD Public Relations 203: NCAR 204
(B): Crown Copyright/Met. Office 205
(AR): Mansell Collection 206 (L): Novosti
297 (BR): Crown Copyright/Met. Office
(AR): Tony Morrison 208 (BL): Novosti
(AR): Crown Copyright/Met. Office 210
(A): Courtesy MOD Public Relations 211
(A): Jerry Mason (B): Courtesy MOD
Public Relations 212 (BL): J. & D. Bartlett/
Bruce Coleman 214 (BL): A. A. Butcher/
Nature Photographers Ltd 214/215 (AC): E.
T. Archive/Tate Gallery, London 215 (AR):
Nat. Severe Storms Lab./NOAA